AL-QAEDAISM
The Threat to Islam, The Threat to the World

First published in 2005 by

ASHFIELD PRESS • DUBLIN • IRELAND

© Richard Whelan, 2005

ISBN: 1 901658 54 6

Typeset by Ashfield Press in 11.5 on 14.5 point Dante
Designed by
SUSAN WAINE

Printed in Ireland by
ßETAPRINT LIMITED, DUBLIN

Al-Qaedaism

The Threat to Islam,
The Threat to the World

RICHARD WHELAN

ashfield
PRESS

Contents

ACKNOWLEDGEMENTS

I would like to thank my friends, neighbours and colleagues who have encouraged me in this unplanned and unexpected project over the last two years. Particular thanks to Kieran Fagan and to Tom Maher for ongoing support, assistance and practical advice.

Special thanks to Prof. Dr. Huseyin Bagci of the Middle Eastern Technical University in Ankara for organising an extremely productive and enjoyable visit to Ankara and to all the people I met there. Thanks also to Prof. Michael Mousseau of Koç University in Istanbul for discussing and amplifying his views on globalisation with me.

My thanks to Dr. Maha Azzam-Nusseibeh, Prof. Dr. Holger Mey, Prof. Dirk Rochtus of The Lessius Institute of Academic Education, and Bob Silano for reviewing earlier drafts of this book and their helpful comments with respect to same. The final manuscript is, of course, solely my own responsibility.

The assistance from the library in the International Institute for Strategic Studies in London and their prompt response to my many requests is much appreciated. On a practical note, the typing of this document was at times difficult and I am grateful for the effort made in that regard by Ailish Fagan, Eva Malley and Gaye Murray, frequently at unsocial hours.

I am also grateful for the contribution made in converting a very rough manuscript to a fine book by the editor, Sean O'Keeffe, proof-reader/indexer Grainne Farren and particularly, my publishers, John Davey and Susan Waine of Ashfield Press. Special thanks also to Terry Prone.

Finally, many thanks to my wife Marian and my twin daughters, Iseult and Sorcha for their forbearance over the last two years, particularly on the numerous occasions when I was present in body but not in spirit.

Introduction

Having studied international politics and strategic syudies for over thirty years, I decided two years ago to write articles on strategic matters for publication by the broadsheets in Ireland. To do such I decided to draw upon indepth analyses and the views of relevant experts together with my own knowledge from my active involvement with a number of international bodies.

This book started as a briefing paper for myself for a short article on al-Qaeda. Over the course of twenty-four months it grew into what you are about to read. A word of caution is in order here. Many years ago, I learned that 'experts' are frequently not as expert as they claim to be, particularly when it comes to dealing with new phenomena such as the global impact of the collapse of communism in the Soviet Union or the current wave of terrorism. This caveat is particularly important when dealing with terrorism, as it is widely accepted that there is a paucity of understanding of terrorism in the academic community worldwide. The study of terrorism is overly policy-oriented and operates in an area between disciplines, such as psychology, history and political science and international relations, which are not accustomed to working together. In addition, in political science, terrorism does not fit well under either the 'realist' or 'liberal' paradigms, so again it has tended to fall between the cracks. (At the core of the realist theory is the belief that international affairs are in essence a struggle for power between states, while the liberal theory focuses on the increasing number of democracies as a positive, but with many dangers and turbulence during the transition to democracy.)

Although there are a small number of real experts in this area, unfortunately most of these are not as well-versed as they might be in Islamic matters and most also disagree on various matters, including whether Osama bin Laden is an engineer or an economist and even what the name 'al-Qaeda' means. (Some believe that it means 'the base', others 'the precept', 'the method' or 'the network'. In fact, the Arabic term 'al-Qaeda' can be translated as any of these things, although Islamic militants clearly see it as meaning 'model' or 'principle' – something one should aspire to, emulate, copy, or follow.)

To understand what I call 'al-Qaedaism' – a totalitarian ideological challenge embracing hyper-terrorism with a perverted interpretation of religion – requires an understanding of terrorism, Islam, Islamism, chemical, biological, radiological and nuclear weapons of mass destruction (WMD), deterrence and various other issues. Most experts operate in their own areas of expertise and few 'cross over' into other areas of expertise. I have, therefore, tried to understand each relevant area and then combine the approaches of all of them into a broad analysis and understanding of al-Qaedaism today.

I should also note that, when many experts write about Islam, they are frequently actually talking about Sunni Islam, the majority tradition in Islam. As the growth in Sunni militancy, which lead to al-Qaedaism, is partly a reaction to Shiite (minority Islam) activism in the wake of the 1979 Iranian Revolution, this is an unfortunate generalisation.

※

The introduction outlines the topic and indicates why I believe al-Qaedaism is now a strategic threat to the world, particularly in view of the fact that expert opinion is coalescing around the view that the proliferation of biological WMD is inevitable.

I show in Chapter 1 that the current wave of terrorism is the fourth such wave, which started around 1979 or 1980. The first wave, which lasted from the 1880s to the 1920s, generally sought political and civil reforms within autocratic states; the second wave, which lasted mainly from the 1920s to the 1930s but continues in some areas to this day, sought national self-determination and freedom from colonial oppression; the first and second waves overlapped to some extent and the second wave then led into the third wave in the 1970s, which was defined by left-wing revolutionary organisations supposedly acting as vanguards for the masses in the Third

World. This period also represents the high point of state-sponsored terrorism. The fourth, current wave, the jihad era, is, as we shall see, potentially the most dangerous of these four waves of terrorism.

Chapter 2 reviews the development of al-Qaedaism, and analyses the people and the concepts, both from the Sunni tradition within Islam and from the West, that helped create this ideology of hatred and aggression. This analysis shows al-Qaedaists to be a totalitarian vanguard of true believers who see all 'others', including most fellow Muslims, as their enemies, who in their eyes are degenerate and devoid of ethical value and who can be slaughtered like animals without compunction.

Chapter 3 discusses the aims of the followers of al-Qaedaism, which include, in the long term, the restoration of the (Sunni) Islamic Caliphate of ancient times and, in the medium term, the replacement of all Islamic governments with Taliban-like regimes. While these dreams are being realised, the al-Qaedaists seek the elimination of the separation of church and state and liberal democracy itself, and significant erosion of women's, human, religious, and civil rights.

In Chapter 4, I review the crisis of Islam in the modern world and the likely continuation of such into the future, in contrast with its glorious past. I consider who is to blame for this crisis and show that many of 'the usual suspects' are innocent. However, this widely perceived crisis has led to a rage amongst many in the Islamic world, usually directed at what they consider the culprit – the West.

In Chapter 5, I consider why the threat from al-Qaedaism has arisen now, and examine various explanations advanced for same. By examining the reasons why this threat has arisen now, it is possible to begin to accurately determine the means of dealing with it, which I do in Chapter 6. The Conclusion summarises my analysis and comments on the action needed to deal with the threat posed by al-Qaedaism.

'Jihad' means 'effort' or 'struggle'. Islamic scholars distinguish between the greater jihad, which is the effort of the believer seeking salvation, change or self-improvement, and the lesser jihad, which refers to the armed defence of the community of believers (*umma*) against outside threats. The latter can according to some but not all Islamic thinkers, include offensive military action to expand the Islamic world. I urge you, as I did, to adopt the approach of the greater jihad in reading this book and in thinking on this issue and to be open to the possibility of changing your views and developing your thinking on this key issue.

RICHARD F. WHELAN
Dublin, July 2005

I

The Jihad Era

'The al-Qaeda worldview, or "al-Qaedaism",
is growing stronger every day.'
JASON BURKE[1]

THIS BOOK EXAMINES what Jason Burke, chief reporter for the
Observer and author of *Al-Qaeda: Casting a Shadow of Terror,* terms
al-Qaedaism and the related US-led war on terror and considers
whether al-Qaedaism is a significant threat to the world and, if so, who is it
from, who is it against, and why has it emerged now?

It is important first of all to define what we are talking about in the
widest sense, as there is some confusion in this area around the various
terms used. Indeed, many of them are inaccurate, misleading or unhelpful.
Firstly, Islam is a religion practised by approximately 1.3 billion people; its
principal population concentration is Asia, not the Middle East/Gulf
region, as many people believe. Islam is not monolithic: it fractured blood-
ily soon after the death of the Prophet Muhammad in 632 and is divided
now by religious, regional and national differences.

The al-Qaedaism threat emanates from the majority Sunni tradition of
Islam and in fact represents as much a threat to minority traditions within
Islam, such as the Shiite, as to the rest of the world. Members of Islamic
minorities number something between 130 million and more than 200 million.

Due to population growth and religious conversions, the percentage of the world's population that is Muslim is expected to grow from approximately 20 percent at present to, according to some estimates, up to 30 percent over the next thirty or forty years.

Secondly, the words 'fundamentalist' and 'fundamentalism' are frequently applied to certain elements within Islam and other religions. Both terms are subject to very different meanings. Within Islam, they usually refer to completely non-violent people who take a literal approach to the Koran and other original sources of their religion and attempt to live their lives accordingly. Some Islamic fundamentalists engage in 'social' violence, relating to what people wear or do, to impose their lifestyle beliefs on others. As such, neither fundamentalist group represents a major threat to the rest of the world. Unfortunately, many references to al-Qaeda are couched in the form of 'fundamentalist' Islam or 'fundamentalist' threat, which is both misleading and inaccurate. I instead use the term 'militant' or 'al-Qaedaist' to distinguish activists such as those in al-Qaeda and similar groups from non-militant (although sometimes socially violent) fundamentalists and others who practise Islam.

Thirdly and finally, we need to define 'Islamism', which is a very important term with regard to the analysis of groups such as al-Qaeda. I use the definition employed by the International Crisis Group (ICG), for Islamism: that is, Islam in political rather than religious mode. (The ICG is an independent multinational organisation, headquartered in Brussels, that works through field-based analysis and high-level advocacy to prevent and resolve deadly conflict.) I define 'Islamist movements' as being 'those with Islamic ideological references pursuing primarily political objectives'. 'Islamist' and 'Islamic political' are essentially synonymous in this regard.[2]

Frequently, references to Islamism explicitly assume that Islam in political mode is a problem, a threat or a contradiction to democratic norms. Much more frequently, there is an underlying, unstated assumption (which is always much more dangerous) that such is the case; some observers go so far as to assume – incorrectly – that Islamism can be equated with al-Qaedaism. For too long analysts, Western governments and Islamic governments themselves have operated on the assumption that Islamism is unacceptable, as it stands in contradiction to democracy, and so must be banned or suppressed.

This assumption does not stand up to scrutiny. It is the practical form

Islamism takes that is crucial. If it takes the view that 'one man (literally) one vote, one time' is the correct approach, (in other words once they win the election they will allow no further elections) then clearly this is a major problem for the development of freedom and democracy. If the Islamist party, however, accepts that a popular mandate can remove the party from office as well as put it into office and is broadly willing to work within democratic structures, treating such a party as a threat to democracy is in itself a hindrance to the development of democracy.

As we will see in Chapter 5, feelings of rage are widespread amongst many Muslims in the world today. The underlying issues that have generated this rage must be addressed. If Islamic parties are unable to express their aims peacefully through democratic means, they may be be expressed in much more unpleasant fashion through al-Qaedaism.

The ICG says: 'Debate over these issues has become bogged down in a welter of fixed but erroneous ideas. One is the notion that posits a simple chain of cause and effect: absence of political reform generates Islamism, which in turn generates terrorism. This simplistic analysis ignores the considerable diversity within contemporary Islamic activism, the greater part of which has been consistently non-violent. It also overlooks the fact that the rise of Islamist movements in North Africa has not been predicated on the absence of reform but has generally occurred in connection with ambitious government reform projects.'[2]

Graham E. Fuller (a former vice-chairman of the National Intelligence Council at the CIA) comments: 'Whether the United States likes it or not, it simply cannot avoid dealing with the single biggest political movement across the entire Muslim world, Islamism, in all its diversity, differences and ongoing evolution. Everyone knows the Muslim world is rife with grievances, frustrations and anger. Today these grievances are expressed through a vehicle of Islamist rhetoric and ideology. Yet these same grievances were articulated many decades ago through a different ideological vehicle – the radical Arab nationalism led by Gamal Abdel Nasser in the 1950s and 1960s – expressing much of the same strong anti-imperialist bent. When Nasserism failed to produce results, Marxism-Leninism and later Islamism became its natural successor. Thus, even if an ideological vehicle can be suppressed or destroyed, the grievances that create such will not vanish but will simply seek new vehicles. By accommodating rather than suppressing

Islamist expression of many popular grievances, Turkey has set important precedents for the Muslim world.

'Turkey has arguably solved, to the extent that any political problem can be considered permanently solved, the problem of political Islam by a combination of just the right degree of pressures and freedoms to allow a vibrant and healthy Islamic-oriented political party to emerge and even flourish.'[3]

It is vitally important to realise, therefore, that Islamism is not necessarily a negative force in political or democratic terms. Nor does Islamism necessarily lead to support for al-Qaedaism, or activism associated with al-Qaeda or similar groups. The issue is the specific manner in which an Islamist expresses his or her beliefs.

How then does our subject, al-Qaeda and al-Qaedaism, fit in? Jason Burke sees al-Qaeda as: 'less an organisation than an ideology. The Arabic word "Qaeda" can be translated as a "base of operation" or "foundation", or alternatively as a "precept" or "method". Islamic militants always understood the term in the latter sense. In 1987, Abdulah Azzam, the leading ideologue for modern Sunni Muslim radical activists, called for "al-Qaeda Al-Sulbah" ("a vanguard of the strong"). He envisaged men who, acting independently, would set an example for the rest of the Islamic world and thus galvanise the *umma* (global community of believers) against its oppressors.

'Although [Osama] bin Laden and his partners were able to create a structure in Afghanistan that attracted new recruits and forged links among pre-existing Islamic militant groups, they never created a coherent terrorist network in the way commonly conceived. Instead, al-Qaeda functioned like a venture capital firm – providing funding, contacts and expert advice to many different militant groups and individuals from all over the Islamic world.

'Today, the structure that was built in Afghanistan has been destroyed, and [Osama] bin Laden and his associates have scattered or been arrested or killed. There is no longer a central hub for Islamic militancy. But the al-Qaeda worldview, or 'al-Qaedaism', is growing stronger every day. This radical internationalist ideology – sustained by anti-Western, anti-Zionist and anti-Semitic rhetoric – has adherents among many individuals and groups, few of whom are currently linked in any substantial way to [Osama] bin Laden or those around him. They merely follow his precepts, models and methods. They act in the style of al-Qaeda, but they are part of al-Qaeda only in the very loosest sense.'[1]

The key point here is that al-Qaeda is an ideology rather than a tightly controlled terrorist group such as the IRA or ETA. (This, of course, makes the groups associated with this ideology even more dangerous, as such a movement cannot be decapitated or rounded up in a major security operation.)

The US political magazine *FrontPage* held a symposium with five terrorism experts from the Rand think-tank on 18 August 2003. (Rand became famous during the cold war for its research and advice, frequently for the US Air Force, on deterrence and other matters.) The five experts were Brian Jenkins, Bruce Hoffman, John Parachini, William Rosenau and Gregory Treverton. Their answers to the first question from the magazine as to whether al-Qaeda was a monolithic entity or not are revealing:

HOFFMAN: 'Al-Qaeda is an ideology more than an army; a transnational movement and umbrella-like organization, not a monolithic entity. Al-Qaeda's strength has always been its ability to function on multiple operational levels. It uses professional terrorists, closely linked to the al-Qaeda command-and-control nucleus, for spectacular, highly lucrative strikes such as 9/11, the 1998 embassy bombings, and the attack on the *USS Cole* etc. In some instances it uses affiliated or associated groups it has trained, armed or otherwise inspired such as the Jemmah Islamiya, the predominantly Indonesian/Malayan/Filipino group responsible for the October 2002 Bali bombings, or the Sudanese group al Ittihad al Islamiya, which committed the attacks against Israeli targets the following month in Kenya. And it uses the so-called "local walk-ins" – individuals or groups with no previous direct, demonstrable al-Qaeda connection, but who are inspired, motivated or animated by [Osama] bin Laden and his implacable message of enmity against the West, the United States and Zionism. Because al-Qaeda is neither monolithic nor leaves a single, identifiable "footprint", nor has one set modus operandi, the movement itself is all the more formidable and resilient.

ROSENAU: 'Al-Qaeda is a worldview, not an organization. Before 9/11, some parts of the US intelligence community described al-Qaeda as a hierarchical, cellular terrorist group with [Osama] bin Laden at the centre, barking out orders to his "troops" in the field and plotting attacks around the world. This mistaken perception was a hangover from cold-war era thinking about terrorism, in which groups like the Japanese Red Army, the Red Army Faction, and Action Directe were organized into tight cells that received orders from their leadership. Al-Qaeda is nothing like that, although as I mentioned there is certainly a 'hard core' around [Osama] bin Laden involved in strategy, financing, and security.

'Like the anti-globalisation movement, al-Qaeda is made up of a politically, nationally and ethnically diverse group of militants who don't agree on everything but subscribe in general terms to an ideology. [Osama] bin Laden's genius was in packaging and promoting an ideology that found enormous appeal among some elements of the Muslim world, and that allowed militants engaged in local struggles to reconceptualise their fights as part of a broader global struggle against Crusaders, Christendom, Jews, etc. Ironically, this Islamist/Salafist/fundamentalist ideology shares many features with Marxism-Leninism – an ideology that al-Qaeda professes to despise (e.g. a belief in a revolutionary "vanguard", the goal of "liberation" from various economic and class oppressions, etc).

'There is no question that this ideology appeals only to a fringe – but that fringe may have millions of members. Our failure to confront this ideology, and to work with those in the Muslim world who are promoting alternatives, is the biggest failure of our global campaign against terrorism. The State Department, the Pentagon, the National Security Council and other agencies are all trying to come to grips with this. With the exception of limited tactical psychological operations (e.g. dropping leaflets), we don't seem able to take action that can de-legitimise this ideology.

PARACHINI: 'Al-Qaeda has evolved from a loosely aligned network of militant Islamic terrorists who shared the formative experience of expelling Soviet forces from Afghanistan to a movement with adherents around the world enabling a global reach. Al-Qaeda has never been a monolithic entity, but a movement populated by Islamic militants from around the globe who answered the call to wage jihad in Afghanistan. Different radical Islamic groups around the world now view their local struggles against national governments, rival ethnic or religious groups, in a broader context. Core followers of Osama bin Laden either originate from the countries with one of these local struggles or have developed contacts with them during and since the conflict with the Soviets.

'The core followers stimulate local actions with inspiration, money,

planning, logistics, and sometimes personnel. The local or regional operatives build upon this contact. Thus, regional or local attacks are cast in a
global context by their perpetrators, and operatives functioning on a global basis have local targets that give purpose to the broader, almost cosmic
struggle.

JENKINS: 'Al-Qaeda is more than an organization. It is an ideology, a
galaxy of extremists, and an enterprise for turning Islam's discontents
into commitment for its brand of jihad. The pre-9/11 al-Qaeda was
chaired by Osama bin Laden, and comprised a consultative council, separate divisions devoted to specific functional areas – training, operations,
education, etc – a global network of paid operatives, centralized training,
an extensive recruiting network, and a large population of trained veterans. Al-Qaeda maintained relations with and offered training and other
forms of assistance to members of like-minded groups, although these
groups have kept their own organisational structures. Since 9/11, al-
Qaeda appears to have adapted to a more hostile operating environment
with greater clandestinity, a smaller physical infrastructure, and more
decentralized operations relying on already dispersed Afghanistan veterans and affiliated groups.

TREVERTON: 'I share the view that al-Qaeda is a loose network. It is
worth remembering, for all its "virtual-ness", that it began with terrorists
from around the world face-to-face in Afghanistan. Now, shards of that
network remain, or local "affiliates" with overlapping agendas. We are, I
think, sometimes misled by our notion of "network", which we think of
as tightly coupled, something like old-fashioned holiday lights wired in
series, so that if one went out, they all went out.' [4]

Based on the above, I focus in this book on the overall strategic threat from
what I term 'al-Qaedaists' – members of groups associated with al-Qaeda –
rather than on the al-Qaeda organisation per se. Destroying the al-Qaeda
organisation would not end the threat from al-Qaedaism: the broader issues
underlying support for al-Qaedaism would still need to be addressed and
resolved.

Al-Qaedaists can be divided broadly into three groups. The first – the
militant core in al-Qaeda and some affiliated groups – is the most dangerous and cannot be negotiated with. They view their relations with the West
– and others – as constituting all-out war. Their war, as we will see, is against

almost the entire world, including Sunni Muslims who do not agree with them, all Muslim minorities, (including the Shiites), Jews and Christians, as well as members of all other religions in the world and atheists.

The second group – those who are affiliated with al-Qaeda and broadly share the international aims of al-Qaedaism – are mainly provoked by national or local issues. They can be negotiated with, and a mixture of 'hard' and 'soft' power can be used to focus them on national and local issues and to detach them from the core of al-Qaeda and thereby reduce the threat they pose. (Hard power refers to the use of military force, while soft power, a term coined by Joseph Nye, refers to all other forms of influence, including diplomatic, economic, financial and cultural means.)

The third group – local 'walk-ins' and those who support the broad ideology of al-Qaedaism but have not yet become activists (and there are millions of them) – can only be detached from the core by soft-focused power, such as a 'Marshall Plan for Islam' (discussed in Chapter 6), applied over a lengthy period of time.

Now, let us define terrorism and place the current terrorist wave in its proper historical perspective. As Audrey Kurth Cronin has put it: 'Terrorism is intended to be a matter of perception and is thus seen differently by different observers.' After a discussion on the different characteristics of terrorism, she concludes: 'Thus, at a minimum, terrorism has the following characteristics: a fundamentally political nature, the surprise use of violence against seemingly random targets, and the targeting of the innocent by non-state actors.'

With respect to the historical perspective, she goes on to say: 'David Rapaport has described modern terrorism such as that perpetuated by al-Qaeda as part of a religiously inspired "fourth wave". This wave follows three earlier historical phases in which terrorism was tied to the break-up of empires, decolonisation, and leftist anti-Westernism. Rapaport argues that terrorism occurs in consecutive if somewhat overlapping waves.

'In the nineteenth century, the unleashing of concepts such as universal suffrage and popular empowerment raised the hopes of people throughout the Western World, indirectly resulting in the first phase of modern terrorism. Originating in Russia, as Rapaport argues, it was stimulated not by state repression but by the efforts of the czars to placate demands for economic and political reforms, and the inevitable disappointment of popular expectations that were raised as a result. The goal of terrorists was to engage in attacks on symbolic targets to get the attention of the common people and thus provoke a popular response that would ultimately overturn the prevailing political order. This type of modern terrorism was reflected in the activities of groups such as the Russian Narodnaya Volya (People's Will) and later in the development of a series of movements in the United States and Europe, especially in territories of the former Ottoman Empire.

The dissolution of empires and the search for a new distribution of political power provided an opportunity for terrorism in the nineteenth and twentieth centuries. It climaxed in the assassination of Archduke Franz Ferdinand on 28 June 1914, an event that catalysed the major powers into taking violent action, not because of the significance of the man himself but because of the suspicion of rival state involvement in the sponsorship of the killing. World War I, the convulsive systemic cataclysm that resulted, ended the first era of modern terrorism, according to Rapaport. But terrorism tied to popular movements seeking greater democratic representation and political power from coercive empires has not ceased. Consider, for example, the Balkans after the downfall of the former state of Yugoslavia. The struggle for power among various Balkan ethnic groups can be seen as the final devolution of power from the former Ottoman Empire. This post-imperial scramble is also in evidence elsewhere – for example, in Aceh [in Indonesia], Chechnya and Xinjiang [in China], to mention just a few of the trouble spots within vast (former) empires. The presentation of a target of opportunity, such as a liberalizing state or regime, frequently evokes outrageous terrorist acts.

According to Rapaport, a second, related phase of modern terrorism associated with the concept of national self-determination developed its greatest predominance after World War I – and indeed continues to the present day. These struggles for power are another facet of terrorism against larger political powers and are specifically designed to win political independence or autonomy. The mid-twentieth-century era of rapid decolonisation spawned national movements in territories as diverse as Algeria, Israel, South Africa and Vietnam. An important by-product was ambivalence towards the phenomenon in the international community, with haggling over the definition of terrorism reaching fever pitch in the United Nations by the 1970s.

'The question of political motivation became important in determining international attitudes toward terrorist attacks as the post-World War II backlash against the colonial powers and the attractiveness of national independence movements led to the creation of a plethora of new states, which were often born out of violence. Arguments over the justice of international causes and the designation of terrorist struggles as "wars of national liberation" predominated, with consequentialist philosophies excusing the killing of innocent people if the cause in the long run was "just". Rapaport sees the US intervention in Vietnam, and especially the subsequent American defeat by the Vietcong, as having catalysed a "third wave" of modern terrorism; the relationship between the Vietnam war and other decolonisation movements might just as easily be considered as being part of the same phase, however. In any case, the victory of the Vietcong excited the imaginations of revolutionaries throughout the world and, according to Rapaport, helped lead to a resurgence in terrorist violence. The Soviet Union underwrote the nationalist and leftist terrorist agendas of some groups, depicting the United States as the new colonial power – an easy task following the Vietnam intervention – and furthering an ideological agenda that was oriented towards achieving a postcapitalist, international communist utopia. Other groups, especially in Western Europe, rejected both the Soviet and capitalist models and looked admiringly toward nationalist revolutionaries in the developing world. Leftist groups no longer predominate, but the enduring search for national self-determination continues, not only in the areas mentioned above but also in other hot spots such as the Basque region [in Spain], East Timor, Sri Lanka and Sudan.

'Terrorism achieved a firmly international character during the 1970s and 1980s, evolving in part as a result of technological advances and partly in reaction to the explosion in the influence of the international media. International links [between terrorist organisations] were not new, but their centrality was. Individual, scattered national causes began to develop into international organizations, with links and activities increasingly across borders and among differing causes. This development was greatly facilitated by the covert sponsorship of states such as Iran, Libya and North Korea, and of course the Soviet Union, which found the underwriting of terrorist organizations to be an attractive tool for accomplishing clandestine goals while avoiding potential retaliation for the terrorist attacks.

'The 1970s and 1980s represented the high point of state-sponsored terrorism. Sometimes the lowest common denominator among the groups involved was the concept against which they were reacting – for example, "Western imperialism" – rather than the specific goals they sought. The most important innovation, however, was the increasing commonality of international connections among the groups. After the 1972 Munich Olympics massacre of eleven Israeli athletes, for example, the Palestinian Liberation Organization (PLO) and its associated groups captured the imaginations of young radicals around the world. In Lebanon and elsewhere, the PLO also provided training in the preferred techniques of twentieth-century terrorism, which included airline hijacking, hostage-taking and bombing.

'Since the September 11 attacks, the world has witnessed the maturation of a new phase of terrorist activity, the jihad era, spawned by the Iranian Revolution of 1979 and by the Soviet defeat in Afghanistan soon afterwards. The powerful attraction of religious and spiritual movements has overshadowed the nationalist or leftist revolutionary ethos of earlier terrorist phases (though many of those struggles continue), and it has become the central characteristic of a growing international trend. It is perhaps ironic that, as Rapaport observes, the forces of history seem to be driving international terrorism back to a much earlier time, with echoes of the behaviour of "sacred" terrorists such as the Zealots-Sicarii [a Jewish religious terrorist group active in Palestine c. 66–72 AD] clearly apparent in the terrorist activities of organizations such as al-Qaeda and its associated groups. Religious terrorism is not new; rather, it is a continuation of an ongoing struggle between those with power and those without it. Internationally, the main targets of these terrorists are the United States and the US-led global system.

'Like other eras of modern terrorism, this latest phase has deep roots. And, given the historical patterns, it is likely to last at least a generation, if not longer. The jihad era is animated by widespread alienation combined with elements of religious identity and doctrine: a dangerous mixture of forces that resonate deep in the human psyche.'[5]

Audrey Kurth Cronin and others have pointed out that currently four types of terrorist groups are active worldwide: left-wing terrorists, right-wing terrorists, separatist/ethno-nationalist terrorists and finally religious (or 'sacred') terrorists. Most experts agree that, as Kurth Cronin notes, 'All four types of terrorist organizations are capable of egregious acts of barbarism. But religious terrorists may be especially dangerous to international security for at least five reasons.

'First, religious terrorists often feel engaged in a Manichaean struggle of good against evil, implying an open-ended set of human targets: anyone who is not a member of their religion or religious sect may be 'evil', and thus fair game. Although indiscriminate attacks are not unique to religious terrorists, the exclusivity of their faith may lead them to dehumanise their victims even more than most terrorist groups do, because they consider non-members to be infidels or apostates – as perhaps, for instance, al-Qaeda operatives may have viewed the Muslims killed in the World Trade Centre.

'Second, religious terrorists engage in violent behaviour directly or indirectly to please the perceived commands of a deity. This has a number of worrying implications: the whims of the deity may be less than obvious to those who are not members of the religion, so the actions of violent religious organizations can be especially unpredictable. Moreover, religious terrorists may not be as constrained in their behaviour by concerns about the reactions of their human constituents, as their audience lies elsewhere.

'Third, religious terrorists consider themselves to be unconstrained by secular values or laws. Indeed, the very target of the attacks may be the law-based secular society that is embodied in most modern states. Their driving motivation, therefore, is to overturn the current post-Westphalian state system – a much more fundamental threat than, say, ethno-nationalist terrorism aiming to carve out a new secular state or autonomous territory.

'Fourth, religious terrorists often display a complete sense of alienation from the existing social system. They are not trying to correct the system, making it more just, more perfect, and more egalitarian. Rather, they are trying to replace it. In some groups, apocalyptic images of destruction are seen as a necessity – even a purifying regimen – and this makes them uniquely dangerous, as was painfully learned on September 11.

'Fifth, religious terrorism is especially worrisome because of the dispersed popular support for it in civil society. On the one hand, groups such as al-Qaeda are able to find support from some Muslim nongovernmental foundations throughout the world, making it a truly global network. On the other hand, in the process of trying to distinguish between the relatively few providers of serious support for terrorist groups from the majority of genuinely philanthropic groups, there is a real risk of igniting the holy war that the terrorists are seeking.

'In sum, there are both enduring and new aspects to modern terrorism. The enduring features centre on the common political struggles that have characterized major acts of international terrorism. The newest and perhaps most alarming aspect of this phenomenon is the increasingly religious nature of modern terrorist groups. Against this historical background, the unique elements in the patterns of terrorist activity surrounding September 11 stand out in stark relief.

'By the late 1990s, four trends in modern terrorism were becoming apparent: an increase in the incidence of religiously motivated attacks, a decrease in the overall number of attacks, an increase in the lethality of attacks, and the growing targeting of Americans. Statistics show that, even before the September 11 attacks, religiously motivated terrorist organizations were becoming more common. The acceleration of this trend has been dramatic: according to the RAND–St Andrews University Chronology of International Terrorism, in 1968 none of the identified international terrorist organizations could be classified as 'religious'; in 1980, in the aftermath of the Iranian Revolution, there were two (out of sixty-four), and that number had expanded to twenty-five (out of fifty-eight) by 1995.

'Careful analysis of terrorism data compiled by the US Department of State reveals other important trends regarding the frequency and lethality of terrorist attacks. The good news was that there were fewer such attacks in the 1990s than in the 1980s: Internationally, the number of terrorist attacks in the 1990s averaged 382 per year, whereas in the 1980s the number per year had averaged 543. But even before September 11, the absolute number of casualties of international terrorism had increased, from a low of 344 in 1991 to a high of 6,693 in 1998. This jump in deaths and injuries can be partly explained by a few high-profile incidents, including the bombing of the US embassies in Nairobi and Dar-es-Salaam in 1998, but it is significant that more people became victims of terrorism as the decade proceeded. More worryingly, the number of people killed per incident rose significantly from 102 killed in 565 incidents in 1991 to 741 killed in 274 incidents in 1998. Thus, even though the number of terrorist attacks declined in the 1990s, the number of people killed in each one increased.

'Another important trend relates to terrorist attacks involving US targets. The number of such attacks increased in the 1990s, from a low of 66 in 1994 to a high of 200 in 2000. This is a long-established problem: US nationals have consistently been the most targeted group since 1968. But the percentage of international attacks against US targets or US citizens rose dramatically during the 1990s, from about 20 percent in 1993-95 to almost 50 percent in 2000. This is perhaps a consequence of the increased role and profile of the United States in the world, but the degree of increase is nonetheless troubling.

'The increasing lethality of terrorist attacks was already being noticed in the late 1990s, with many terrorism experts arguing that the tendency towards more casualties per incident had important implications. First, it meant that, as had been feared, religious or "sacred" terrorism was apparently more dangerous than the types of terrorism that had predominated earlier in the twentieth century. The world was facing the resurgence of a far more malignant type of terrorism, whose lethality was borne out in the larger death toll from incidents that increasingly involved a religious motivation. Second, with a premium now apparently being placed on causing more casualties per incident, the incentives for terrorist organizations to use chemical, biological, nuclear, or radiological weapons would multiply. The break-up of the Soviet Union and the resulting increased availability of Soviet chemical, biological, and nuclear weapons prompted experts to argue that groups that were seeking more dramatic and deadly results would be increasingly drawn to these weapons. The 1995 sarin-gas attack by the Japanese cult Aum Shinrikyo in the Tokyo subway system seemed to confirm this fear. More recently, an examination of evidence taken from Afghanistan and Pakistan reveals al-Qaeda's interest in chemical, biological and nuclear weapons.

'In addition to the evolving motivation and character of terrorist attacks, there has been a notable dispersal in the geography of terrorist acts – a trend that is likely to continue. Although the Middle East continues to be the locus of most terrorist activity, Central and South Asia, the Balkans and the Transcaucasus have been growing in significance in this regard over the past decade. International connections themselves are not new: international terrorist organizations inspired by common revolutionary principles date to the early nineteenth century; clandestine state use of foreign terrorist organizations occurred as early as the 1920s (e.g. the Mussolini government in Italy aided the Croat Ustasha); and complex mazes of funding, arms, and other state support for international terrorist organisations were in place in the 1970s and 1980s. During the cold war, terrorism was seen as a form of surrogate warfare and seemed almost palatable to some, at least compared to the potential prospect of major war or nuclear cataclysm. What has changed is the self-generating nature of international terrorism, with its diverse economic means of support allowing terrorists to carry out attacks sometimes far from the organisation's base. As a result, there is an important and growing distinction between where a terrorist organization is spawned and where an attack is launched, making the attacks difficult to trace to their source.

'Reflecting all of these trends, al-Qaeda and its associated groups and individuals are harbingers of a new type of terrorist organization. Even if al-Qaeda ceases to exist (which is unlikely), the dramatic attacks of September 2001, and their political and economic effects, will continue to inspire groups that have similar motivations – particularly if the United States and its allies fail to develop broad-based, effective counter-terrorist policies over the long term. Moreover, there is significant evidence that the global links and activities that al-Qaeda and its associated groups perpetuated are not short-term or anomalous. Indeed, they are changing the nature of the terrorist threat as we move further into the twenty-first century. The resulting intersection between the United States, globalisation, and international terrorism will define the major challenges to international security.'[5]

A key concern with the new terrorism is the willingness and the desire to inflict mass casualties on targeted populations. As Kumar Ramakrishna puts it: 'Moreover, the religious-messianic motivation of the new terrorists appears to encourage the perpetration of mass casualties and indiscriminating terror. Previous terrorist organizations, whether motivated by political, nationalist anti-colonial, or revolutionary goals, were careful to refrain from indiscriminate attacks on civilians, precisely because they recognised that ultimately, (as Peter L. Bergen put it in "Picking up the pieces: what we can learn from – and about – 9/11", *Foreign Affairs*, volume 81, no.2, March-April 2002) "wanton violence could be counterproductive" and they needed popular support to attain their political aims. Al-Qaeda, on the other hand, because it is ideologically predisposed to see all Americans, civilians and combatants alike, as infidels, seems to have little compunction in targeting non-combatants. Moreover, the messianic orientation of the al-Qaeda leadership appears to explain their lack of discrete, negotiable political demands, apart from the stated intention of eliminating Western and American influence from Muslim lands as a prelude to setting up truly Islamic governments there. Hence, as Stephen Simon and Daniel Benjamin argue in their article "The Terror", published in *Survival* (Vol. 43, No. 4, Winter 2001–2002), the worrying new characteristic of the new terrorism is "the absence of a plausible political agenda", which is correlated with the "increased lethality of attacks" due to the "absence of constraints on violence". This lack of concern for mass civilian casualties is certainly one key reason why the horrific September 11 terrorist strikes were mounted. Nevertheless, despite his primordial hatred of infidels that justifies the use of virtually unlimited force against them, Osama bin Laden remains an utterly rational man: he is an experienced commander who possesses considerable operational experience from the Afghan jihad against the Soviets. In this context, Osama bin Laden, shrewdly judging the American public to be unwilling to bear major sacrifice – an assessment which he appears to have developed as a consequence of President Clinton's decision to withdraw US forces from Somalia in 1993 following the combat deaths of eighteen servicemen – deliberately seeks to generate very high levels of fear and anxiety amongst the American public. He probably holds that, at some point in the al-Qaeda campaign – probably after another series of spectacular mass-casualty strikes – the people will compel the American government to disengage from the Muslim world. The desire to target and destroy the will of the American people by employing extra-normal means of destruction against them is also the reason why al-Qaeda has sought to acquire WMD capabilities and may be plotting other "modalities of mass destruction" (MMD).

'In sum, while the essence of al-Qaeda's grand strategy of avoiding American strength and hitting American weakness is in fact familiar, the enhanced capacity of terrorists to rain death and destruction on societies, the increasingly pronounced vulnerability of societies to such attacks, and the religious-messianic predisposition of the terrorists to mass-casualty terrorism make this phenomenon distinct from previous terror waves.'[6]

A number of experts have correctly focused on the detailed planning and implementation of the September 11 attack to show that Western technology can, and will be used very effectively against it by these new terrorists.

To quote Ramakrishna again: 'This ability to tap the vast information resources of the World Wide Web enables terrorist organizations to "adapt their structure and strategy, including their use of violence, to their environment and to the degree and kind of pressure that governments can bring to bear against them". (David Tucker, in "What is New about the New Terrorism and How Dangerous is It?" *Terrorism and Political Violence*, Vol. 13, No. 3, Autumn 2001): This suggests that the well-educated new terrorists, many of whom seem to possess backgrounds in science and engineering, can think up creative ways of inflicting mass casualties quite apart from simply relying on Weapons of Mass Destruction (WMD). In other words, modern societies must be alert not merely to the threat of WMD use by terrorists but also to various MMD. Thomas Homer-Dixon[64] points out in this regard that "modern societies are filled with supercharged devices packed with energy combustibles and poisons, giving terrorists ample opportunities to destructive ends. To cause horrendous damage, all terrorists must do is figure out how to release this power and let it run wild or, as they did on September 11, take control of this power and retarget it." Homer-Dixon identifies, for instance, large gas pipelines running through urban areas, the radioactive waste-pools of nuclear reactors, and chemical plants as providing "countless opportunities for turning supposedly benign technology to destructive ends."'

'Not only has globalisation significantly increased the capacity of terrorists to wreak havoc, it has also enhanced the vulnerability of modern societies to the new terrorism in two ways. First, states have increasingly porous borders. People movements in and out of countries in recent decades have been greatly facilitated by the increasing convenience and affordability of air travel, and this has had direct implications for the current conflict with al-Qaeda. On the one hand, Muslim-diaspora communities incorporating small but significant minorities of radical elements have sprung up in America and in European countries. Moreover, in the case of the Middle East and Southeast Asia, the movement of thousands of Muslims between these regions and the centres of radical Islamic teaching in South Asia both during and after the Afghan jihad against the Soviet

Union, have resulted in the exposure of scores of moderate Muslims from Morocco to the Philippines to radical Islamic ideas.

'Furthermore, it should not be forgotten that the Internet contributes to the ideological permeability of modern societies, as the tenets of radical Islamic thinking can be disseminated effortlessly across national boundaries via cyberspace. Apart from what James Rosenau once called the "penetrated" nature of the modern state, globalisation processes have rendered modern societies extremely vulnerable to the new terrorism in another critical way. As Homer-Dixon has argued, a modern state represents not merely an extremely complex and densely packed network of cities, highways, railways, airports and power grids but, more importantly, a "tightly coupled, very unstable and highly non-linear psychological network." This network is wired together tightly by "Internet connections, satellite signals, fibre-optic cables, talk radio, and twenty-four-hour television news." These tight interconnections greatly expedited the rapid outward spread of the shock of the September 11 attacks. Consequently, al-Qaeda's strikes had their "biggest impact" on the "collective psychology" of Americans and their "subjective feelings of safety and security". In other words, the complex psychic network that makes up modern societies "acts like a huge megaphone, vastly amplifying the emotional impact of terrorism." Because al-Qaeda, as we have seen, seeks to physically target the American public, this novel feature of modern globalised societies significantly enhances its potential impact.'[6]

For fifteen years, strategic experts have been warning of the danger of terrorists using nuclear, radiological, biological, or chemical weapons of mass destruction. Only in the last few years, however, have terrorism experts begun to fully appreciate the significance of 9/11 in terms of terrorists' desire to inflict mass casualties and the related danger of Western technology and infrastructure being used as MMD to achieve such. The worry after 9/11 in the strategic-studies community is that matching the recent revolution in military affairs is a revolution in terrorism affairs, the latter reflecting a trend of smaller groups of terrorists that are anxious and willing to cause mass casualties and now clearly having the intention to do so – lacking only the capability. This is a fundamental change in the terrorism scene. What has been termed hyper-terrorism would involve terrorists using

WMD or MMD to inflict catastrophic casualties on civilian populations in targeted countries.

The Bush National Security Strategy, issued in September 2002, included the comment that: 'given the goals of rogue states and terrorists, the United States can no longer solely rely on a reactive posture as we have in the past. The inability to deter a potential attacker, the immediacy of today's threats, and the magnitude of potential harm that could be caused by an adversary's choice of weapons do not permit that option. We cannot let our enemies strike first.'[7]

Whatever about the need to preempt rogue states, a much disputed assertion, there is a valid point here with respect to terrorists. The key, and new, strategic development is the perceived inability to deter a non-state hyper-terrorist group that is intent on causing mass casualties. With no country or natural targets to hold hostage to their good behaviour, deterrence cannot be fully applied to such groups, unlike, say, the Soviet Union, which faced a catastrophic counter-strike if it had used WMD against the West.

To pose such a strategic threat – and clearly hyper-terrorism using WMD or MMD is a strategic threat – a terrorist group has to have the following characteristics: the intent to acquire and use WMD or MMD to inflict mass casualties, a global reach and a reasonable level of global support, and a reasonable-sized group of people prepared to commit suicide to achieve their aims. Unfortunately for the rest of the world, al-Qaedaism meets these three requirements.

With respect to the first characteristic, in 1998 Osama bin Laden issued a statement on 'the Nuclear Bomb of Islam', which said that 'it is the duty of Muslims to prepare as much force as possible to terrorise the enemies of God.'[8] In August 2001, [Osama] bin Laden received two key former officials from Pakistan's nuclear-weapons programme at his secret headquarters near Kabul. Over the course of three days of intense conversations, he and his second-in-command, the Egyptian surgeon and organisational mastermind [of al-Qaeda] Ayman al-Zawahiri, quizzed Sultan Basahiruddin Mahmood and Abdul Majeed about chemical, biological and, in particular, nuclear weapons.'[8] 'In the end, US intelligence agencies concluded that Mahmood and Majeed provided [Osama] bin Laden with a blueprint for constructing nuclear weapons.'[8]

In October 2004, it was reported that Osama bin Laden had sought religious justification from a senior Saudi Arabian theologian for a mass-casualty attack on the United States. This is believed to have resulted in the publication of a religious fatwa called 'Rules for the Use of WMD Against the Infidels' by Sheikh Nasser bin Hamad Al-Fahd, who is currently under arrest in Riyadh.

In addition to this clear interest in nuclear weapons, a ranking Taliban source declared with respect to Osama bin Laden that 'his priority is to use biological weapons'.[9] This intention has been reiterated on a number of occasions subsequently.

Expert opinion and understanding evolves. While the threat of any type of WMD in the hands of terrorists was originally seen as potentially catastrophic, it is now believed that the use of chemical and radiological WMD is likely to be much less destructive than that of biological and nuclear WMD and that the world should therefore focus in particular on the control of the latter two types of WMD. (I ignore here the psychological effects of the use of WMD, which are likely to vastly exceed the actual death and destruction caused by an attack, as Brian Michael Jenkins of RAND has pointed out.[10]) This change in focus has led to an understanding amongst the experts that biological WMD will be impossible to control fully and that, as a result, there is a very high likelihood of biological WMD being obtained by al-Qaeda. It is very significant that al-Qaeda had the very particular objective of acquiring biological WMD one or two years before expert opinion had fully appreciated the difficulties involved in controlling the diffusion of such WMD.

As Christopher Chyba and Alex Greninger say: 'Biotechnological capacity is increasing and spreading rapidly. This trend seems unstoppable, since the economic, medical and food-security benefits of genetic manipulation appear so great. As a consequence, thresholds for the artificial enhancement or creation of dangerous pathogens – disease-causing organisms – will steadily drop. The revolution in biotechnology will therefore almost inevitably place greater destructive power in the hands of smaller groups of the technically competent: those with skills sufficient to make use of the advances of the international scientific community. This future is being driven not primarily by military programmes, but rather by open, legitimate private and academic research.

'Lessons from the past half-century of relative success in blocking nuclear proliferation cannot be easily applied to the twenty-first-century challenge of biological proliferation. Neither cold-war bilateral arms control nor multilateral nonproliferation provide good models for how we are to manage this new challenge. *Much more than in the nuclear case, civilisation will have to cope with, rather than shape, its biological future. In the biological realm, we are entering an unprecedented world.*'[11] (Emphasis added.)

Four developments in the 1990s have led to this serious challenge to the world: an increase in the number of new infectious diseases (one per year on average for the previous two decades), the rise of mass-casualty terrorism, violations of the 1972 Biological and Toxic Weapons Convention (BWC), and dramatic advances in biotechnology.

An increasing number of experts now see this threat as a major one for the world. As Julian Perry Robinson and Matthew Meselson put it: 'The community of states may still be prepared to confer a qualified legitimacy on nuclear weapons – consistent with the NPT's [Nuclear Non Proliferation treaty] norms, obligations and ambitions – if they are needed to keep the peace between great powers. This conclusion is unlikely to be granted to CBW (chemical and biological weapons), not least because of their relative accessibility to non-state actors.' They continue: 'the rise of biotechnology ... poses a special problem, as it will inevitably develop means for manipulating cognition, development reproduction and heredity. Therein lie unprecedented and, in time, widely accessible possibilities for violence, coercion, repression or subjugation.' ... 'If left unchecked, biological weapons could become the most potent of all instruments for expressing enmity.'[12]

It is notable that in July 2001 the US government withdrew from the negotiations on an international protocol for compliance with the BWC, declaring it to be 'inherently unverifiable' due to past violations by Iraq, the Soviet Union and others, which violations they considered impossible to detect by 'normal' means.

The threat from biological weapons is therefore now seen in terms of the defence of public health rather than in inappropriate analogies to other WMD. Dealing with this threat will require a broad range of measures to make biological terrorism more difficult, including disease surveillance and response, anti-proliferation measures, increased security for dangerous stocks, the development of and stockpiling of vaccines, and the development and implementation of last-move defences (such as dealing with drug resistance on an organism-by-organism basis).[11]

Chyba and Greninger conclude: 'Broad-based and publicly acknowledged bio-defence research would aim to globalise dissuasion, convincing non-state terrorist groups that they cannot hope to counter the entire array of defences that the world's legitimate bio-defence research community has arrayed against them. With research on de facto "last-move" defences [a defence against the evolutionary counter-measures of natural microbes], the bio-defence community should thereby endeavour to circumvent, or at least mitigate, an otherwise endless biological [offence-defence] arms race.'[11]

It is therefore clear that we are facing into a potentially very difficult situation in this area, particularly with respect to biological WMD.

A number of experts believe that the threat of a nuclear attack is also quite serious. One, Dr Graham Allison, Director of the Belfer Center for Science and International Affairs at the John F. Kennedy School of Government in Harvard University, quotes the conclusion of Eugene Habiger, who ran the nuclear anti-terror programs for the US Department of Energy until 2001, on nuclear terrorism: 'It is not a matter of *if*, it's a matter of *when*.'[8] He then quotes the legendary investor Warren Buffett on a nuclear terrorist attack as 'The ultimate depressing thing. It will happen. It's inevitable. I don't see any way that it won't happen.'[8]

Allison's own conclusion is stark: 'On the current course, nuclear terrorism is inevitable. Indeed, if the US and other governments keep doing what they are doing today, a nuclear terrorist attack on America is more likely than not in the decade ahead. With a ten-kiloton nuclear weapon stolen from the former Soviet arsenal and delivered to an American city in a cargo container, al-Qaeda can make 9/11 a footnote. And if not al-Qaeda, one of its affiliates can step up, using a weapon built from HEU (highly enriched uranium) from Pakistan or North Korea or from a research reactor in Uzbekistan.'[8]

Acquiring any type of WMD and using them enables al-Qaedists to potentially inflict mass casualties on their enemies, as would an MMD attack which was appropriately directed. As the International Institute for

Strategic Studies (IISS) put it: 'Al-Qaeda spokesman Suleiman Abu Ghaith has said that there can be no truce until the group has killed 4 million Americans, whereupon others could convert to Islam.'[13] This al-Qaeda spokesman's statement is worth quoting at length: 'We have not reached parity with them. We have the right to kill 4 million Americans – 2 million of them children – and to exile twice as many and wound and cripple hundreds of thousands. Furthermore, it is our right to fight them with chemical and biological weapons so as to inflict them with the fatal maladies that have afflicted the Muslims because of the [Americans'] chemical and biological weapons.'[14] Dr Allison points out that nuclear attacks on four major US cities, if properly targeted, would achieve this objective of killing 4 million Americans.[8] Recent claims (made on the flagship CBS news programme *60 Minutes*) that Osama bin Laden had obtained religious approval for the use of WMD would fit with the consistent approach taken by al-Qaedaists in getting spurious religious justification for 9/11 and other terrorist attacks.

So al-Qaedaism clearly meets the first requirement to be a strategic threat to the world: its members have the clear intent to acquire WMD or to use MMD to inflict mass casualties. Secondly, al-Qaedaism clearly has global reach, having carried out attacks in the United States, Asia, Africa and Europe. The flat, dispersed and franchised structure of al-Qaedaist groups gives them global support, with many of their activists new to the game. This makes the detection of and protection against terrorist attacks particularly difficult for the police and the intelligence community. Finally, al-Qaedaists have shown in 9/11 and other attacks an ability to get groups of people to commit suicide on a coordinated basis, with the practical intent of causing mass casualties. Therefore, al-Qaeda in the broadest sense meets the definition of a hyper-terrorist group: all it lacks is the actual possession of WMD or the more lethal usage of MMD. It is this unique configuration in al-Qaedaism of globally supported terrorist capabilities, a willingness to commit suicide, and a desire and intent to inflict mass casualties on its enemies that makes it a strategic threat to the world.

The Bush National Security Strategy, while it does not name al-Qaeda, clearly confirms this view and understanding and has acted forcefully upon it. The EU in its Security Strategy, which does name al-Qaeda, takes the same view, placing terrorism and the proliferation of WMD as the first two key threats to the EU. It goes on to say that 'taking these different elements together – terrorism committed to maximum violence, the availability of WMD, organised crime, the weakening of the state system and the privatisation of force – we would be confronted with a very radical threat indeed.'[15]

This threat also meets the definition of terrorism arrived at for the UN by the High-level Panel on Threats, Challenges and Change, set up by Kofi Annan in 2003. Annan stated that the panel had agreed the definition of terrorism as 'any action intended to kill or seriously harm civilians or non-combatants, with the purpose of intimidating a population or compelling action by a government or international organisation.'[16] The formal definition of terrorism by this body is 'any action, in addition to actions already specified by the existing conventions on aspects of terrorism, the Geneva Convention and Security Council Resolution 1566 (2004), that is intended to cause death or serious bodily harm to civilians and non-combatants, when the purpose of such an act, by its nature or context, is to intimidate a population or to compel a government or an international organisation to do or to abstain from doing any act.'[17]

This new strategic threat is fully appreciated in the strategic-studies community and in the United States but is not fully appreciated in Europe or the rest of the world, for a variety of reasons, including the negative reaction to the Bush National Security Strategy and particularly its reference to pre-emptive war, the polarisation arising from the debate on, and the invasion of, Iraq, the inability to find stocks of WMD as expected in Iraq, and the lengthy historic experience of Europe and the rest of the world with conventional terrorism.

Most outside the United States have delinked terrorism from WMD and any threat with respect thereto. There is also an understandable but historically lethal tendency to ignore emerging threats until it is almost too late.

If al-Qaedaism was a major threat at one stage, is it still such a threat now? There are three reasons for raising this question: the defeat of al-Qaeda and the Taliban regime in Afghanistan, the absence of a second 9/11, and the views of a number of experts that al-Qaeda has had its day and militant Islamism is in decline. This latter thesis was advanced by Gilles Kepel in his book *Jihad: The Trail of Political Islam,* which was published, with unfortunate timing, shortly after 9/11.

For a series of reasons set out below, particularly the depth of the rage against the West in the Islamic world, the great success al-Qaedaism has had in using modern technology to disseminate its propaganda, the continuing terrorist attacks, and the persistent crisis in the Islamic world, I believe that we will continue to confront this threat for some time, even if Osama bin Laden is killed and most al-Qaedaist activists are killed or captured.

An up-to-date independent assessment of this issue was contained in an essay on international terrorism in the *Military Balance,* published by the IISS in October 2004.[18] 'Overall, risks of terrorism to Westerners and Western assets in Arab countries appeared to increase after the Iraq war began in March 2003. With the military invasion and occupation of Iraq, the United States demonstrated its desire to change the political status quo in the Arab world to advance American strategic and political interests. Al-Qaeda seeks, among other things, to purge the Arab and larger Muslim world of US influence. Accordingly, the Iraq intervention was always likely in the short term to enhance jihadist recruitment and intensify al-Qaeda's motivation to encourage and assist terrorist operations. The May 2003 attacks in Saudi Arabia and Morocco, the gathering of foreign jihadists in Iraq, the November 2003 attacks in Saudi Arabia and Turkey, and the March 2004 bombings in Madrid confirmed this expectation.

'The Afghanistan intervention that began in October 2001 offensively hobbled, but defensively benefited, al-Qaeda. While al-Qaeda lost a recruiting magnet and a training, command and operations base, it was compelled to disperse and become even more decentralised, 'virtual' and invisible. Conservative intelligence estimates indicate that al-Qaeda is present in more than sixty countries, and that at least 20,000 jihadists were trained in its Afghanistan camps since 1996. Although half of al-Qaeda's thirty senior leaders and perhaps two thousand rank-and-file members have been killed or captured, a rump leadership is still intact and over eighteen thousand potential terrorists are at large. Naturally, only a small number of that total are likely to be hard-core terrorists; a substantially larger number would be peripheral support players, providing technical, logistical or financial assistance; and the remainder might merely be operationally inactive individuals who support al-Qaeda's political and religious agenda but who remain susceptible to becoming active terrorists on precisely that account. This breakdown is roughly analogous to the configuration of more traditional terrorist organisations or insurgencies. To fairly characterise al-Qaeda's pool at any given moment, one would have to add to this number an unspecified increment of those recruited directly through the enlistment of local groups – which in turn recruit on their own – since the Afghan training camps were eliminated in late 2001. It is probable that recruitment generally has accelerated on account of Iraq.

'Al-Qaeda's cells still appear to operate semi-autonomously, maintaining links through field commanders to leaders who are probably in Pakistan's "tribal areas" near the Afghan border. On account of its offensive limitations, al-Qaeda must now relinquish substantial operational initiative and responsibility to local talent, which post-attack investigations have revealed usually include jihadists trained in Afghanistan. Still, experienced al-Qaeda middle managers can provide planning and logistical advice, material and financing to smaller groups, as they did in Saudi Arabia, Morocco and Indonesia, and probably Turkey and Kenya. Al-Qaeda is the common ideological and logistical hub for disparate local affiliates, and [Osama] bin Laden's charisma, presumed survival and elusiveness enhance the organisation's iconic drawing power. Galvanised by Iraq, if compromised by Afghanistan, al-Qaeda remains a viable and effective "network of networks".

'The Madrid bombings in March 2004 suggested that al-Qaeda's network had fully reconstituted, set its sights firmly on the United States and its closest Western allies in Europe, and established a new and effective modus operandi. While al-Qaeda remained a generally even flatter and less hierarchical organisation than it had been prior to the Afghanistan intervention, US agencies developed intelligence suggesting that certain functions – in particular, bomb-making – may be more centralised and therefore potentially more efficient and sophisticated than earlier believed. Al-Qaeda will keep trying to develop more promising plans for terrorist operations in North America and Europe. *These potentially involve weapons of mass destruction or disruption, which al-Qaeda is known to want to develop but is not believed to possess yet in operational form.* [Emphasis added.] Meanwhile, soft targets encompassing Americans, Europeans and Israelis, and aiding the insurgency in Iraq, will do. Given the group's maximalist objectives and transnational ubiquity and covertness, stiff operational counter-terrorist measures, inter-governmentally coordinated, are still acutely required. Progress will come incrementally. It is likely to accelerate only with currently elusive political developments that would broadly depress recruitment and motivation, such as the stable democratisation of Iraq or resolution of the Israeli-Palestinian conflict. A survey of the activity of al-Qaeda and its affiliates in separate geographical areas indicates that the magnitude and complexity of the counter-terrorism challenge remain substantial.

'Western Europe. Radical Islam appears to be on the rise in Western Europe. Furthermore, the sources of European Muslims' grievances – customarily "diaspora" concerns involving political conditions in their countries of origin, such as Algeria – are increasingly social, economic and political marginalisation in host countries. This "universalisation" of Muslim complaints dovetails with al-Qaeda's anti-Western and pan-Islamic agenda. It follows that jihadist recruitment seems to be increasing in Western Europe. In addition, Europe's southern exposure to the Maghreb has become an acute point of vulnerability, given the heavy involvement of North African operatives – Moroccans and Tunisians as well as Algerians – in terrorist attacks, notably those that occurred in Madrid in March 2004. There remain residual threats from more old-style ethno-nationalist terrorist groups such as the Basque separatists of *Euskadi ta Askatasuna* and various Irish groups. But the high political costs of their increasing violence since September 11 appear to have disinclined them to do so. The principle threat to Europe is now transnational Islamic terrorism, which potentially entails mass-casualty attacks that the old groups eschewed.

'Central Asia. Several hundred Taliban and al-Qaeda holdouts – including Taliban leader Mullah Omar and al-Qaeda leaders [Osama] bin Laden and al-Zawahiri – remain at large in the "tribal areas" of northwestern Pakistan near the Afghan border. Both groups appear to be able to win fresh recruits among Deobandi madrassa [radical Sunni religious schools] graduates, and to benefit from some assistance from anti-American Islamist warlord Gulbuddin Hikmatyar's militia, and at least passive tactical support from elements within Pakistan's Inter-Service Intelligence agency.'[18]

Another expert, Kumar Ramakrishna, also agrees that the threat from al-Qaeda has not gone away: 'Even if the [global anti-terror] coalition succeeds in disrupting al-Qaeda cells across the world; even if the transnational terrorist funding flows are interdicted, and even if radical Muslims are somehow denied capabilities to produce and deliver WMD, the threat would not necessarily be eradicated. Globalisation has expedited what Thomas Friedman calls the "democratisation" of finance, technology and information. Consequently, a fanatically determined radical Islamic core that is scattered throughout the world – but leveraging on communications technology to coordinate activities and manpower movement – can, over time, generate new cells, reconstruct disrupted logistics and funding networks while clandestinely restoring access to WMD capabilities.'[6]

Bruce Hoffman, an authority on terrorism from Rand, had this to say on the subject: 'In conclusion, whatever the future holds for [Osama] bin Laden and al-Qaeda, it is indisputable that they have had a seismic effect on the United States and the entire world. [Osama] bin Laden is in fact one of the few people alive who can claim to have fundamentally changed the course of history. And, in this respect, the epic battle that he launched is not over yet. The multiyear planning period of all previous al-Qaeda spectaculars alone suggests that it is too soon to write off either [Osama] bin Laden or his jihadists. Accordingly, some monumental new operation may have been set in motion before 9/11 that is now slowly and inexorably unfolding. Indeed, because of the destruction of the Taliban and because of what al-Qaeda sees as America's global 'war on Islam', the movement's sense of commitment and purpose today is arguably greater than ever.'[19]

UN bodies agree with these independent assessments, especially with respect to WMD. The IISS, reviewing the UN 'Report of the High-Level Panel on Threats, Challenges and Change', had this to say: 'The United States, in particular, should welcome the frank and unequivocal acknowledgement which the report makes of the possible use of nuclear, chemical and biological weapons.'[17]

Further, in February 2005, according to the *Irish Times:* 'In New York a UN team monitoring sanctions on al-Qaeda predicted yesterday that there would be an escalation in the brutality of terrorist attacks and warned that the network remains determined to strike around the world. Al-Qaeda still have a strong interest in acquiring chemical, biological, radiological and nuclear weapons, and it can only be "a matter of time" before a successful [WMD] attack occurs, the report said.'[20]

The strategic threat from al-Qaedaism clearly has not gone away. In fact,

a November 2004 *Adelphi* paper from the IISS concluded: 'The new terrorist threat is strategic, and it has spurred a worldwide mobilisation of intellectual and material resources comparable to that required by a world
war.'[21]

So the world is truly involved in a war with al-Qaedaism. But where has this
war, and the strategic threat posed by al-Qaedaism, come from? In particular, what makes al-Qaedaists capable of inflicting mass casualties on people
who are, by any normal legal or moral definition, completely innocent?

2

The Development of al-Qaedaism

'This vanguard constitutes the strong
foundation *(al-Qaeda al Sulbah)* for the expected society.'
ABDULLAH AZZAM

FOLLOWING THEIR DISPERSAL after the war in Afghanistan, al-Qaeda, which consists of the core al-Qaedaism militants, are now best seen as an umbrella organisation for a wide variety of terrorist groups and entities which share the same broad objectives or beliefs. Amongst those terrorist groupings are at least eighteen thousand trained in Afghan training camps since 1996 who have spread to more than sixty countries world-wide, either absorbing or liaising with groups such as the Egyptian Islamic Jihad, the Islamic movement of Uzbekistan, Abu Sayyaf in the Philippines, the Armed Islamic Group (GIA) of Algeria, Al-Ittihaad Al-Islamiya in East Africa, Ansar Al-Islam and other groups in Iraq, many groups in Kashmir, Jemaah Islamiah in Indonesia, and many others including the Taliban in Afghanistan. All commentators now agree that Osama bin Laden is best seen as a figurehead or rallying point for such groups rather than their outright leader.

A number of experts maintain that the total number of activists trained in core al-Qaeda camps in the Sudan, Yemen, Afghanistan and elsewhere now totals over one hundred thousand. The head of Germany's intelligence service put that number at about 70.000 at the World Economic Forum in Davos in January 2003.

Whatever their number, al-Qaedaists see themselves as a tiny vanguard of true believers. Everyone else in the world – all other Sunni Muslims who do not fully accept their 'guidance' and support them, Shiite and other Muslim minorities, all Muslim rulers (described as 'Muslim hypocrites'), Jews and Christians (frequently identified, targeted and referred to, as they are the peoples of the two religions which, in the eyes of the militants, were superseded by Islam), Hindus and Buddhists and the rest of the world – are enemies in their eyes. Minority sects in Islam (who number between 10 and 16 percent of the total Muslim population, i.e. between 130 million and more than 200 million people) such as the Shiites (the largest minority) are described by al-Qaedaist spokesmen as 'a sect of idolatry and apostasy' and considered to be 'the most evil creatures under the heavens'. To al-Qaedaists, the rest of the world, including most Muslims, other than their tiny vanguard, are considered to be *jahiliyya* – those involved in unbelief and cultural barbarism. This term was originally applied to the pagan period in the Arabian peninsula before the arrival of Islam. Applying the term to Muslim leaders and people was a revolutionary idea that was introduced by certain Islamist ideologists in the mid-twentieth century – which went against 1,300 years of Islamic thinking and tradition.

All people involved in such *jahiliyya* are subject to military jihad and may be killed without compunction. In terms of where such thinking has come from, it has been said by John Calvert that '[Osama] bin Laden's ideological vision must be seen as *an extreme manifestation* of a particular syndrome of Muslim reaction to the Western-dominated political and cultural order that has been over fifty years in the making. The word "syndrome" is apt, because the Muslim reaction is less a product of direct ideological influence (though individual thinkers and texts have had their effect) than of a cluster of disparate articulations of Islamic-oriented thought and practice that adhere fundamentally to two basic propositions.

'The first of these holds that the secular civilisation sponsored by the West is degenerate and devoid of ethical value, in sharp contrast to the civilisation based on the divinely revealed truth of Islam. The second proposition holds that secular culture in the Muslim world, including the allegedly corrupt regimes that uphold it, must be resisted vigorously and, if need be, forcefully. As is clear from the 9/11 attacks, some representatives of this syndrome, including Osama bin Laden and his close associate, the (Egyptian) Ayman al-Zawahiri, have decided to take their battle directly to the Western source of the perceived pollution of the Muslim world. Islam, according to those who adhere to these propositions, has engaged since its inception in a cultural struggle against forces that have attempted to sap its will, either forcefully, through conflict, or surreptitiously, by means of cultural contamination. Consequently, the tendency among such individuals has been to conceive of history simply as the waxing and waning of the authentic Islamic essence, and to conflate the mission of the Prophet Muhammad and the struggle of the contemporary period.

'Nor are these propositions the tap-root only of the present syndrome. Islamic history is replete with examples of movements that have rallied around the core principles of Islamic exceptionality and "jihad in the path of God". What distinguishes modern understandings of these propositions from earlier articulations is their purpose, which has been to fortify Muslim identity against the political and cultural encroachments of the West. This discourse of Muslim self-assertion, which in the West goes by the title "Islamism", is in dialectical relation to the civilisation that it seeks to rebuff. Against the Western hegemony of what constitutes the "good life", Islamists represent Islamic tradition not in terms of privatised religion but *as a comprehensive way of life concerned with all aspects of spiritual, political, social and cultural existence.'* [Emphasis added.]

'[Sayyid] Qutb (a foundational thinker to al-Qaedaism) underscored his denial of the legitimacy of the Egyptian republic by equating its moral universe with that of the *jahiliyya*. Traditionally, *jahiliyya* referred to the condition of unbelief and cultural barbarism current among the Arabs of the Arabian peninsula prior to the advent of the Prophet. *Jahiliyya*, in this sense, had a precise temporal meaning that distinguished Islam from the pre-Islamic period of degeneracy. Qutb, however, applied the term to those governments and societies in his own time (the 1940s and 1950s) which, in his view, functioned without the benefit of divine guidance. In Qutb's words: 'We are today in a state of jahiliyya similar to that which existed during the first period of Islam; perhaps it is a little darker. Everything that surrounds us, people's beliefs, ideas, habits and art, rules and law – is jahiliyya'.

[42]

According to Qutb, all societies in the world, without exception, were to be classified as jahili for their wilful ignorance of God's design for creation. These included, in his estimation, the "pagan" societies of India, Southeast Asia and regions of Africa, all Christian and Jewish societies, whose corrupted scriptures advanced the false notion of the separation of church and state, and atheistic communist societies. But Qutb broke new ground by including in this category the societies and governments of the so-called Muslim world: 'Although they believe in the unity of God, they hand over the legislative attribute of God to others and submit to their authority. . . . God most High says concerning such rulers: "Those who do not judge according to what God has revealed are unbelievers" (Koran 5:44).'[22]

In broad terms, therefore, al-Qaedaism despises the world, and particularly the United States as its key power, not simply for what it does but, crucially, for what it is. Al-Qaedaism, and the foundational Egyptian thinker behind many of its core ideas, Sayyid Qutb, as well as some Iranian and other Shiite militants, sees the United States in particular as the 'Great Satan' because of its supposed degeneracy and debauchery, its separation of church and state, and its supposed Judaeo-Christian ethos. The United States is not attacked or seen as a major threat by al-Qaedaists simply because of its actions or inaction, but rather for what it is: namely the 'seducer' of innocent Muslims.

The chart on the following page, the 'Tree of Influence', sets out the *people* who have had a significant influence on the development of al-Qaedaism.

It can be seen however that the biggest influence on al-Qaedaism has not been any individual thinker, ideologist or activist but the pervasive failure of Islam, in non-religious areas, for many hundreds of years, and its currently perceived appalling future, with both counterposed against a very successful and illustrious past. This failure has been identified within Islam for a considerable period of time and has led to many of the developments reviewed below.

IBN TAYMIYYA (1268–1328)

Ibn Taymiyya was an Islamic legal scholar, a theologian and a political

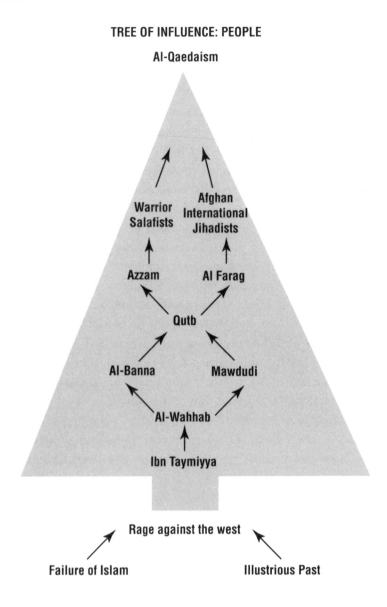

TREE OF INFLUENCE: PEOPLE

Al-Qaedaism

Warrior Salafists

Afghan International Jihadists

Azzam

Al Farag

Qutb

Al-Banna

Mawdudi

Al-Wahhab

Ibn Taymiyya

Rage against the west

Failure of Islam

Illustrious Past

figure. His thinking has had a direct impact on the Wahhabi movement, Sayyid Qutb and Muhammad Al Farag. He is seen by many as the spiritual father of revolutionary Sunni Islam, the wellspring of al-Qaedaism.

He lived in a tumultuous period in Islamic history which saw the fall of Baghdad to the Mongols in 1258 and the conquest of the Abbasid Empire. He and his family were forced to flee to Syria. He was a professor of

Hanbali law, the most conservative of the four Sunni schools of law.

His core beliefs include the view that there is an extremely close connection between society, religion (Islam) and the state; a rigorous, literalist interpretation of the Koran and other sacred sources; a belief that the community at Medina in the eighth century was a perfect model for an Islamic state; the need for a purification of Islam and for a return to the period of Muhammad and the first four Caliphs to restore Islam's glory; and a sharp distinction between the Dar Al-Islam ('the land of Islam') and the Dar Al-Kufr or Dar Al-Harb ('the land of unbelief or war').

The use of fatwas against unbelievers who are thus excommunicated is one of his key negative heritages and was directed by him at the invading Mongols, despite their conversion to Islam, as they continued to follow the legal code of Genghis Khan rather than the Sharia, or Islamic law. He considered them to be no better than the polytheists of pre-Islamic *jahiliyya*. This made them a lawful target of jihad: Muslim citizens thus had the duty to revolt against them and to wage military jihad against them until death.

Since then, many, including the assassins of Anwar Sadat in Egypt and various al-Qaedaists have used this precedent, issuing fatwas to call for jihad against Islamic rulers and elites, and against the West. They can then draw their own rigid distinctions and impose their own definition of true belief and unbelief, level the charge of unbelief, proclaim the excommunication of their targets and then call for jihad to the death on these unfortunates.

MUHAMMED IBN ABD AL-WAHHAB
(1703–87 OR 1703–92)

Wahhabism started in Saudi Arabia as one of the earliest Sunni attempts to reverse the decline of Islam. It was led by Muhammad ibn Abd al-Wahhab, who united the warring Arabian tribes and eventually established a modern state in Arabia. He himself preached a return to faith and obedience to the fundamental teachings of Islam, eliminating modernisation and its influences and combining same with discipline, piety and a sense of sacrifice. His son-in-law, Muhammad Ibn Saud, gave his name to modern Saudi Arabia.[49] Wahhabism is now the dominant religious influence in Saudi Arabia and has been exported by it to many Islamic countries. In essence, its tradition is religiously and politically conservative rather than revolutionary. Saudi Arabian activism through Wahhabi-oriented schools worldwide has, however, sometimes led to unintended consequences, such as the eventual alliance between Osama bin Laden and the Taliban, which has now turned against the leaders of Saudi Arabia, as well as the development of *jihadi madrasas* ('jihad' schools) in many Islamic states.

As John L. Esposito puts it: "Although originally associated with Saudi Arabia, Wahhabi Islam or Wahhabism has come to be used popularly, although inaccurately, as a blanket term for Islamic fundamentalism, religious extremism, and radicalism. For this reason, some prefer the terms Salafi or Salafiyya movement. This has the advantage of both reflecting the activists' claim to be returning to the pristine Islam of Muhammad and the first generation of Muslims (*salafi,* or pious ancestors) and of indicating, more accurately, that this ultraconservative, rigid and exclusivist worldview is common to many groups and organizations. Saudi Arabia's Wahhabi Islam is but one strand. Ultimately, both Wahhabi and Salafi can be misleading, as they are used as umbrella terms that incorporate diverse ideologies and movements, medieval and modern, non-violent and violent.

Since the late twentieth century, the term 'Wahhabi' has been applied to militant movements that have taken up arms against existing governments. This particular labelling is not all that new. In nineteenth-century colonial India, the British labelled indigenous, anti-imperialist, Islamic-revivalist movements 'Wahhabi'. In recent years, Wahhabi Islam has been identified not only with the Taliban and Osama bin Laden's al-Qaeda but also with Islamic opposition movements in other areas, in particular Russia, the Caucasus, Chechnya, Dagestan, and Central Asia.

The Wahhabi vision went international in the 1960s in response to the threat posed by Arab nationalism and socialism. It was fuelled by petrodollars, especially the wealth from skyrocketing revenues after the 1973 oil embargo. Saudi Arabia and other monarchies were threatened in particular by Nasserism and in general by radical Arab socialist governments that came to power promising a social revolution for the masses and condemning conservative Arab monarchies. Under the leadership of Prince (later King) Faisal, the Saudis championed a pan-Islamic policy against Nasser's 'secular, socialist' pan-Arabism, with its ties to 'atheistic communism' in the Soviet Union and Eastern Europe. Saudi Arabia asserted its global Islamic leadership as custodian of Islam's two holiest sites and made common cause with other Muslim governments in the struggle against Nassser and his disciple, Libya's Muammar Qaddafi.

The Saudi government also developed close ties with major Islamic movements such as the Muslim Brotherhood and the Jamaat-i-Islami. Despite significant differences, they shared a religious vision based on a return to the fundamentals of Islam and an antipathy to common enemies. Saudi Arabia gave asylum to Muslim Brothers such as Muhammad Qutb, the brother of Sayyid Qutb, who fled Nasser's suppression of the Brotherhood in the mid-1960s. The Saudi government and other Gulf countries provided significant funding for Islamic movements and conferences. Petrodollars became a major enabling mechanism for the movements to internationalise and spread organizationally, to translate the writings of al-Banna, Qutb, Mawdudi, and later to produce audiotapes to be distributed around the world, creating an international Islamist discourse. In addition, many Islamists from other countries, well educated and possessing needed professional and technical skills, were employed in the Gulf and could send funds back to their homelands to support mainstream and clandestine movements. Saudi funding to Islamic groups worldwide accelerated dramatically after the Iranian revolution [in 1979] in order to counter the challenge from Iran's alternative revolutionary (Shiite) Islamic system. Iran's call and support for a global (Sunni and Shiite) Islamic revolution and its funding of Shiite groups in the Middle East and South Asia to counter Saudi influence threatened Saudi Arabia's Islamic leadership.

Saudi initiatives produced a rapid growth of Islamist groups and the dissemination of their worldview and fundamentalist interpretation of Islam in many countries. The Islamists' informal alliance with the Saudis and their acceptance of refuge or patronage was in fact a marriage of convenience, since many regarded the monarchy to be an un-Islamic form of government and were critical of the un-Islamic behaviour and corruption of many royals.

Many of those benefiting from Saudi largesse learned that it came with a hefty price tag, the purification or eradication of local belief, practice and culture. Particular targets for purification are Sufism and Shiism. Much as Saudi armies destroyed major Shiite shrines in the nineteenth century, Saudi aid agencies have been responsible for the destruction or reconstruction of many historic mosques, libraries, Koran schools and cemeteries in Bosnia and Kosovo because their Ottoman architecture, decorations, frescos, and tombstones did not conform to Wahhabi iconoclastic aesthetics that regard statues, tombstones or artwork with human representations as idolatry and polytheism. To the extent that the Taliban reflected this puritanical, militant mentality – seen in their strict ban on television and music, their insistence on the veiling and public segregation of women, their use of religious police to enforce Islamic behaviour, and their destruction of Buddhist monuments – they have been labelled Wahhabi. However, Saudi and Taliban strict controls on some modern technology such as the Internet or satellite dishes have often been driven less by religious concerns than by security concerns. They certainly cannot represent a complete rejection of modern technology; Islam has not proven to be an obstacle in their use of other modern communications technology, weapons and transport."[23]

This Wahhabi ideology has usually found fertile soil in cultures or societies where economic development is weak and moral and political decay are rampant. Its claim that returning to a basic, more moral way of life will restore law and order (and the former glory of Islam) can be very attractive to those experiencing poverty and political repression. Wahhabism has had a direct impact on many Islamic thinkers and ideologists, and on al-Qaedaism.

HASAN AL-BANNA (1906–49)

Al-Banna set up the Muslim Brotherhood in Egypt in 1928 with the aim of strenghtening an Islamic society that was going through a serious crisis. Al-Banna was a teacher, a pious, educated man with a traditional Sunni Islamic religious background and a knowledge of Western thought. He primarily blamed the problems in Egypt and the Islamic decline on European imperialism and Egyptian elites who had westernised. He took the view that nationalism in Egypt had failed and sought an alternative approach.

Crucially, as John L. Esposito says: 'He rejected the preference for the spiritual jihad over a military one. Since Muslim lands had been invaded, he said, it was incumbent on all Muslims to repel their invaders, just as it was an Islamic imperative for Muslims to oppose rulers who block the establishment of Islamic governments.'[23]

He shared many of the views of Mawlana Mawdudi (founder of the Jammat-i Islami in Pakistan) whom we will consider next.

Esposito continues: 'The following represents the main points of the worldview that the two men shared:

1 Islam is a total, all-encompassing way of life that guides each person and his or her community and political life.
2 The Koran, God's revelation, and the Sunnah of the Prophet and the early Muslim community are the foundations of Muslim life, providing the models that guide daily actions.
3 Islamic law (Sharia) provides the ideal and blueprint for a modern Muslim society not dependent on Western models.
4 Departure from Islam and reliance on the West are the causes for Muslim decline. A return to the straight path of Islam will restore the identity, pride, success, power and wealth of the Islamic community in this life and merit eternal reward in the next.
5 Science and technology must be harnessed and used. This must be achieved within an Islamic context, not by dependence on foreign Western cultures, to avoid the westernisation and secularisation of society.
6 Jihad, to strive or struggle, both personally and in community, in ideas and in action to implement Islamic reform and revolution, is the means to bring about a successful Islamisation of society and the world.

'Both men posited a struggle between the forces of God and Satan, good and evil, darkness or ignorance and light. Each envisaged his organisation as a vanguard, a righteous community that would serve as a dynamic nucleus for true Islamic reformation within the broader society.'²³

As it has been applied by Sayyid Qutb and other Egyptian ideologists, the heritage of Al-Banna has had quite a negative effect. This is particularly the case with respect to his focus on the lesser military jihad over the greater spiritual or personal jihad. The Muslim Brotherhood, which Al-Banna set up, has been influential not only in Egypt but also in the Sudan, Jordan, Syria and a number of other states. It has taken the Brothers many years to live down the fact that Sayyid Qutb was a member. It has now, however, recovered much of its previous strength.

This unusual body currently combines aspects of a religious movement practising Islamic preaching or missionary activity, a strong social move-

ment, an extremely robust network of charitable education and sports associations and a – currently illegal – political party. It is presently accorded no
legal status either as a political party or as an association and so exists outside the law. At the same time, the state tolerates it and the Egyptian press
reports its activities.

Many of the Brothers have been abandoning revolutionary tactics for a
more social-democratic approach, working within the institutions of the
state rather than trying to overthrow them. This is particularly the case in
Egypt.

As the ICG puts it: 'This evolution of Egyptian Islamism is not unequivocal and some scepticism is in order. In rejecting Qutb's outlook, the
Muslim Brothers – the largest movement in Egypt today – initially referred
to Al-Banna's less radical perspective, and they have since followed a non-
violent and gradualist strategy. In subsequently incorporating the idea of
democracy into their discourse, the brothers departed from Al-Banna's
views, but this has not been fully acknowledged, still less accompanied by
an explicit repudiation of the illiberal and anti-democratic strand of Al-
Banna's thoughts. For this reason, it is liable to be interpreted as a pragmatic
and temporary adaptation to democracy rather than a wholehearted conversion to it. And conserving its purpose as a missionary movement –
Da'wa – the brothers have remained vulnerable to the government's charge
that theirs is a religious organisation, which it would be inappropriate to
legalise as a political party.'[2]

MAWLANA MAWDUDI (1903–79)

Mawdudi founded the Jamaat-i-Islami in Pakistan in 1941, again in a Muslim
society in crisis. Malise Ruthven explains: 'The intellectual father of modern Islamism was Sayyid Abu Ala (Mawlana) Mawdudi (1903-79), founder of
the Jama'at-i-Islami, an organization whose agenda is similar to that of the
Muslim Brotherhood in Egypt. Although Mawdudi claimed that Islam was
entirely self-sufficient, being God's final revelation to humankind, which
superseded all other religions and philosophies, he was strongly influenced
by the intellectual climate of the 1930s, particularly the writings of Alexis
Carrel, a popular French writer who would later be discredited for his support for the Vichy government. Carrel's animadversions on the "corrup-

tions" of modern living found their way into Mawdudi's denunciations of the West as a sewer of vice and wickedness. Impressed by the totalitarian movements in Russia, Italy and Germany, he [Mawdudi] compared Islam favourably with communism and fascism as a movement with the potential to mobilise the masses. The Jama'at-i-Islami, with himself as *amir* (commander), had more than a hint of *Fuhrerprinzip* about it. He insisted, however, that the Islamic movement would be free from the destructive features of the totalitarian ideologies because its leadership would be people of proven virtue.

'As Olivier Roy stresses, the Islamist political theory developed by Mawdudi and adapted and brought forward by Sayyid Qutb in Egypt is trapped in what might be called a "vicious circle of virtue". Because the Islamist model is predicated on the belief in government by morally impeccable individuals who can be counted on to resist temptation, it does not generate institutions that are capable of functioning autonomously. Political institutions function only as a result of the virtue of those who run them, but virtue can become widespread only if society is already Islamic. Mawdudi believed that the proper observance of Islamic norms – a prerequisite for belonging to the Jama'at-i-Islami – was a guarantee of personal integrity. Unlike the members of secular movements, the Islamists would not be corrupted by power.

Mawdudi believed that the law had been revealed to Muhammad for all time and for all humanity: 'The Koran does not claim that Islam is the true compendium of rites and rituals, and metaphysical beliefs and concepts, or that it is the proper form of religious attitudes of thought and action for the individual (as the word "religion" is nowadays understood in Western terminology). Nor does it say that Islam is the true way of life for the people of Arabia, or for the people of any particular country or for the people preceding any particular age (say the Industrial Revolution). *No! Very explicitly, for the entire human race, there is only one way of life which is right in the eyes of God and that is al-Islam.'* [Emphasis added.]

'It follows that, in the true Islamic state, for which Mawdudi coined the term "theo-democracy", the representatives of the people may be co-opted into the national assembly rather than elected, on the grounds that truly virtuous people will not always put themselves forward for election. As Yousef Choueiri has observed, Mawdudi's theo-democracy is an "ideological state in which legislators do not legislate, citizens only vote to reaffirm the permanent applicability of God's laws, women rarely venture outside their homes lest social discipline be disrupted, and non-Muslims are tolerated as foreign elements required to express their loyalty by means of paying a financial levy" (the *Jizya*).

'A prolific journalist and writer, Mawdudi, was not trained as a traditional *alim* (religious scholar), but he retained close links with the conservative *ulama* (plural of Alim) of India. Although he was initially opposed to the idea of Pakistan, which he saw as being dominated by leaders with an unacceptably secular outlook, once Pakistan became a reality in 1947 he worked ceaselessly to convert the homeland of India's Muslims into a fully fledged Islamic state. Mawdudi has been described (by Wilfred Cantwell Smith) as "much the most systematic thinker of modern Islam". Adapting, without acknowledgment, the Marxist idea of "permanent revolution", Mawdudi argued that jihad was the ultimate political struggle for the whole of humankind. His tract on jihad merits quoting at length:

"For Islam is not concerned with the interest of one nation to the exclusion of others and does not intend to advance one people to the exclusion of others. It is not at all interested what state rules and dominates the earth, but only in the happiness and welfare of humanity. Islam has a concept and a practical program, especially chosen for the happiness and progress of human society. Therefore Islam resists any government that is based on a different concept and program, in order to liquidate it completely. . . .

Its aim is to make this concept victorious, to introduce this program universally, to set up governments that are firmly rooted in this concept and this program, irrespective of who carries the banner of truth and justice, or whose flag of aggression and corruption is thereby toppled. *Islam wants the whole earth and does not content itself with only a part thereof. It wants and requires the entire inhabited world.*" [Emphasis added.]

'Mawdudi's writings became available in Arabic translation in the 1950s. They exercised an important influence on Sayyid Qutb, the principal ideologue of the Muslim Brotherhood in Egypt.'[24]

Jamaat-i-Islami blamed the Muslim decline in South Asia on the imperialist adventures of European powers, particularly the UK and France, and on the growth in Hindu power and nationalism.

As well as influencing Qutb and, through him, militants in Egypt and

North Africa, Mawdudi's thinking has had an important impact in Malaysia, Indonesia, Turkey, Afghanistan and the Sudan. His approach to jihad, picked up by many others, has been particularly negative.

SAYYID QUTB (1906–66)

Sayyid Qutb, described by many as the godfather of militant jihad, took the ideas of Al-Banna and Mawdudi and built upon and radicalised them. Unfortunately, many in the Islamic world understand the thinking of al-Banna and Mawdudi (who had many positive features) only through the writings and eyes of Qutb.

Qutb's influence on militant Sunni Islamists has been profound, although some al-Qaedaists disagree with his interpretations of the Koran, as they believe him not to have been a religious expert. Despite these differences, his impact has been dramatic; it has led directly to the ideological strains in al-Qaedaism which are most dangerous to Islam and the world.

After a modern education, Qutb studied at a college in Egypt set up by reformers to train teachers in a modern curriculum. He was initially a great admirer of the West and Western literature and was a prolific author, publishing more than forty books, many of which were translated into English and Persian, and still widely read.

As Malise Ruthven puts it: 'One of his stories, "Ashwak" ("Thorns") is a veiled account of his disappointment in love, after which he resolved to remain a bachelor. Coming from a rural background in Upper Egypt, he was shocked by the unveiled women he met at work in Cairo. Unwilling to choose a bride from such "dishonourable" women yet unable for lack of family connections to meet a woman "of sufficient moral purity and discretion," he remained celibate for the rest of his life – a condition he shared with the founder of modern Islamic radicalism, Jamal al-Din al-Afghani.

'In 1948 he obtained a generous government grant to investigate American instructional methods and curricula in primary and secondary education. . . . Qutb's visit to the United States deserves to rank as the defining moment or watershed from which the "Islamist war against America" would flow.'[24]

Qutb moved to America in 1949. His experiences there, especially with women, made him determinedly anti-Western. 'Of American culture, and

Americans generally, he remained determinedly disdainful. 'Jazz' he told his fellow Egyptians, 'is (their) favourite music. It is the type of music invented by blacks to please their primitive tendencies and desire for noise.'"[24]

He returned to Egypt, joined the Muslim Brotherhood and edited its official journal until it was banned. Four days before the coup that eventually brought him to power, Nasser visited Qutb at his home in Cairo. The Muslim Brotherhood supported Nasser initially but eventually fell out with his government. He was jailed by Nasser in 1954; after being released briefly, he spent the rest of his life in prison. He was badly tortured and kept in terrible conditions and hanged in 1966.

Some of his prison writings have become extraordinarily famous and very influential. Key passages include the following:

'The beauty of the new Islamic system cannot be appreciated until it takes concrete form. To bring it about, there must first be a revival in one Muslim country, enabling it to attain the status of world leadership. To achieve this aim, there must be a vanguard which holds to a steady course, marching through the vast ocean of *jahiliyya* which has encompassed the entire world. It must remain aloof from this all-encompassing *jahiliyya* while also keeping some ties with it. The role of the vanguard is to read the landmarks and signposts on the road, so that it will recognise the starting place, the nature and the responsibilities of this journey as well as its ultimate purpose.

'The first generation [of Muslims] did not approach the Koran for the purpose of acquiring culture and information, nor for the purpose of taste or enjoyment. None of them came to the Koran to increase his sum total of knowledge for the sake of knowledge itself or to solve some scientific or legal problem or to remove some defect in his understanding. He rather turned to the Koran to find out what the Almighty Creator had prescribed for him and for the community in which he lived, for his life and for the life of the group. *He approached it to act on what he heard immediately, as a soldier on the battlefield reads "Today's Bulletin" so that he know what is to be done . . . At most he would read ten verses, memorise them and then act upon them.'* [Emphasis added.]

'Here the fabric of traditional exegesis, according to which any one statement in the Koran must be balanced by all the others, is completely cut away. The Koran, whose claims to literary and aesthetic perfection are regarded by pious Muslims as self-validating, has often been treated as a kind of fetish. This is how it came to be regarded in many premodern societies, where the book itself was invested with magical potency, becoming a kind of votive object. But it is strange to find the sophisticated Qutb endorsing such a seemingly unscholarly approach to the divine text. As we have seen, he was no philistine: his contempt for Americans lay in his perception of *their* philistinism. In the hands of his less sophisticated disciples, his "soldiers on the battlefield", however, the text would become an operational manual, a seventh-century time bomb.

'Qutb cannot, however, be exonerated for the misuse to which the divine text would be put by his disciples. The sections on jihad in *Signposts on the Road* are explicit in rejecting any idea of the struggle as spiritual or defensive. Qutb accuses writers who argue that jihad is purely defensive as being apologetic and defeatist, of succumbing to the "wily attacks of the orientalists" who distort the concept of Islamic jihad. These people confuse two issues: the statement that "there is no compulsion in religion" (Koran 2:256) and the historical fact that Islam expanded by eliminating all the obstacles that stood between the people and Islam, preventing them from accepting the sovereignty of God. These two principles, Qutb says, are not related. The causes of Islamic jihad should be sought in the very nature of Islam and its role in the world, its high principles, which have been given by God. It was for the implementation of these principles that God appointed Muhammad, declaring him to be the last of all prophets and messengers. Anyone who understands Islam will know that jihad is not a "defensive movement" in the narrow sense of what is technically called a "defensive war".

[As Qutb notes:] '*It is a movement to wipe out tyranny, and to introduce true freedom to mankind, using whatever resources are practically available in a given human situation.* [Emphasis added.] If we insist on calling Islamic Jihad a defensive movement, then we must change the meaning of the word "defence" to mean "the defence of man" against all those forces that limit his freedom. These forces may take the form of beliefs and concepts, as well as political systems, based on economic, racial and class distinctions. At the advent of Islam, the world was full of such systems, just as the present-day *jahiliyya* abounds in various systems.'

Qutb continues: 'When we take this broad meaning of the word "defence", we understand the true character of Islam in that it proclaims the universal freedom of every person and community from servitude to every other individual or society, the end of man's arrogance and selfishness, the establishment of the sovereignty of Allah and his lordship throughout the world, and the rule of the divine Sharia [Islamic law] in human affairs ... When Islam calls for peace, its object is not a superficial peace which requires only that the part of the earth where the followers of Islam are residing remain secure. *The peace of Islam means that* din *[the law of the society] be purified for Allah, that all people should obey Allah alone, and every system that permits some people to rule over others be abolished.*' [Emphasis added.][24]

'It is most important to note that there are currents of thought whose origins are not acknowledged in his text. The message of revolutionary anarchism implicit in the wish that "every system that permits some people to rule over others be abolished" owes more to radical European ideas going back to the Jacobins than to classical or traditional ideas about Islamic governance. Similarly the revolutionary vanguard that Qutb advocates does not have an Islamic pedigree, though historically there have always been tribal forces that sought to "purify" Islam from religiously improper accretions. The vanguard is a concept imported from Europe, through a lineage that also stretches back to the Jacobins, through the Bolsheviks and latter-day Marxist guerrillas such as the Baader-Meinhof gang.

'The idea of a vanguard or revolutionary elite that acts in the name of future generations, rebuilding society in line with higher, transcendent truth (whether that truth be conceptualised in terms of the general will, the historical destiny of the proletariat, or the nation) is common to most modern radical political movements. Qutb legitimises his call to arms by reference to the classical Islamic tradition. As we have seen, this appeal to the example of the Prophet Muhammad and the early caliphs cannot be dismissed as spurious. The classical tradition was formed during the period of expansion that accompanied the Arab conquests. As I have suggested, Islam – in the mainstream Sunni tradition, if not always for the Shiite minority – is "programmed for victory". Its religious institutions were predicated upon the attainment of imperial power. "Can anyone say" Qutb asks rhetorically, referring to Islam's first great territorial expansion under Muhammad's "rightly guided" successors, "that if Abu Bakr . . . had been satisfied that the Roman [that is, Byzantine] and Persian powers were not going to attack the

Arabian peninsula, they would not have striven to spread the message of Islam throughout the world? How could the message of Islam have spread in the face of such material obstacles, the political tyranny of an absolutist state, the socio-economic system based on races and classes, and supported by the military might of tyrannical governments? It would be naive to assume that a call to free the whole of humankind throughout the world may be effected by preaching and exposition of the message alone. Indeed, because there is no compulsion in religion, it strives through preaching and exposition when there is freedom of communication and when people are free from all extraneous pressures. But when the above-mentioned obstacles and practical difficulties are put in its way, it has no recourse but to remove them by force so, when it is addressed to the people's hearts and minds, they are free to accept or reject it with open minds." The totalitarian menace is clear: anything that stands in the way of Qutbist preaching constitutes an obstacle to religious freedom.'[24]

'But Qutb and his disciples deliberately eschewed a spiritual interpretation of Islam. For them it was much more than religion: it was the blueprint for the correct social order, the model for the ideal society ordained by God. In the struggle against imperialism and neo-colonialism, the spiritual jihad must give way to the jihad of the sword. To internalise the message, to spiritualise it as the Sufis had always done and as the Isma'ilis (both Muslim minorities) did after the collapse of the legitimist (Fatimid) caliphate, was to accept defeat. The pre-Kantian metaphysical deity demanded action as well as prayer. In Qutb's fiery rhetoric, the Enlightenment and the political and economic power flowing from it are simply "a mask for the crusading spirit", a new attempt by the old enemy, Christendom, to crush the believers.'[24]

Qutb could have avoided being hanged by the Egyptian authorities if he had moderated his position. He refused to do so and it is probable that he knowingly accepted what he saw as his martyrdom. In retrospect, it was a significant political act, one which al-Qaedaists involved in suicide missions such as 9/11 have emulated and will continue to emulate.

Leonard Binder attempts to analyse Qutb's thinking: 'Qutb's ontological Islam is thus linked to the "ownmost being" of the believing Muslim, in a manner that urges him to act out, to realise, to practise that faith as an expression of his being, and not with regard to the practical political or

[57]

social consequences of that act. When we consider once again that the absolute foundation of Islam, and of the freedom of the individual Muslim to act, is the *hakimiyya* (sovereignty) of God, then the characteristic Islamic act becomes the defiance of *jahiliyya* activity. Thus is the groundwork laid for acts of martyrdom which appear to be suicidal and/or hopeless acts of political terrorism.'[26]

To quote Gilles's overall evaluation on Qutb: 'The weakness in Qutb's theory lay in the latitude he allowed for the interpretation of exactly what the Prophet's experience had been and how it should be reproduced in the context of the twentieth century. Qutb died before he could clarify his views on this important point, and those who claimed his mantle – ranging from sectarian cranks who wrote off the whole of society as "impious" to militants who reserved this adjective exclusively for regimes in power – found themselves in a state of ideological confusion that in the long run did great damage to the Islamist movement.'[27]

Qutb legacy on many concepts, especially jihad, martyrdom and the vanguard, has been quite negative and clearly totalitarian both in theory and in the way in which it has been applied.

DR ABDULLAH AZZAM (1941–89)

Abdullah Azzam was a Palestinian member of the Muslim Brotherhood and reportedly a founder of Hamas. He had strong academic and Islamic credentials. He was infamous for his fiery and captivating speeches and particularly for his support for global jihad and militant confrontation. A saying for which he is rightly infamous summarised the core of his views: 'Jihad and the rifle alone: no negotiations, no conferences, and no dialogues.'[27]

After Sayyid Qutb, he is one of the most important of all the exponents of the modern jihadist movement. In 1967, he escaped from his hometown, Jenin, when it fell into Israeli hands during the Six-day War. He was friendly with the family of Sayyid Qutb as well as with Shaikh Umar Abd al-Rahman, who later became the spiritual leader of Islamic Jihad in Egypt.

He was a teacher in King Abdul Aziz University in Jeddah, where Osama bin Laden was one of his students. After the Soviet invasion of Afghanistan, he focused all his attention on the jihad there and moved to Pakistan to help in the struggle against the Soviets. He is said to have worked with the CIA to recruit volunteers and support for Afghanistan, and toured the United States in the 1980s in that effort.

Malise Ruthven explains: 'His writings make it perfectly clear that the Afghan war was part of a wider programme of Islamic irredentism. The struggle to expel the Soviets was simply the prelude to the liberation of Palestine and other "lost" territories, including Al-Andalus (Spain).

> "The jihad in Afghanistan is the right of every able Muslim in order to turn communism away, and the Afghan jihad has been judged to be a *fard'ain* (individual obligation), like prayer and fasting, which a Muslim is not permitted to neglect. . . . Jihad is now ... incumbent on all Muslims and will remain so until the Muslims recapture every spot that was Islamic but later fell into the hands of the *kuffar* [infidels]. Jihad has been a *fard'ain* since the fall of Al-Andalus, and will remain so until all other lands that were Muslim are returned to us . . . Palestine, Bukhara, Lebanon, Chad, Eritrea, Somalia, the Philippines, Burma, Southern Yemen, Tashkent and Al-Andalus ... The duty of jihad is one of the most important imposed on us by God. ... He has made it incumbent on us, just like prayer, fasting and alms *[zakat]*. Such duties are divine obligations."

'The forbidding of jihad is *kufr*, which strays from faith ... Central to Azzam's preaching were the themes of martyrdom and sacrifice. Expatiating upon the well-known *hadith* [early traditions] that the 'ink of the scholar is worth more than the blood of the martyr', he insists that the two fluids are of equal value:

> "The life of the Muslim *umma* is solely dependent on the ink of its scholars and the blood of its martyrs ... so that the map of Islamic history becomes coloured with two lines: one of them black, with the ink of the scholar's pen; the other one red with the martyr's blood. It is even more beautiful when the two become one, so that the hand of the scholar which expends the ink and moves the pen is the same as the hand which expends its blood and moves the *umma* to action. The extent to which the number of martyred scholars increases is the extent to which nations are delivered from their slumber, rescued from their decline and awakened from their sleep. History does not write its lines except with blood. *Glory*

does not build its lofty edifice except with skulls. Honour and respect cannot be established except on a foundation of cripples and corpses. Empires, distinguished peoples, states and societies cannot be established except with examples of such as these martyrs. By the likes of these martyrs, nations are established, convictions are brought to life and ideologies are made victorious. . . . Indeed, those who think that they can change reality, or change societies, without blood sacrifices and wounds, without pure, innocent souls, do not understand the essence of our religion. They do not understand the method of the best of Messengers (may Allah bless him and grant him peace)." [Emphasis added.]

'In the same tract, Azzam celebrates the heroic examples of Abu Bakr (the first caliph, who reigned from 732 to 734 and fought the apostate tribes in Arabia and brought them back into the fold of Islam) and Ahmad ibn Hanbal (780–855), founder of the law school to which Wahhabism is heir, who resisted torture in opposition to the doctrine that the Koran was 'created' in time. [This opposition is a key Sunni tradition.] The implication is clear: when the *umma* goes astray and espouses false doctrines, God sends an individual or small group of people who will rescue it from perdition and restore it to the path of truth. The members of this small elite, says Azzam,

> "are the ones who carry convictions and ambitions. And an even smaller group from this band are those who flee from the worldly life in order to spread and act upon these ambitions. And an even smaller group from this elite, the cream of the cream of the cream, are those who sacrifice their souls and their blood in order to bring victory to these ambitions and principles. It is not possible to reach glory except by traversing this Path."'[24]

"The Jihad initially began as a few drops, until Allah decided to ignite the sparks within this blessed people and explode the Jihad, blessing with it the land of Afghanistan and the rest of the Muslims until its good encompassed the whole world. Some thought that the Earth had become devastated and that this umma had been drained of the thirst for martyrdom. Therefore, Allah exploded the Jihad on the land of Afghanistan and the groups of youths from the Islamic world marched forth to Afghanistan in search of jihad and martyrdom. Indeed this small band of Arabs, whose number did not exceed a few hundred individuals, changed the tide of the battle, from an Islamic battle of one country, to an Islamic world-jihad movement, in which all races participated and all colours, languages and cultures met; yet they were one, their direction was one, their ranks were one and the goal was one: that the Word of Allah is raised the highest and that this religion is made victorious on the Earth."

Azzam's tract includes a famous *hadith* from the collection of Al-Tirmirdhi detailing the rewards the martyrs can expect in paradise:

"Indeed the martyr has seven special favours from Allah: all his sins are forgiven at the first spurt of his blood, he sees his place in Paradise as his blood is shed (before his soul leaves the body), he tastes the sweetness of *iman* (faith), he is married to seventy-two of the Beautiful Maidens of Paradise, he is protected from the Punishment of the Grave, he is saved from the Great Terror (on the Day of Judgement), there is placed upon his head a crown of honour, a jewel which is better than the whole world and everything in it, and he is granted permission to intercede for seventy members of his household to bring them into Paradise and save them from the Hell Fire."[24]

'Smuggled into the discourse, however, wearing, as it were, an Afghan burqa, is an idea that is rarely found in the Saudi-Hanbali tradition to which Azzam formally lays claim. It is the notion, adopted from Sayyid Qutb, of a dedicated vanguard or elite, the 'cream of the cream of the cream' of Islamic youth, spearheaded by the Arabs, that will bring about the restoration of the *umma* at its fullest extent, recovering the lost domains of Palestine, Bukhara (the former Islamic Amirate, now part of Uzbekistan) and Spain.

'Qutb's ideas, as suggested earlier, were "invisible" adaptations of the revolutionary or political vanguardism to be found in both Bolshevism and fascism. The quest for social justice that Azzam and other members of the movement, including Ayman al-Zawahiri, share with Qutb and with Shiite ideologues, such as Ali Shari'ati, owe much to Marxist and social ideas, though it is only Shari'ati who openly acknowledges and critiques them.

'But the fascist parallels go deeper than the Marxist ones. In his explicit hostility to reason (alluded to in the reference to Ahmad ibn Hanbal's struggle – now seen as heroic in the Sunni tradition – against the Mu'tazilite doctrine of the "created" Quran), it is not Marx, grandchild of the Enlightenment, but Nietzsche, an anti-rationalist like the anti-Mu'tazilite Al-Ash'ari, whom Azzam echoes. The attachment to the lost lands of Palestine, Bukhara and Spain (unlike a rational and humane concern for Palestinian rights) is, like Mussolini's evocations of ancient Rome, nostalgic in its irredentism, its "obliteration of history from politics". The invocation of religion is consistent with the way fascism and Nazism used mythical modes of thought to mobilise unconscious or psychic forces in the pursuit of power, a task made easier in a population sanctified by a millennium of Islamic religious programming. Georges Sorel, sometimes seen as the intellectual father of fascism, declared that "use must be made of a body of images which, by intuition alone, and before any considered analyses are made, is capable of evoking as an undivided whole the mass of sentiments which corresponds to the different manifestations of the war undertaken by socialism." Mussolini, to whom Sorel in his later years lent his support, saw fascism as "a religious conception in which man is seen in his immanent relationship with a superior law and with an objective Will that transcends the particular individual and raises him to conscious membership of a spiritual society." Along the same lines, Alfred Rosenberg, the Nazi ideologue, stressed the other-worldly, spiritual aspect of Hitler's racial theories: "The life of a race does not represent a logically developed philosophy, nor even the unfolding of a pattern according to natural law, but rather the development of a mystical synthesis, an activity of soul, which cannot be explained rationally."

'It would be too reductive to redefine Islamism as "Islamo-fascism", but the resemblances are compelling. The social, political and cultural contexts in which the two ideologies have flourished are different. Fascism took root during the 1920s and 1930s in European societies that had already experienced a long exposure to modern thought and industrialization. None of the countries that adopted fascism had suffered from foreign occupation or direct colonial rule. The ideological bases of the two movements do, however, share common features. Fascism reacted both to the uncertainties of liberalism and to the chiliastic post-Enlightenment modernism of communism by seeking refuge in nostalgia and by refusing to acknowledge the contingent nature of the contemporary realities brought about by historical and social change. In the words of a recent analyst, Adrian Lyttleton:

"Abandoning the concept of class and class struggle, fascism masquerades as the representative of all classes, conceived as a single national unit; fascism obliterates history from politics and fills the space with nature; fascism appropriates the concept of revolution, applies it to its own activism, and declares revolution to be nothing other than one manifestation of the universal war.'"

'This formulation can be adapted for significant parts of the modern Islamic world, including Afghanistan, where it is tribalism rather than "class" that is abandoned in order to facilitate, by concealing, the extension of tribal power under the guise of a national-religious purpose; while for "the concept of revolution" may be substituted the "reversion" or "return" to Islam under the leadership of the vanguard of the pure. In the Islamist discourse, the space filled under fascism by "nature" is taken by the religion itself, conceived of as *din al-fitra*, the "religion of nature" or *al-tariqa al-mutawasita*, the "middle way" between the "extremes" of Left and Right, communism and capitalism.'[24]

Azzam was a very significant influence on Osama bin Laden, an influence that was strongly totalitarian. They worked closely together for a number of years, recruiting, funding and training volunteers for Afghanistan, and creating medical and engineering support structures. Backed by Osama bin Laden's money and organisation, Azzam became a leading exponent of militant jihad.

Azzam made powerful enemies, however, and he was eventually murdered, along with two of his sons, in a car bomb in Peshawar, Pakistan, in November 1989. There are various views on who might have been responsible for the attack. It is clear, however, that, prior to Azzam's assassination, Osama bin Laden had turned away from his close relationship with him and had begun to fall under the influence of two Egyptian militants, Shaikh Abd al-Rahman and Dr al-Zawahiri. Azzam may have been murdered on Osama bin Laden's orders. As often happens in such circumstances, the presumed culprit has been using the words and ideas of the dead man to his advantage. For example in the video Osama bin Laden released in November 2001, after the US bombing of Afghanistan had begun, he quoted directly Azzam's endorsement of terrorism (*Irhab*) against the Soviets:

'We are terrorists, and terrorism is our friend and companion. Let the West and East know that we are terrorists and that we are terrifying as well.

We shall do our best in preparation to terrorise Allah's enemies and our own. Thus terrorism is an obligation in Allah's religion.'[24]

Azzam's legacy, particularly with respect to jihad, martyrdom and the vanguard, is directly reflected in al-Qaedaism, and is clearly totalitarian.

MUHAMMED AL-FARAG

John L. Esposito explains the importance of Farag in the development of al-Qaedaism: 'A clear and at times chilling articulation of the new jihadist culture and its indebtedness to the past can be found in the writing of Muhammad al-Farag, a member of the radical [Egyptian] organization Islamic Jihad, who articulated its ideology in [the book] *The Neglected Duty*. Farag drew heavily from Al-Banna, Mawdudi, and especially Ibn Taymiyya and Sayyid Qutb. He takes the ideas of Ibn Taymiyya and Qutb with respect to jihad and pushes their application to its radical conclusion regarding the condition of the Muslim world and Egypt in particular.

Farag believed that the decline of Muslim societies was made possible by those who had lulled the community into believing that jihad was non-violent; the restoration of the Muslim world to the straight path of Islam hinged on reclaiming the true meaning of jihad, the forgotten or neglected requirement of Islam. Farag maintained that jihad was the sixth pillar of Islam [along with going on the Hajj to Mecca, bearing witness, prayer, alms-giving and fasting], forgotten or obscured by the majority of *ulama* [traditional religious scholars of Islam] and Muslims: 'Jihad . . . for God's cause (in the way of Allah), in spite of its importance for the future of religion, has been neglected by the *ulama* ... of this age. ... There is no doubt that the idols of this world can only disappear through the power of the sword.'

As in the time of Muhammad, Farag maintained, this was the task of a minority, a vanguard who must be prepared to fight against unbelief and apostasy, and be ready to suffer and die for their faith. Looking at the state of the *umma,* and especially Muslim governments, he concluded that unbelief and apostasy were endemic diseases:

'The Rulers of this age are in apostasy from Islam. They were raised at the tables of imperialism, be it Crusaderism, or Communism, or Zionism. They carry nothing from Islam but their names, even though they pray and fast and claim to be Muslim.'

The punishment for their apostasy is loss of all rights, including their right to life. Given the authoritarian and corrupt nature of regimes and their societies, a true Islamic state could not be established through non-violence but only through radical surgery, militant jihad, and the overthrow of apostate rulers.

'We have to establish the rule of God's religion in our own country first, and to make the Word of God supreme. ... There is no doubt that the first battlefield for jihad is the extermination of these infidel leaders and to replace them by a complete Islamic order.'

Islamic Jihad and Farag saw the bulk of Egyptians as basically good Muslims who were caught between the land of Islam, or peace, and the land of war, living in un-Islamic states, governed by un-Islamic laws and being only nominal Muslims. Holy war against Egypt's 'atheist' state and ruler was both necessary and justified – an obligation for all true believers. The creation of an Islamic state required the eradication of Western law, the implementation of Islamic law and the toppling of regimes through armed revolution.

As quoted in Saad Eddin Ibrahim, *Egypt, Islam and Democracy*, Farag stated: 'This state is ruled by heathen laws despite the fact that the majority of its people are Muslims. These laws were formulated by infidels who compelled Muslims to abide by them. And because they deserted jihad, Muslims today live in subjugation, humiliation, division and fragmentation. ... The aim of our group is to rise up to establish an Islamic state and restore Islam to this nation. ... The means to this end is to fight against heretical rulers and to eradicate the despots who are no more than human beings who have not yet found those who are able to suppress them with the order of God Almighty.'

'[Muhammad] Farag's book *Neglected Duty* [1986] and Islamic Jihad's ideological worldview were just another stage in the spread of jihad across the Muslim world, promulgating the rationale for extremist movements and the growth of networks that would later, as a result of the jihad in Afghanistan, form part of a global jihad. Their narrow, extremist interpretation of Islam and jihad was one side in the struggle within Islam between extremist and moderate Muslims, and it demonstrated yet again the capacity of religious scriptures and tradition to be interpreted, reinterpreted and misinterpreted.'[23]

WARRIOR SALAFIYYA, or SALAFIYYA JIHADIYYA

Warrior Salafiyya, one of two different trends in the Salafiyya movement, forms a significant inner core of al-Qaedaists today. The name 'Salafiyya' comes from the term for the 'pious ancestors' of Muslims, i.e. the first generation of Muslims.

The movement, set up in the late nineteenth century by the Persian scholar Jamal al-Din Al-Afghani and the Egyptian scholar Muhammed Abduh, was essentially a modernist movement promoting Islamic renewal using Western ideas and methods. After World War I, it evolved into a conservative and anti-Western movement and tended to align itself with the then-resurgent Wahhabism of Saudi Arabia.

The ICG explains: 'The Salafiyya movement today is widely perceived as oriented to Saudi Arabia and closely associated with, if not identical to, Wahhabism.' [It] 'is fundamentalist and very conservative. It is also disinclined to acknowledge or attach value to national identities and emphasises instead the supra-national Islamic identity and community. For the mainstream of the movement, dominated by religious scholars, *ulama* . . . and so sometimes called the *Salafiyya Ilmiyya* (the "scholarly" or "scientific" Salafiyya), the impulse to violence is rooted in its ambition to dictate, control and correct individual behaviour, and takes the form of occasional punitive actions against individuals or groups regarded as "bad Muslims". This form of violence is notably found in Algeria and Morocco, especially in the shanty towns and run-down housing estates on the edges of big cities; however deplorable, it poses little threat to North African governments or western interests.

'Recourse to violence as a primary strategy is the defining characteristic of a particular wing of the Salafiyya movement known as the *Salafiyya Jihadiyya* (the 'fighting' or 'warrior' Salafiyya). It originated in the war against the Soviet-backed regime in Afghanistan and took root across North Africa as Arab veterans of that conflict returned home. Extremely conservative if not reactionary, the '*Salafiyya Jihadiyya*' typically attacks Western targets in a campaign rationalised in traditional doctrinal terms as a conventional jihad in defence of the Islamic world against Western aggression.'[28]

The Warrior Salafiyya movement tends to justify and rationalise its activity by drawing on the ideas of Sayyid Qutb and particularly by using the concept of *kufr* declaring or denouncing someone or something as infidel and therefore as being open to death in the course of jihad.

Two events turned some members of the resistance in Afghanistan into core militants of al-Qaedaism. The first was the defeat of the Soviet Union in Afghanistan: its withdrawal was completed on 15 February 1989. The second was the invasion of Kuwait by Iraq on 2 August 1990. The first event is widely understood, the second less remarked upon.

Most Islamic movements condemned the annexation of one Muslim country – Kuwait – by another – Iraq. When the United States and its coalition (acting under a full UN mandate) were granted access to Saudi Arabian territory to expel the invaders of Kuwait, however, almost all Islamic militant movements and significant elements of the population in the Middle East and the Gulf region turned against the United States, and, in many cases, the Saudi monarchy as well. (The United States and Saudi Arabia had already reduced their support for the jihad in Afghanistan following the Soviet withdrawal.)

Suddenly, the two key supporters of the Afghan resistance were seen in a negative light by the members of that resistance. This feeling quickly turned into animosity towards the Saudi Arabian ruling family and a belief that the UN-sanctioned war to remove Iraq from Kuwait, and reverse the annexation of a UN member state, was another Christian/Crusader/Jewish plot to control Islam.

Gilles Kepel makes a crucial point here: 'The international brigade of jihadi veterans, being outside the control of any state, was suddenly available to serve radical Islamist causes anywhere in the world. Since they were no longer bound by local political contingencies, they had no responsibilities to any social group either. They reflected neither the interest of the devout bourgeoisie nor those of the young urban poor, even though their militants were drawn from both classes. They became the free electrons of jihad, professional Islamists trained to fight and to train others to do likewise: they were based in Pakistani tribal zones, in smugglers fiefdoms over which [the Pakistani capital] Islamabad exercised next or no authority, and in Afghan Mujahedin encampments. Around the most heavily involved militants gathered clouds of sympathisers, many of whom were in trouble in their own countries and were unable to obtain visas to Western nations; they were stuck in Pakistan and obliged to survive in the direst circumstances. Young Islamists from all over the world came to join these men and learned the terrorist trade from them; some emerged later as perpetrators of a series of attacks in France in 1995. Above and beyond the cause they claimed to serve, they constituted a pool of manpower that could be used by the secret services of a number of states who might find it opportune to manipulate unattached extremist militants.

'This milieu was cut off from social reality; its inhabitants perceived the world in the light of religious doctrine and armed violence. It bred a new, hybrid Islamist ideology whose first doctrinal principle was to rationalise the existence and behaviour of militants.'[27]

Some of these individuals were Warrior Salafiyya; others were freebooters addicted to violence and an unconventional life.

The problem of what to do with militants who are suddenly 'out of a job' has been seen after many conflicts. In Afghanistan, this was a serious issue. Many of the militants and their supporters had no state to which they could return – or in which they would be accepted – and the problem was 'exported' by those states. They had no way of getting a visa to the West and so were stuck in the tribal areas of Pakistan. They therefore formed a core of militants for al-Qaedaism – one which was capable of anything, as it had no loyalty to anybody other than itself, no loyalty to conventional Islam, and no family or social structures to moderate its extremes.

❦

From all of these individuals and movements emerged al-Qaedaism, 'fronted' by Osama bin Laden and his deputy, Ayman al-Zawahiri. Much has been written about Osama bin Laden, and I do not intend to retread old ground, but a few points in relation to him are worth restating.

Osama bin Laden is the seventeenth son of a billionaire whose family was quite close to the royal family in Saudi Arabia. At the last count, he had four wives. He came from a very privileged background and had a privileged education. Osama bin Laden turned against the royal family in Saudi Arabia after they refused his offer of help in dealing with the Iraqi invasion of Kuwait. Despite his own propaganda, he appears to have performed poorly in the fight against the Soviets in Afghanistan, as did the core al-Qaeda group itself.

In 23 August 1996, during Bill Clinton's presidency, Osama bin Laden released a famous declaration of jihad against the Americans occupying the land of the two holy places. He talked in the statement about the sufferings the 'Zionist-Crusader' alliance had inflicted upon Muslims in various countries around the world, and clearly invited readers to draw a parallel between the Prophet Muhammad's flight to Medina and Osama bin Laden's flight to the mountains in Afghanistan – a propaganda theme he has since repeated consistently.

In this declaration, as Gilles Kepel notes, he 'goes on to stigmatise the deep injustice in Saudi Arabia. *Above all he champions the claims of the higher social strata of the kingdom (his own class), referring to them as the 'great merchants' to which the state is 'indebted', who are suffering from the 'devaluation of the rial'* [the Saudi Arabian currency] *and so on*. Mainly he addresses himself to the devout middle class (and to some of the princes) in the hope of detaching them from the ruling dynasty.' (Emphasis added)[27]

Some of his later declarations have a much greater 'leftist' leaning and are intended to appeal to the secular Left at home and abroad.

In February 1998, Osama bin Laden created the International Islamic Front against Jews and 'Crusaders' and signed the founding charter of this organisation with the man who became his deputy, Ayman al-Zawahiri, and a number of others.

Though Osama bin Laden was not legally or religiously entitled to do so, in this short text he issued a fatwa stipulating that 'every Muslim who is capable of doing so has the personal duty to kill Americans and their allies, whether civilians or military personnel, in every country where this is possible.'[27]

His propaganda activities have been significantly underplayed in the West. He is clearly winning the propaganda war, particularly in the Middle East and the Gulf region, and in other Islamic areas around the world. It is frequently forgotten, in this context, that the original inner core of al-Qaedaists set up four departments: religious affairs, finance, military and (crucially) the media. Osama bin Laden has made great use of propaganda and the media since then.

Trained as an economist many of his speeches encourage his followers to target 'economic nodes' in the West.

Osama bin Laden's second-in-command is Ayman al-Zawahiri, an Egyptian surgeon who became leader of Islamic jihad and then folded much of this organisation into Osama bin Laden's al-Qaeda group. Al-Zawahiri is seen by many as Osama bin Laden's mentor and successor. He was born in 1953 into a wealthy, conservative religious family, joined the Muslim Brotherhood after the Egyptian defeat in the Six-day War in 1967, and quickly became involved in Islamic Jihad, rising quickly to be one of its leaders. After the assassination of President Anwar Sadat, he, along with many others, was arrested in Egypt.

As the ICG puts it: 'An important element of al-Zawahiri's outlook is ascribed by some Egyptian Islamists to his experience in prison. Independent Islamist commentator Fahmi Howeidi told the ICG: "Al-Zawahiri left Egypt because he had been tortured, humiliated; he hated the whole world after that. Al-Zawahiri was a product of a repressive system."'[2]

After leaving Egypt, he emigrated to Saudi Arabia and then to Afghanistan, where he worked as a field surgeon. He met Dr Abdullah Azzam (whose career is discussed above) there. He became much closer to Osama bin Laden over the years and in 1992 moved with him to Sudan. He returned to Afghanistan in 1996. It is widely believed that he masterminded a significant number of terrorist attacks, including the killing of fifty-eight European tourists in Luxor in Egypt in 1997. He is also believed by many to have been the organiser behind the 9/11 attacks.

Many commentators believe that, if Osama bin Laden was killed, al-Zawahiri would take over his role and would, if anything, be a much more dangerous opponent than Osama bin Laden: he lost both his wife and his only son in a US air strike in Afghanistan in November 2001.

Al-Zawahiri has for some time been the key ideologist for al-Qaedaism in the Muslim world. His experiences in Egypt led him to the view that international jihad was the only solution to what he saw as the pervasive failure of Islam. When he failed to convince Islamic Jihad in Egypt of this, he joined up with Osama bin Laden's group, taking some of the members of Islamic Jihad with him.

After the bombing of the Egyptian Embassy in Islamabad in 1996, while still the leader of the Islamic Jihad movement, he published an important treatise entitled 'Shifa Sudur Al-Mu'minin' ('The Cure for Believers' Hearts'). This was a justification for the attack, following significant criticism of the attack from various Islamic sources. This treatise has become the justification for al-Qaedaist attacks and militant actions in general.

In the treatise, he ranks the main issues facing the Islamist movement in order of priority, with Palestine top of the list. As Maha Azzam puts it: 'The view expressed is that all Arab and Islamic regimes, including the PLO, had sold out by the mere fact that they accepted the authority of the United Nations and the very idea that any Jew might remain in any part of Palestine. . . For example, he sees the Saudi regime as traitorous because of its ties with the US government, which supports Israel.

'Subordinate to the first point is a struggle against the oppressive regimes that fight the Muslims (i.e. Islamists) through physical and intellectual means. It is secondary because al-Zawahiri sees these regimes as clients of the infidels, Christians and Jews – something that is clearly prohibited in Islamic law (a view he recently reiterated in another treatise serialised in the Al-Quds newspaper in London), and which therefore places them outside the fold of Islam.

'He dismisses their [the victims of the Islamabad bombing's] description in the Egyptian media as innocent civilians by saying that the fact that they worked for the Egyptian government makes them party to the crimes of that government and therefore a legitimate target.'

'This point is crucial because, as al-Zawahiri became the theorist for the new al-Qaeda movement, he translated that concept of personal liability to the group's view of Western governments. Logically, this theory could be presented as follows: Civilians in the West elect and pay for their governments. They are therefore responsible for the actions of these governments – in essence they are the decision makers – and thus they negate their status under Islamic law as innocent non-combatants and become legitimate targets.

'Thirdly, al-Zawahiri propounds the twin ideas of the greater good and the need to react to exceptional circumstances. Ideologically, he is grappling with two major problems. The first is the clear and absolute prohibition of suicide under Islamic law. As this is one of the strongest taboos in Islam, he cannot find any theological backing except for the idea of martyrdom in the Christian sense. The cases he uses are instances in early Islam where some

Muslims were captured by the 'idolaters'. They were asked, on pain of death, to recant, but refused to do so. He views their refusal as an act of suicide for the glory of God. Since these early martyrs were not condemned for their actions by the early Muslims and great theologians, he argues that an Islamist can commit suicide for the greater good. That provides the movement with the legitimacy for suicide attacks, which 1,500 years of Islamic theology would view as heretical.

'The second problem is that he needs to justify collateral damage. Having dismissed the innocence of civilians, he is left with Muslims and children who might be unintentional victims of these attacks. Again he is struggling against the main corpus of Islamic theology, which is clear in its rejection of such collateral damage. To counter this, he claims that Muslims are facing exceptional circumstances, with an overpowering enemy and weak resources, and that these exceptional circumstances allow for a more lax interpretation of the law.

'It was this political theory that formed the basis and justification for the attacks on the World Trade Centre. The United States supports Israel and is therefore the enemy. No US civilian can be deemed innocent because they elect and pay for their government, and while killing children and Muslims is normally not acceptable, the exceptional circumstances of the current situation, where the Muslims (i.e. Islamists) are fighting superior forces, allows for an exception to these rules. Finally, because these attacks are for the greater good of Islam, there can be premeditated suicides, which would otherwise be deemed to be heretical.

'The implication of this political theory is a complete separation between the Islamists and the 'enemy', which now includes all Muslims who are in any way connected to non- Islamist regimes in the Islamic world as well as all citizens of Western countries that recognise the state of Israel, even if at times they support Muslim causes in Afghanistan or Bosnia. The 'other' then becomes a perfectly legitimate target in the war for the glory of Islam.

'It is important to note that this is a completely new departure for the Islamist movement. This theory is neither based on the main school of Islamic theology (including Wahhabism) nor on the often-misunderstood Ibn Taymiyya. Although intellectually weak, al-Zawahiri has nevertheless provided al-Qaedaism and those Islamists who wish to follow it with a theoretical legitimisation for ruthless political action.

'The reaction on the Muslim street clearly shows that this new ruthless form of confrontation has found fertile ground for general support. In many ways, this is not surprising: al-Qaeda is merely echoing the rejectionist views of Nasser, which were very popular in the 1960s and 1970s.

'At the same time the undemocratic and oppressive nature of the Arab regimes in particular feeds a general antipathy among their populations.

'That is not to say that the mainstream on the Muslim street accepts all aspects of this new ideology. What we have is a small movement of dedicated revolutionaries with a clear exclusive political theory that exploits a greater feeling of disaffection.

'For the Muslim street ... al-Qaeda is seen as the only movement that scored a successful blow against the combined enemy. Nothing succeeds like success, and the Western and Arab media have portrayed the twin towers attack as a success.' [29]

To a propagandist like Osama bin Laden and an ideologist such as al-Zawahiri, this media reaction has confirmed their importance to the Muslim street and in the Muslim world generally.

❧❦

The table on the following page presents the second 'Tree of Influence', showing the concepts that have been appropriated and modified by al-Qaedaists, and have led to the type of thinking outlined above.

I JAHILIYYA

As set out above, al-Qaedaism has taken this term, which was previously applied to the pagan period in Arabia (before the advent of Islam), and applied it to any group, country or time which suits the purposes of al-Qaeda. Essentially, therefore, any group, people, country or culture can be deemed 'barbarians' or 'barbaric' – which implies that the relevant people are not proper Muslims and so may be struck down, just as the Prophet Muhammad struck down the original *jahiliyya* in Arabia and built a glorious Islamic state upon its ruins.

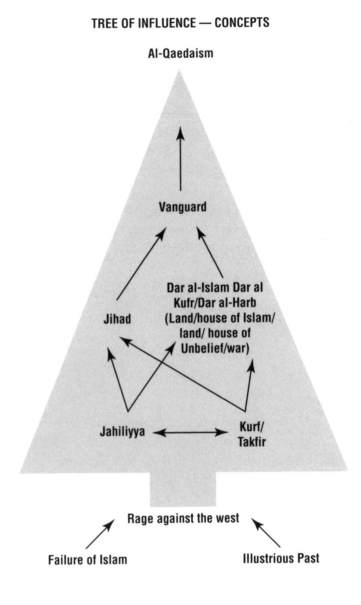

TREE OF INFLUENCE — CONCEPTS

Al-Qaedaism

Vanguard

Jihad

Dar al-Islam Dar al Kufr/Dar al-Harb (Land/house of Islam/ land/ house of Unbelief/war)

Jahiliyya ⟷ Kurf/ Takfir

Rage against the west

Failure of Islam

Illustrious Past

2 KUFR AND TAKFIR

Using these words is an extraordinarily serious accusation in Islamic doctrine. The word *takfir* derives from the word *kufr*, which means 'impiety'.

Takfir refers to a person who is or claims to be a Muslim but is declared 'impure' and then excommunicated in the eyes of the Community of the Faithful. Interpreting Islamic law literally, such a person can no longer benefit from the protection of Islamic law and accordingly, 'his blood is forfeit' and he is condemned to death. [27]

Takfir has always been a sentence of last resort, and the *ulama,* who are the only ones authorised to pronounce *takfir,* after taking significant prescribed legal precautions, have always been very reluctant to use it. This is because, if it was used improperly, it would quickly lead to discord and sedition in the ranks of Islam, which is to be avoided at all costs.[27]

Sayyid Qutb died leaving his own detailed thoughts on *jahiliyya* – and the use of takfir – unclear and therefore open to misuse – a situation that al-Qaedaism has capitalised upon.[27]

3 JIHAD

Although I have already commented on various aspects of jihad already, a number of key points need to be drawn out.

Malise Ruthven explains: 'Jihad, as is now widely known, means "struggle": it has the same root as *Ijtihad,* the interpretative "effort" needed to fathom the law as revealed by God and his Prophet. According to a well-known *hadith,* jihad is the "monasticism" of faith.' 'Every nation has its monasticism and the monasticism of this nation is the jihad'. Muhammad disapproved of asceticism: there was to be 'no monkery' in his community. Jihad held the place occupied by asceticism in early Christianity. On an individual level it meant the struggle against evil. An often-cited Hadith equates the 'lesser jihad' with war, the 'greater jihad' with spiritual and moral endeavour. According to the story, when the Prophet returned from a raiding party, he said: 'We have now returned from the smaller jihad to the greater jihad'. When asked what he meant by the greater jihad, he replied: 'The jihad against oneself.' Peters points out, however, that this tradition is not included in any of the authoritative compilations, a fact that has allowed the militant Islamists to reject it as spurious.'[24]

For centuries and for many in the Islamic world, the greater jihad (struggling with the self) has been the more important jihad. The leaders and members of al-Qaeda and its related groups focus exclusively on the lesser jihad of war to avoid facing the much harder self-examination of the greater jihad.

The second area where al-Qaedaism has reinterpreted jihad is with respect to the individual and group responsibility involved. For many centuries, the lesser jihad had been seen as a group or community issue rather than an individual one. Al-Qaedaism and its supporters have obviously been anxious to reverse that and so they consistently emphasise the belief that jihad is essentially an individual obligation and not one that can be discharged by the state, group or community. This puts pressure on individual Muslims to fall into line and become actively involved in the movement – or at the very least support the approach of those who get involved in militant activity.

Thirdly, they wish to change the lesser jihad so as to remove the normal immunity of non-combatants, women, children and Muslims.

There is no doubt that majority opinion in Islam believes that 9/11 and similar catastrophes caused by the lesser jihad of war run completely contrary to the laws of Islam. As Malise Ruthven explains: 'Dr S. F. Milani, citing numerous Koranic passages, stated unequivocally that the concept of jihad (meaning "struggle", often translated as "holy war") can never justify Muslims attacking civilian targets. The greater jihad, following the teachings of the Prophet, was a struggle against evil. The lesser jihad, armed struggle, only applied to Muslim self-defence. "Even if a state of war exists between a non-Islamic and a Muslim country, no Muslim is permitted to assault, attack or harm any non-Muslim civilian who does not physically participate in the fighting." The balance of educated Islamic opinion, reflected in statements throughout the Islamic world, was unequivocal in condemning these atrocities as contrary to the laws of Islam.'[24]

Al-Qaedaism is anxious to maintain that there is a Judeo-Christian conspiracy against Islam, as this implies that Islam is under attack and therefore that jihad is allowable in self-defence. Because of decades of anti-Zionist, anti-Israel and anti-Semitic attacks, along with blatant anti-Americanism and anti-Westernism together with low levels of literacy in much of the Middle East and Gulf region, the propensity to believe any conspiracy theory about the United States or Israel, and about Jews or Christians, is extraordinarily high. This has provided al-Qaedaism with fertile soil to convert a defensive jihad into an aggression that can be used against almost anyone because of a presumed, but non-existent, conspiracy against Islam.

In addition there are many references in the original Islamic sources to jihad. Some of them can be read in an expansionist mode and have been so applied over the centuries. It is a simple matter for al-Qaedaism to use these references to further justify its militant activities.

4   DAR AL-ISLAM, DAR AL-KUFR AND DAR AL-HARB

The division of the world in two between Dar al-Islam ('the Land of Islam') and Dar al-Kufr ('the Abode of Unbelief') or Dar al-Harb ('the Abode of War') is a brilliant underpinning for al-Qaedaism's repeatedly stated propaganda that the West is actively conspiring to destroy Islam and is therefore not just a land or abode of unbelief but in fact a land of war, in opposition to Islam.

Originally, the two 'Dar's had a neutral meaning. Over time, pious Muslims would have carried out the fundamentalist act of *hijra* or emigration from the Dar al-Kufr to the Dar al-Islam either physically, by moving to an isolated locality, or simply by means of a personal spiritual retreat from Dar al-Kufr or worldly values and practices.

The radical, recent interpretation of *hijra* by al-Qaedists goes further, calling for not only spiritual and physical separation from unbelief but also jihad against it.

5   VANGUARD

The al-Qaedaist vanguard compares itself to the Companions of the Prophet Muhammad in order to justify its actions. The 9/11 hijackers adopted the term *kunyas*, familiar names adopted by Arabs, referring back to the time of the Prophet's Companions, being the heroic age of Islam. One of the *Suras* [common term for the basic units of the Koran] the 9/11 hijackers were urged to recite was *Surat al-Anfal* ('the Spoils of War'), which was said to have been revealed to the Prophet directly after the battle of Badar in 624, the first major victory of the Muslims over the Meccans. Al-Qaedaists see this period as providing a close parallel for the current era.[24] 'They too see themselves as a small, isolated band fighting against impossible odds.'[30]

'They look back in history and see how, during the earliest days of Islam, the small embattled group of Muslims was able to triumph over its Meccan enemies against overwhelming odds with the help of God and to defend the nascent Islamic state. In due course that state became the kernel of the Arab empire and world civilisations that followed in its wake. In line with this attitude of heroic nostalgia the inner circle of al-Qaeda refers to the attacks of 9/11 as the "Manhattan Ghazwa" or raid, comparing it to the raids that brought about the first Muslim conquests'.[24]

Vanguards always turn against their own if their own is not sufficiently committed, radical or pious. The experiences of such groups in Algeria provide a number of examples in this regard.

The ICG presents a clear picture: 'Inside *Al-Salafiyya Al-Jihadiyya* [a warrior-Salafist group in Algeria], there were two tendencies: one decreed the regime to be impious, the other went further in considering that the entire society should undergo the punishment reserved for apostates in the event that it did not follow their lead. ... Under Djamel Zitouni's [very militant leader of Groupe Islamique Armé (GIA) Afghan veteran led armed rebel group in Algeria] predecessors in 1993/94, the GIA had already begun to expand the concept of *takfir* to embrace elements of society, not merely the "impious" state. In the districts it controlled, it [the GIA] imposed a "re-Islamisation" of society and punished with death civilians who defied its injunctions, such as woman who refused to wear the *hijab*, hairdressers who ignored orders to close their shops, and newsagents who continued to sell the national newspapers. ... In February 1997, Benhadjar's group [a more radical GIA splinter group] split away to form the Islamic League for Preaching and Jihad (*Ligue Islamique pour le Da'wa et le Djihad'lidd*).

The first massacres [carried out by the GIA] date from this period. While much remains unclear, it seems that the initial attacks – in Medea [in Algeria] in late 1996 – targeted families that were loyal to the Islamist cause but were opposed to the extremism of Zitouni, Zouabri [extreme GIA leader who succeeded Zitouni] and the Al-Muwahhidun grouping. [another GIA extreme splinter group]'[31]

This type of behaviour becomes possible when the vanguard, in its desire to emulate an appropriate historic example, wages jihad on the people of unbelief, as defined by themselves. Inevitably, the vanguard's interpretation of who and what is involved in *jahiliyya* leads to the denunciation of *takfir* and to the deaths of many innocents.

As Jason Burke explains: 'Abdullah Azzam said [in 1987] that: "Every principle needs a vanguard to carry it forward and [to] put up with heavy tasks and enormous sacrifices. This vanguard constitutes the strong foundation (*al-Qaeda Al Sulbah*) for the expected society."

'[Osama] bin Laden and a number of close associates acted on Azzam's suggestion and, probably sometime in 1988 or early 1989, set up a militant group in Peshawar, the frontier city in western Pakistan. They hoped the group would act as a vanguard in the coming struggle. The unity that a common purpose had forced on the disparate groups of Islamic extremists fighting against the Soviets was disintegrating. National and ethnic divisions re-asserted themselves among the volunteers. [Osama] bin Laden's group was formed with the aim of rousing Muslims, through active campaigning or "propaganda by deed", to create an international army that would unite the *umma,* or world Islamic community, against oppression. The group was small, comprising not more than a dozen men, and there was little to distinguish it from the scores of other groups operating, forming and dissolving in Pakistan, Afghanistan and elsewhere in the Islamic world.'[32]

As we have seen, this vanguard has been spectacularly successful on its own terms, 9/11 being a classic "propaganda by deed" attack, designed to increase recruitment into the al-Qaedaism movement and to help fuel further resentment against the West.

This type of vanguard thinking is a major threat not only to the United States but to the world as a whole, and explains why their potential to use WMD should not be discounted.

If US defences against WMD attack are as successful as their defences against 'normal' terrorist attacks have been since 9/11, just as al-Qaedaism struck at softer targets outside the United States in Bali, Madrid and Istanbul, so future WMD attacks may also occur outside the United States. To al-Qaedaists, the overwhelming conventional power of its enemies entitles it to use WMD to achieve its aims, and such unfortunately may be directed at any target no matter how civilian, neutral or innocent such might be to the rest of the world.

It is clear that al-Qaedaism, in terms of its political beliefs and its religious practices, runs counter to almost 1,300 years of Islamic thinking and practice.

In relation to recent events in Egypt, as Esposito points out: 'Islamic Jihad's war is waged against all non-believers, Muslim and non-Muslim alike. Extremist groups like [Islamic] Jihad reject Islam's traditional tolerance of the protected communities of Jews and Christians, 'Peoples of the Book' (*dhimmi*). Like Osama bin Laden, they [members of Islamic Jihad] see Jews and Christians as part of a historic battle or crusade connected with European colonialism and Zionism, and they regard Israel as a Trojan horse of the West, a fifth column within Muslim societies. Once people have been condemned as unbelievers who must be subject to the sword, they forfeit their right to life, security and property. Shaykh Omar Abdel Rahman, spiritual advisor to Islamic Jihad and Gamaa Islamiyya, issued a fatwa sanctioning the killing and plundering of Christians (i.e. European tourists) in Luxor in 1997 because they were 'anti-Muslim'. This outlook has been passed on to other groups in the Arab and Muslim world who believe that international conspiracies, Jewish Zionism, the Christian West, and atheistic communism all intend to divide the Muslim world and destroy Islam. In public protest, they chant: "Holy War against lackeys: Jews, Christians and atheists.' 'No to America! And No to Israel!"' [23]

It is also a serious misunderstanding to assume that al-Qaedaist activists are all pious, old-fashioned, religious Muslims. It is clear that many of the 9/11 hijackers, the mastermind of the 1993 World Trade Centre bombing in New York, and others who have carried out terrorist atrocities for al-Qaedaism visited lap-dancing clubs, go-go bars and other such places – despite al-Qaedaism's stated view that these places are examples of Western debauchery. Those who loudly condemn the hypocrisy of others, which al-Qaedaists do, are often the worst hypocrites themselves.

A review of Olivier Roy's book *Globalised Islam: The Search for a New Umma* in *The Economist* magazine stated: 'As he argues, the culture of suicide attacks as fostered by al-Qaeda and its imitators, and promoted on their websites – has a self-indulgent, me-generation flavour about it. The narcissistic characters who carried out the 9/11 attack were no exception to this.' [33]

The instructions to the 9/11 hijackers are instructive in this regard. Malise Ruthven explains: 'Just over two weeks after the September 11 attack, the FBI released a translation of an Arabic document left behind by Mohammed Atta, generally thought to have been the pilot among the five men who hijacked American Airlines Flight 11 from Boston, the Boeing 767 that crashed into the North Tower of the World Trade Centre. The agents found it in his luggage, which remained in Boston after failing to make the connection from a flight from Portland, Maine, where he had spent the previous night. A similar text was found in the wreckage of United Airlines Flight 93, which crashed in Pennsylvania.

The document, posted on the FBI website and published in translation by the *Washington Post*, has been subjected to a detailed analysis by Kanan Makiya and Hassan Mneimneh. It is a chilling reminder of the way in which sacrifice and violence may be blended in the religious mind: the certainty of death is linked directly to the promise of paradise. The message is profoundly solipsistic; at no point in the document's published excerpts is there any sense of human compassion, beyond concern for the would-be martyr's soul, over the likely consequences of the act. The apocalyptic mind is solipsistic in two respects: the actor who undertakes an apocalyptic mission identifies his action with the will of God; by so doing he leaves to God the moral consequences of his act. There is no hint of justification for the action in the document. It is not a manifesto; nor is it an explanation. The moral and intellectual arguments have been left entirely with God.

The text contains some guidance of a purely practical nature: '[Check] the suitcase, the clothes, the knife, your tools, your ticket. ... your passport, all your papers. Inspect your weapon before you leave.' But this is linked directly to the practice of the 'righteous predecessors', who 'tightened their clothes as they wore them prior to battle. And tighten your shoes well, and wear socks that hold in the shoes and do not slip on them.' By means of an almost magical association, the practical need for tight shoes (or perhaps trainers) required for the deft footwork the hijacker will need on board the aircraft is assimilated with the practice of the righteous predecessors or Companions of the Prophet, who tightened their armour for battle during Islam's heroic age.

Throughout the text, practical instructions alternate with pious invocations in the manner of a medieval devotional manual. The hijacker must always maintain a positive attitude: 'Forget and force yourself to forget that thing which is called the world; the time for pleasure is gone and the time for reckoning is upon us. So therefore you must use these few remaining hours that you have to seek forgiveness from God. You must be convinced that these few remaining hours that you have are few indeed, and after that you will begin living a life of happiness, a life of eternal paradise. Be optimistic, for the Prophet (Peace Be Upon Him) was always positive. Always repeat or remember the verses whose recitations are desirable before death. Remember that God said, "If Allah helps you, no one can vanquish you. If He forsakes you, who can help you after that? So the believers should put their trust in Allah.'

The hijackers are urged on in their endeavour with several other Koranic quotations. For example, they are reminded: 'Obey Allah and His messenger and do not quarrel amongst yourselves lest you lose heart and your momentum disappear. And be steadfast, for God is with the steadfast. You were longing for death before you met it. Now you have seen it with your own eyes.' The hijackers are urged to keep their minds open and responsive.

'You will enter heaven, you will enter a life of eternity. Remember if you encounter any problem how to get out of it. The believer is always put to the test. You will never enter paradise unless the greatest trial confronts you. Make absolutely sure of all your possessions . . . your bag, your clothes and the knives. And your identity documents and your passport and all your papers. Make absolutely sure that no one is following you and be very watchful that you are very clean and also that your shoes are clean.'

Emphasis is placed on ritual purity. Prior to the hijacking, the would-be martyrs are urged to 'perform the dawn prayer with an open heart' and are also told: 'Don't go until you have performed your ablutions for your prayers. Continue the prayer and when you enter the airplane say: "O God open all doors for me." ("*Allahum aftah li kul al-abwab.*")'

In the most sinister of the passages analysed by Makiya and Mneimneh, the hijackers are told what to do if they encounter resistance: 'If God grants any one of you a slaughter, you should perform it as an offering on behalf of your father and mother, for they are owed by you.' Makiya and Mneimneh point out that the word used for 'slaughter' – *dhabaha,* rather than the more familiar *qatala* – 'kill' – connects the act of murdering a passenger to the ritual sacrifice of an animal by slitting its throat.' 'The thought expressed in the document,' say Makiya and Mneimneh, 'is that a civilian passenger attempting to resist his hijackers is a gift bestowed by God upon the man chosen to kill him.' The sense throughout 'is that the would-be martyr is engaged in his action solely to please God. There is no mention of any communal purpose behind his behaviour. In all of the four pages available to us, there is not a word or an implication about any wrongs that are being redressed through martyrdom', whether in Palestine, Iraq or Arabia. Martyrdom does not appear in the document as a favour bestowed by God on the warrior for his selfless devotion to the community's defence. It is, rather, 'a status to be achieved by the individual warrior and performed as though it were his own private act of worship'. The document's author has taken the 'shell of a traditional religious conception' and replaced its original content with 'radically new content which finds its legitimation in the word of God [and] the example of his prophets.' This substitution amounts to 'a deeply subversive form of political and ideological militancy'. 'The idea that martyrdom is a pure act of worship, pleasing to God irrespective of God's specific command, is a terrifying new kind of nihilism,' the authors assert.[34]

In broader terms, the focus of al-Qaedaists on propaganda and, indeed, their proud usage of the term 'terrorist', their definition of 'the vanguard', their contempt for almost all the world's citizens, institutions and states, and their inappropriate and murderous application of many concepts in Islam make them the ultimate totalitarian movement, both in terms of the original understanding of the word by Hannah Arendt, and in the broadest sense of the essence of totalitarianism itself.

Indeed, Arendt has a warning for those within Islam (and elsewhere) whose belief in conspiracies makes them ideal candidates for totalitarian domination: 'The ideal subject of totalitarian rule is not the convinced Nazi or the convinced communist but people for whom the distinction between fact and fiction (i.e. the reality of experience) and the distinction between true and false (i.e. the standards of thought) no longer exist.'[35] She adds: 'What prepares men for totalitarian domination in the non-totalitarian world is the fact that loneliness, once a borderline experience usually suffered in certain marginal social conditions with old age, has become an everyday experience of the ever-growing masses of our century.'[35]

Islamic Caliphate

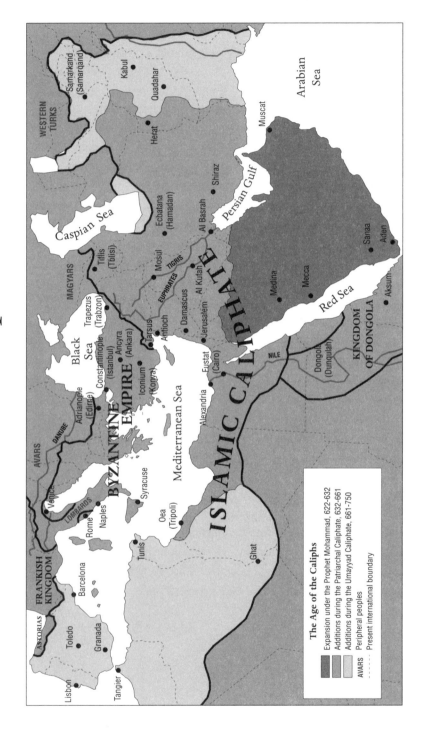

The Age of the Caliphs

Expansion under the Prophet Mohammad, 622-632
Additions during the Patriarchal Caliphate, 632-661
Additions during the Umayyad Caliphate, 661-750
AVARS Peripheral peoples
------ Present international boundary

3

The Objectives of the al-Qaedaists

'The struggle between us and them, the confrontation and clashing began centuries ago, and will continue ... until Judgement Day.'
(OSAMA BIN LADEN, *Al Jazeera TV, 4 January 2004*)

THE FIRST THING they need is an enemy to provide a foil for the terrorist actions of their militants. As Eckhart Tolle puts it: 'Who would the believer be without the unbeliever?'[36]
The Islamic expert Bernard Lewis says: 'Islam as such is not an enemy of the West, and there are a growing number of Muslims, both there and here, who desire nothing better than a closer and more friendly relationship with the West and the development of democratic institutions in their own countries. But a significant number of Muslims – notably but not exclusively those whom we call fundamentalists – are hostile and dangerous, not because we need an enemy, but because they do.'[25] He continues: 'There are still significant numbers, in some quarters perhaps a majority, of Muslims with whom we share certain basic cultural and moral, social and political beliefs and aspirations; there is still a significant Western presence – cultural, economic and diplomatic – in Muslim lands, some of which are Western allies. But there is a surge of hatred that distresses, alarms, and above all baf-

fles Americans. Often this hatred goes beyond the level of hostility to specific interests or actions or policies or even countries, and becomes a rejection of Western civilisation as such, not so much for what it does as for what it is, and for the principles and values that it practises and professes. These are indeed seen as innately evil, and those who promote or accept them are seen as the "enemies of God".'[25]

The long-term objective of al-Qaedaists is the reestablishment of the (Sunni) Islamic Caliphate. The Caliphate was abolished by Kemal Ataturk, the father of modern Turkey in 1924, as he deemed it an anachronistic holdover from the ancient past.

As Paul Berman explains: 'The Caliphate in twentieth-century Turkey was a purely ceremonial office, without power. It was venerable, though. In the early Middle Ages, the Caliphate had been the seat of the Ottoman Emperors, and had descended to the Ottomans from still-remoter times, when it served as the seat of the Arab Empire from the days of Muhammad's Companions.'[37]

The Caliphate had gradually declined in power and prestige from the eleventh century, when the Abbasid rulers had handed power over to their Pretorian guards. The Caliphate was later revived by the Ottoman sultans in the nineteenth century.

Many commentators assume that Osama bin Laden would be the new Caliph. It is of interest in this regard that many inductees into the core al-Qaeda group have sworn an oath of allegiance to him. This restored (Sunni) Islamic Caliphate would be set up on the ruins of Turkey and would include all of the other Islamic states in the Gulf region and the Middle East (including, presumably, all majority Shiite Islamic states, such as Iran, Iraq and Bahrain) and extend to the other areas occupied by the Muslims up to the 'high-water' mark of Islamic expansion in the period after the rule of the Prophet Muhammad. This includes most of Spain and Portugal, France up to just south of the Loire River, the southern portion of Italy, including Sicily, Hungary, the Balkan states, Azerbaijan (which is a majority-Shiite state), Georgia, the Crimea, Anatolia, Kurdistan, and significant parts of Asia and North Africa.

Some Asian al-Qaedaists propose a mini-Caliphate in Asia until the full Caliphate is restored, to embrace Indonesia, Malaysia and at least part of the Philippines.

To achieve such an objective would involve devastating wars, genocide and massive population transfers.

To such thinking, the UN, with its core belief in the sovereignty of individual states, is a threat. This explains the devastating attack on UN personnel in Iraq, the most deadly in the history of the UN, and the earlier plan to bomb the tunnels under the UN building in New York, and the building itself.

A few days after the attack on the UN in Iraq, an al-Qaeda communiqué said that: 'One of the Mujahedin drove with a van full of explosives into the back part of the headquarters at the offices of the personal representative of America's criminal slave, Kofi Annan, the diseased Sergio De Mello, criminal Bush's friend.' The communiqué continued: 'Why cry over a heretic? Sergio Vieira De Mello is the one who tried to embellish the image of America, the Crusaders and the Jews in Lebanon and Kosovo, and now in Iraq. He is America's first man, where he was nominated by Bush to be in charge of the UN after Kofi Annan, the criminal and slave of America, and he is the crusader that extracted a part of the Islamic land [a reference to the UN's help in achieving East Timorese independence].'[14]

This negative view of the UN among al-Qaedaists is not of recent origin. As Paul Berman noted: 'It was Shaykh Rahman's group that bombed the World Trade Centre in 1993 and killed six people, and it was Rahman's group that planned to bomb tunnels and the United Nations in New York.'[37]

Osama bin Laden's video two months after 9/11 again described the Secretary-General of the UN, Kofi Annan, as 'a criminal'. He went on to say that 'the Arab and Muslim leaders who sit at the UN and share its politics place themselves outside Islam. They are Unfaithful, they do not respect the message of the Prophet.' In addition, he said that 'those who claim the legitimacy of international institutions give up the only authentic legitimacy, the legitimacy which comes from the Koran.'

The reestablishment of the Islamic Caliphate is clearly a pipe-dream on the part of the al-Qaedaists. Standing in the way of its achievement are the national views in each country and their military power, together with the power of NATO, Russia, China, India and the United States, and Muslim opinion, both Sunni and Shiite, worldwide. Moreover, if al-Qaedaists ever succeeded in getting control of one country, as the Taliban did in Afghanistan, this would provide an obvious target or hostage to stop the onward march of al-Qaedaism – terrorists are difficult to find, countries are not.

This pipe-dream is not part of an utopian ideology, however. As John Calvert points out: 'It would be incorrect to label radical Islam a utopian ideology, in the strict meaning of that term. Whereas utopias are models of the future based upon speculative discussion and planning, radical Islam is the expression of the collective conviction intuited in the moment. Much like fascism, radical Islam makes the revolutionary process central to its concerns at the expense of a fully thought-out "orthodox" stage when the dynamics of a society settle down to becoming "steady-state", namely when its internal and external enemies have been eliminated and new institutions created. In other words, the mythic horizons of radical Islam do not extend beyond the stage of struggle to envision precisely what a "proper" Islamic state should look like.'[38]

With respect to the internal workings of this new Islamic Caliphate, a reign of terror like that of the Taliban in Afghanistan would be let loose, but on a much vaster scale. In Afghanistan the Taliban promoted their own brand of revolutionary Islam. They imposed their strict Wahhabi-like brand of Sunni Islam on Afghan society basing such on the Orthodox practices of Saudi Arabian Sunni Wahhabism which had evolved on that peninsula since the 18th century. They banned women from school and the workplace, required that men wear beards and women burqas, banned music, photography and television and imposed strict physical punishment on deviators. Their intolerance for any deviation from their brand of Islam expressed itself in the slaughter of many of Afghanistan's Shiite minority (10% of the population), whom they disdained as heretics[25]

As al-Qaedaists refer back to the period of the Prophet Muhammad and his Companions in the eighth century as the ideal world, it is therefore likely that this is what they hope to achieve. What this of course creates is a 'total system for adherents and corresponding total power for leaders'[39], with all that that entails. Minorities, including muslim minorites, would face a catastrophe in such a Taliban-like Caliphate.

As Vali Nasr argues: 'Anti-Shiite sectarianism is an important dimension of the Taliban's and al-Qaeda's political objective, one that their war on the West has largely overshadowed. Pakistani, Sunni, Taliban and al-Qaeda combatants fought together in military campaigns in Afghanistan, most notably in the capture of Mazar-i Sharif and Bamiyan in 1997 [and 1998], which involved the wholesale massacre of the Shiites. Pakistan Sipah-i-Sahabah fighters did most of the killing, nearly precipitating a war with Iran when they captured the Iranian consulate and killed eleven Iranian diplomats. Sectarian Sunni fighters in Iraq will draw on the ideological and organisational resources of the broader network of Sunni militancy that developed over the past decade and has been ensconced in society and politics in the greater Middle East, impacting sectarian relations where those resources originate, in Afghanistan and South Asia.'[40]

This sectarianism is little known or understood. 'After the Taliban captured Mazar-i Sharif in 1997, they declared that the Shiites were not Muslim and not welcome. They gave the Shiites the option of converting to Sunnism, emigrating to Iran, or as was the fate of some 2000 – death.'[40]

All this is not just of theoretical or historic interest. The attack on the UN in Iraq and many of the more horrendous terrorist attacks there, particularly against the Shiite population, have been attributed to or claimed by the al-Qaeda affiliate Ansar al-Islam. This organisation was based in northern Iraq before the American invasion of the country and is reputed to have had connections with both Iranian and Iraqi intelligence operatives.·[41]

The spiritual leader of Ansar al-Islam, Mullah Mustapha Kreikar, who is currently in exile in Norway, confirmed that 'the fight against the Americans in Iraq was the same as that against the Soviets in Afghanistan'. He went on to say that 'the resistance is not only a reaction to the American invasion, it is part of the continuous Islamic struggle since the collapse of the Caliphate. *All Islamic struggles since then are part of one organised effort to bring back the Caliphate.*'[14] (Emphasis added.)

The key issue then to the vanguard of al-Qaedaists is what to do now to achieve this long-term objective of reestablishing the Sunni Islamic Caliphate. Obviously, to achieve this objective, each Islamic government or regime needs to be overthrown. How, then is the key issue? The answer from the al-Qaedaists is to remove Western influence and support from Islamic countries and then it is assumed by the al-Qaedaists that these countries will quickly fall into their hands.

The actions to date of the vanguard of al-Qaedaism fit in perfectly with this short- to medium-term objective. Step by step, country by country, this, they assume, would eventually lead to the re-establishment of the Caliphate.

Achieving this objective would involve the deaths of huge numbers of Muslim rulers, army and police personnel, and innocent civilians. This is completely justifiable to al-Qaedaists as Paul Berman explains: 'The vanguard had to recognise that the false Muslims or "hypocrites" who ruled the Muslim world were not Muslims at all. It was because Islam is not divisible into crucial aspects and less crucial aspects, and a partially Islamic life is not an Islamic life. ... Qutb judged these people to be *jahili* barbarians, exactly like the polytheists in Arabia before the time of Muhammad. To struggle against those people was right and just – a struggle with full force, too, and not with moderation or reservations. To live a proper Islamic life meant engaging in that kind of struggle, the jihad for Islam.'[37]

It is difficult to imagine what it would mean in such thinking to treat the vast majority of the Muslim population of the world, apart from the tiny vanguard of their own movement, as Jahili barbarians. Sayyid Qutb himself said "their efforts will come to nought. They shall have no protection whatsoever against God's punishment, which is bound to come, keen as they may be to avoid it."[37]

The new Palestine that would be set up as part of this process would involve the elimination of the state of Israel and the death or expulsion of all Jews there, as well as the death and expulsion of all secular and Shiite Muslims living in the area – many millions of people.

Sayyid Qutb also predicted the violent and suicidal activities of al-Qaeda against their own and others in his section on 'Martyrdom and Jihad' in his commentary on Surah 2: 'The Surah tells the Muslims that, in the fight to uphold God's universal Truth, lives will have to be sacrificed. Those who risk their lives and go out to fight, and are prepared to lay down their lives for the cause of God, are honourable people, pure of heart and blessed of soul. But the great surprise is that those among them who are killed in the struggle must not be considered or described as dead. They continue to live as God Himself clearly states.

'To all intent and purposes, those people may very well appear lifeless, but life and death are not judged by superficial physical means alone. Life is chiefly characterised by activity, growth and persistence, while death is a state of total loss of function, of complete inertia and lifelessness. But the death of those who were killed for the cause of God gives more impetus to the cause, which continues to thrive on their blood. Their influence on those they leave behind also grows and spreads. Thus after their death they remain an active force in shaping the life of their community and giving it direction. It is in this sense that such people, having sacrificed their lives for the sake of God, retain their active existence in everyday life. ... There is no real sense of loss in their death, since they continue to live.'[37]

This is not just old-fashioned thinking: 'In the first week of the war against the Taliban regime in Afghanistan, a young Afghan warrior was quoted in a British newspaper. "The Americans," he said, "love Pepsi-Cola, but we love death.'[42]

It is clear that the level of ruthlessness shown by al-Qaeda in its activities to date includes a complete lack of concern for the slaughter of innocent bystanders, including Muslims. As Bernard Lewis notes: 'The first major example was the bombing of two American embassies in East Africa in 1998. In order to kill twelve American diplomats, the terrorists were willing to slaughter more than two hundred Africans, many of them Muslims, who happened to be in the vicinity. In its issue immediately after these attacks, an Arabic-language fundamentalist magazine called *Al-Sirrat al-Mustaqim*, published in Pittsburgh, Pennsylvania, expressed its mourning for the "martyrs" who gave their lives in these operations and listed their names, as supplied by the office of al-Qaeda in Peshawar, Pakistan. The writer added an expression of hope "that God would ... reunite us with them in paradise."'[25] In addition a total of 4,574 people were injured in these two bombings, again most of them Muslims, in order to injure 15 Americans.

All this suggests that a key part of the world's battle against al-Qaedaism should be directed at helping the majority of Muslims who are effectively fighting for their lives against this vanguard, members of which feel free – indeed, compelled – to kill anyone who gets in their way.

But in supporting the majority of Muslims, whom precisely does the West support? Unfortunately, liberal or pluralist Islam is a minority activity in most Islamic states, with one or two exceptions – Turkey being one example and Indonesia another.

In most cases, however, the active battle within Islam is almost completely between militant al-Qaedaists and the current establishment. As Emmanuel Sivan puts it: 'Indonesian circumstances are unique; the success of liberal Islam in this country is, quite simply, exceptional. Elsewhere in the Muslim world, the popular conditions of Indonesia do not exist. The regimes have a unitary-populist, if not plainly tyrannical outlook; the religious tradition is not pluralistic; and liberals lack communicating and organising skills. The liberal message in the Middle East and North Africa is as learned and sophisticated as that in Indonesia, yet it is a voice calling in the desert. The clash within Islam thus pits the radicals against the powers that be. And this, sadly, is the only struggle that counts.'[43]

The reestablishment of the Sunni Islamic Caliphate does not only impact on current Islamic states. To al-Qaedaists the Caliphate also embraces any state, region or area that was once Islamic. Europe is therefore a direct target in this effort.

What many in the EU would consider imperialism – the Muslim advances in Spain, Portugal, France, Italy and Eastern Europe in ancient times – is considered by al-Qaedaists to have been 'liberation' from apostasy and more importantly 'bringing the true God to European heretics'. Al-Qaedaists therefore consider what many in the EU see as freedom from oppression and occupation as in fact imperialism and, worse still, an imperialism that flies in the face of God and resists his bounty. According to such thinking, the re-establishment of the Islamic Caliphate of old is quite simply liberation from oppression.

Spain, however, clearly cannot hand back its 'occupied territories' to a group of al-Qaedaists. Nor will Spain – or any other European country – tolerate the re-establishment of an Islamic Caliphate which would stretch through the Middle East and Gulf into North Africa, Europe and Asia.

In the meantime al-Qaeda's other aims include the following:

- *The elimination of the separation of church and state*
  Sayyid Qutb considered the modern separation of church and state as 'hideous schizophrenia'. In Turkey in 1924, Ataturk separated the functions of church and state. This was considered by Qutb as an attempt to 'exterminate' Islam. Secular Turkey, continuing such 'extermination' efforts, is therefore a key target for attack by groups associated with al-Qaeda.

Many observers misunderstand how al-Qaedaists view the separation of church and state. To them there can be no separation: there is no distinction between the state and Islam – Islam is all.

- *The destruction of democracy itself*
  Al-Qaeda seeks the end of democracy because of its ability to seduce Muslims from the 'true path', as defined by al-Qaedaism. Many al-Qaedaist militants and the key thinkers they admire consider Western civilisation degenerate, devoid of any ethical value and ready to collapse. It is notable that even the possession of a voter-registration card in Afghanistan or Iraq in 2004 was considered a crime punishable by death by the al-Qaedaists.

  Writing on Iraq in 2003, the al-Qaedaist theoretician Yussuf Al-Ayyeri said: 'What threatens the future of Islam, in fact its survival, is American democracy.' Lest that be misunderstood, in December 2004 Osama bin Laden issued a fatwa declaring democracy to be a violation of Islam and calling on the Iraqis not to allow a government based on the votes of their people, but rather to institute one based on divine will. Abu Musab al-Zarqawi followed this up with the statement: 'We have declared a fierce war on this evil principle of democracy and those who follow this wrong ideology.'

- *The ending of women's liberation*
  Women's liberation as practiced in the West is considered by al-Qaedaists to be a sign of complete moral degeneracy and contrary to their understanding of the teachings of the Prophet Muhammad. To Al-Qaedaists, a man may take many wives, and women are possessions who have few rights and no entitlement to education, work or the practice of a profession. Their allies the Taliban in Afghanistan displayed this in extreme form, publicly executing women who dared visit the hairdresser. As Gilles Kepel put it: 'Women were compelled to wear burqas in public and were forbidden to take jobs, with the result that many of those women who had lost their husbands, fathers and brothers in the war were forced to beg in the streets surrounded by their starving children.'[27]

- *The elimination of Christians and Jews*

    In al-Qaedaist thinking, Christians and Jews should realise that the error in their religions was fully exposed on the establishment of Islam and should have conceded the latter's 'greater truth'. If they do not accept this, they may be killed if they do not accept conversion. As Bernard Lewis puts it: 'The Christians, whom Muslims recognised as having a religion of the same kind as their own, and therefore as their primary rivals in the struggle for world domination – or, as they would have put it, world enlightenment. Christendom and Islam are two religiously defined civilisations that were brought into conflict not by their differences but by their resemblances.

    'The oldest surviving Muslim religious building outside Arabia, the Dome of the Rock in Jerusalem, was completed in 691 or 692. The erection of this monument, on the site of the ancient Jewish Temple and in the vicinity of Christian monuments such as the Holy Sepulchre and the Church of the Ascension, sent a clear message to the Jews and, more importantly, the Christians: Their revelations, though once authentic, had been corrupted by their unworldly custodians and were therefore superseded by the final and perfect revelation embodied in Islam, just as the Jews had been overcome and superseded by the Christians, so the Christian world was to be replaced by the Muslim faith and the Islamic Caliphate. To emphasise the point, the Koranic inscriptions in the Dome of the Rock denounce what Muslims regard as the principal Christian errors: 'Praise be to God who begets no son, and has no partner' and 'He is God, one, eternal. He does not beget, He is not begotten and He has no peer.' (Koran CXII). This was clearly a message to Christendom in its birthplace. A millennium later, the stationing of American troops in Arabia was seen by many Muslims, notably Osama bin Laden, as a similar challenge, this time from Christendom to Islam.

    'In the Muslim perception, the Jews and later the Christians had gone astray and followed false doctrines. Both religions were therefore superseded, and replaced by Islam, the final and perfect revelation in God's sequence.'[25]

This thinking, which has been twisted out of recognition by al-Qaedaism, is not just of theoretical or theological interest. When the Taliban killed a French UN aid worker in Afghanistan in early 2004, their communiqué said simply: 'We killed the Christian.' Usually al-Qaedaist communiqués are more circumspect and use the word 'Crusader', which in their eyes means Christians who are assumed to be conspiring against Islam or invading Muslim lands. Osama bin Laden has not always been so circumspect, however. In a 1998 interview with Al-Jazeera television, he said: 'Every grown-up Muslim hates Americans, Jews and Christians. It is our belief and religion.'[42]

It is crucial to note that these al-Qaedaist views, which they have clearly acted upon, are still minority views within Islam. The crucial point for the West is not to give undue credence to such ideas or to act as though they are the views of all who adhere to the Islamic faith.

- *The destruction of the secular Turkish republic*
A key historic development for both Osama bin Laden and Sayyid Qutb was Ataturk's formal dissolution of the Ottoman Empire and the secular reforms he subsequently carried out in Turkey in 1924. As part of this modernisation, Ataturk ended the Islamic Caliphate, which as part of various Arab and Ottoman empires had ruled much of the Sunni Islamic world since the time of the Prophet Muhammad's Companions. Atuturk went on to separate Islam from the state and declare a purely secular state in Turkey. Paul Berman notes: 'Ataturk showed that Islam was vulnerable in fact and not just in theory. And what would happen if, thanks to people like Atuturk and their Jewish supporters and the Christians from the West, Islam was pushed into a corner of society separated from the state? True Islam would become partial Islam; and partial Islam does not exist. Atuturk's assault, grim as it was, had already led to a new battle, even grimmer than the first. It was "a final offensive which is actually taking place now in all the Muslim countries. ... It is an effort to exterminate this religion as even a basic creed, and to replace it with secular conceptions having their own implications, values, institutions and organisations."'[37] Both

Osama bin Laden and Qutb considered this development to be a catastrophe for Islam – which explains why Osama bin Laden frequently refers to it.

It might be asked how, in practical terms, al-Qaedaism can hope to win all these battles against such odds. Firstly it needs to decide who to attack initially. There has been great debate among militant Islamists for about twenty years as to what the target of their attacks should be. Should it be the government and its armed forces in their own country or should they target the West? Governments in the Middle East and the Gulf region have been termed the 'near enemy' in this regard, while the West generally, and the United States in particular, is termed the 'far enemy'.

Al-Qaedaists eventually decided to target the far enemy, in particular the United States. This was a brilliant propaganda and operational move. Instead of disparate groups fighting disparate national enemies, by concentrating on just one, the various militant groups could enjoy a unity of focus, propaganda, and eventually support.

As Rand terrorism expert, Brian Michael Jenkins, put it: 'What Osama bin Laden and his associates contributed to this potent but unfocused force was a sense of vision, mission and strategy that combined the twentieth-century theory of a unified Islamic polity with restoration of the Islamic Caliphate that, at its height, stretched from Spain to India. This vision had operational utility. It recast the numerous local conflicts into a single struggle between an authentic Islam and a host of corrupt satraps who would collapse without the backing of the West – the United States in particular. It therefore provided a single, easily agreed-upon enemy, whose fate, when confronted with a unified Islamic struggle, would be the same as that of the Soviet Union. By erasing the boundaries between individual countries and their conflicts, al-Qaedaism could draw upon a much larger reservoir of human resources for the larger battle. In addition to the thousands of veterans of the war against the Soviet Union, al-Qaedaism now had thousands of new recruits to train.'[10]

A key underlying tactic here is to create a belief system through propaganda and militant actions which convinces significant numbers of Muslims that the West is an enemy and therefore must be confronted and defeated. If significant numbers of Muslims can be so convinced, a clash of civilisations becomes more likely, irrespective of what the West thinks or does.

Al-Qaedaists use their websites as a significant tool in this regard: 'The persistent reappearance of the al-Neda Website is another example of al-Qaeda's unremitting recruitment and morale-strengthening efforts. The site, which is published in Arabic only, continues to disseminate its anti-American and anti-Western messages. Three basic themes are emphasised:

- The West is implacably hostile to Islam.
- The only way to address this threat and the only language the West understands is the logic of violence.
- Jihad is the only option.

'The theory of jihad in particular is elaborated in great detail, with continued exhortations to Muslims that Islam involves commitment to spread the faith by the sword. In addition, regular summaries are posted of news affecting the Islamic struggle against the West, including al-Qaeda's own accounts of ongoing fighting and skirmishing with American and allied forces both in Afghanistan and Pakistan, along with a selection of suggested readings, including books by approved authors. Justification is also provided for the 9/11 attacks, with video clips and other messages praising the operation and citing Islamic legal arguments to justify the killing of civilians.'[19]

Successful attacks such as 9/11 and other attacks attributed to al-Qaedaists in Europe, Iraq, Afghanistan and elsewhere clearly help attract support in the wider Islamic population: for one thing, al-Qaedaists are seen as the only group that is successfully attacking the 'far enemy'. Their view of the world is receiving much more support now than it did only a few years ago, and significantly more than it did fifteen years ago, when the al-Qaedaist campaign effectively started. As Jason Burke has put it: '[Osama] bin Laden's aim is to radicalise and mobilise. He is closer to achieving his goals than the West is to deterring him.'[1]

The message targeted at local audiences in the Middle East and the Gulf region is particularly brilliant. It stresses that the action against the West and the United States, whether in that area or elsewhere, is defensive, as it is the aggressive West that is trying to complete the crusading project started during the Crusades to the Middle East more than one thousand years ago – and continued by the West in the colonial period. This propaganda, which continually uses the term 'crusades' and 'colonialism', is highly effective, particularly insofar as it is directed towards the citizens of states who have diverted their people from their own appalling situation at home by continually beaming anti-American, anti-Western, anti-Zionist and anti-Semitic propaganda at them. The invasion of, and continued military action in, Iraq clearly adds huge potency to this message, as do the events in and coverage of the US military's abuses in Abu Ghraib Prison and the extra-legal detention of suspected al-Qaeda members at the US base in Guantánamo Bay.

Al-Qaeda's strategy of focusing on the far enemy is not always consistent, however. In an al-Qaeda tape broadcast by Al-Jazeera on 21 May 2003, several Arab states, including Saudi Arabia, Kuwait, Qatar, Bahrain, Egypt, Yemen and Jordan, were deemed apostate for collaborating with the United States and other Western powers in the war against Iraq. It is clear, however, that the key target is the far enemy: to al-Qaedaists, political reform and liberalisation among the 'near enemy' is irrelevant. Osama bin Laden has rejected political reform by the 'near enemy'as an excuse for not pursuing jihad. In a taped speech broadcast by Al-Jazeera television on 4 January 2004, he stated that parliaments and democracy are an affront to religion, which he said must govern all worldly affairs.

With respect to the 'far enemy', the United States is the primary target. The reason for this is that, when the United States has been defeated, al-Qaedaists assume that the West, in particular the EU, will collapse like a house of cards. This makes sense to al-Qaedaists for a number of reasons. Firstly, by focusing on the United States, particularly after the divisions between Europe and the United States about the war in Iraq and the Bush administraion's National Security Strategy, Osama bin Laden may be hoping to obtain allies, either active or passive, beyond the Islamic world.

In an article entitled '[Osama] bin Laden May Be Fishing for Allies on Europe's Secular Left' published in the *Los Angeles Times,* Brian Michael Jenkins, a terrorism expert from Rand, outlines the view that a recently broadcast message from Osama bin Laden was directed not at his usual Muslim audience but at the Left in Europe. This message appeared to try to divide Europe from the United States by offering European countries sanctuary if they 'do not attack Muslim nations'.

The tape had many extreme-Left, anti-American comments in it and very little Islamic commentary. As Jenkins points out: 'More recently, Italy's new generation of Red Brigades applauded the 9/11 attacks and called for an alliance between European and Middle Eastern terrorists.' He continues: 'The goal is to portray America and those who remain in its orbit as the real axis of evil. … The jihadists' broad themes – whether addressing Muslims or European radicals – are the same. The terrorists cast themselves as self-less heroes out to end the suffering of the innocent, as unceasing warriors against Western imperialists, as champions of the downtrodden and as undying opponents of an evil Israel. This selection of specific issues remains opportunistic.

'Bin Laden's recent message to Europeans is: don't shed European blood for the gang in the White House. This message conveniently ignores the fact that al-Qaedaists have done the killing in Europe. A talented com-municator, [Osama] bin Laden has this time crafted his words to sell his product – violent opposition to America and the West – to the widest pos-sible audience.'[44]

Whether or not it is due to the propaganda of al-Qaedaism, there is no doubt that the divisions between Europe and the United States are wide at present, with minimal support from European countries for US actions in Iraq.

The second reason for al-Qaedaists to attack the United States first is that the latter presents the perfect propaganda target for al-Qaedaism. As a superpower which uses military force and supports Israel, all its negative actions can be magnified, while inconvenient facts like UN approval and EU support for military action in Afghanistan and elsewhere can be ignored or turned into conspiracies against Islam. The United States is a much better target than, say, a more diffuse EU, because of the former's superpower activist role, its presumed leadership role of globalisation, and of course widespread anti-Americanism.

But how could al-Qaedaists possibly hope to defeat the United States? Kumar Ramakrishna explains this very clearly: 'It intends to do so by first deposing moderate Muslim governments, and this in turn requires elimi-nating the American support that helps sustain such regimes. It is against this wider political background that we must examine more carefully the so-called 'new terrorism' and discern what is indeed 'new' and what is not.

In this respect, it must be noted that, in military-strategic terms, al-Qaeda is waging a guerrilla war against the West and in particular against the United States. This guerrilla war has a transnational character and is not confined to any particular state because the constituency of which Osama bin Laden seeks to win support is not a specific Muslim population but rather the 1.2 [now 1.3] billion-strong Muslim *umma* or nation, which transcends state and ethnic boundaries.

'It must be emphasized, however, that while this transnational guerrilla war may be quite unlike a conventional, geographically delineated guerrilla conflict, as theorized by Mao Zedong and Vo Nguyen Giap [the North Vietnamese military leader], it nevertheless remains in essence a guerrilla war: like Giap before him, Osama bin Laden knows that he cannot engage American forces directly, as he does not have the military strength to do so. Hence, like Giap, he intends to defeat America by targeting not its military might but rather what he perceives to be its critical vulnerability, or soft underbelly: the American public. While [Osama] bin Laden and Giap may share similar views about what Clausewitz called the 'centre of gravity' of the United States, however, there is a critical difference between the operational strategies each used to target this weak spot. Giap sought to achieve his political goal of the reunification of Vietnam by undermining public support within America, but he never tried to break the resolve of the American people by sponsoring mass terror attacks within the American 'theatre of operations'. Rather, Giap sought gradually to erode American popular will by stubbornly remaining undefeated within Vietnam. Technically speaking, therefore, Giap adopted an indirect approach against America in two ways: at the strategic level, by bypassing the armed forces and targeting the public will and, within the American theatre, by not striking physically at Americans but rather by seeking to produce a debilitating psychological effect on them by indefinitely prolonging the Vietnam War. On the other hand, while bin Laden, like Giap, seeks to bypass the armed forces of the United States and strike at the will of the American public, he, unlike Giap, is willing to strike physically at Americans, as the September 11 attacks clearly proved. Bin Laden is thus fighting against American civilians indirectly, at the strategic level, and directly, at the operational, theatre level.

'While the essence of al-Qaeda's grand strategy of avoiding strength and attacking weakness is familiar enough, there are nonetheless precisely three features of the terrorism it employs which can be considered as novel: the enhanced capacity of the terrorists to plan and carry out attacks, the increased vulnerability of modern societies to terrorist strikes, and the religious-messianic motivation of the terrorists, which appears to predispose them to mass-casualty strikes.'[6]

This image of al-Qaedaists involved in a guerrilla war targeting American civilians, using MMD (modalities of mass destruction) or WMD, or both, with full religious blessing, and rushing to paradise to the greater delights that await them there, is the stuff of nightmare fantasy. Only one element of the nightmare is currently missing, however: the WMD weapon, or the MMD opportunity.

The defeat of the Soviet Union in Afghanistan by a wide range of resistance movements led Osama bin Laden to believe that the core al-Qaeda group alone had successfully defeated that superpower. This assumption ignored the poor combat record of al-Qaeda against Soviet troops, the efforts of all the other resistance movements, the impact on the Soviet Union of the Star Wars programme in the United States (which brought home to Soviet leaders that they could not compete with the United States economically or technologically), the growth of the Solidarity movement in Poland, and the attractiveness of the liberal-democratic model to citizens of the Eastern Bloc. Bin Laden also ignored the importance of the assistance given to the Mujahedin by the United States and Pakistan in helping to defeat the Soviet Union in Afghanistan.

Osama bin Laden has made a further strategic error in this regard: that the United States is less strong than the Soviet Union was at the time of its involvement in Afghanistan and is in effect a 'paper tiger' whose people would revolt against its government when an attack such as 9/11 took place.

But would al-Qaedaists be willing to carry through such a vicious, bloody and indiscriminate guerrilla war? The answer, as is clear from the analysis to date, is 'yes'. The key question is: why do many Muslims support the al-Qaedaists in this campaign?

4

The Crisis
Within Islam

Whereas Muslims make up just 20 percent of the world's total population,
they constitute more than 50 percent of the 1.2 billion [now 1.3 billion]
people living in abject poverty.

ANWAR IBRAHIM, *former deputy prime minister of Malaysia*[45]

MUCH OF THE MUSLIM WORLD has failed, over a period of
many centuries, to modernise itself to meet the needs and
wishes of its people. Over the last few years, a large number
of studies have been carried out, in the Middle East and the Gulf region in
particular, to assess their relative performance in relevant areas.

In terms of economic development, literacy and many other widely
accepted standards and norms, the Middle East and the Gulf region have
lagged behind every other area of the world, with the exception of Africa.
This, despite the fact that many of the countries in the region have significant oil reserves to fund their development. In short, this area of the world
has had the resourses to modernise and look after its people but has signally failed to do so.

In a chapter entitled 'A Failure of Modernity" from a book on *The Crisis
of Islam*, one commentator chronicles the dismal statistics relating to a
broad variety of areas: 'Almost the entire Muslim world is affected by poverty and tyranny. Both of these problems are attributed, especially by those

with an interest in diverting attention from themselves, to America. ... Globalisation has become a major theme in the Arab media, and it is almost always raised in connection with American economic penetration. The increasingly wretched economic situation in most of the Muslim world, compared not only with the West but also with the rapidly rising economies of East Asia, fuels these frustrations. American paramountcy, as Middle Easterners see it, indicates where to direct the blame and the resulting hostility.

'The combination of low productivity and high birth rates in the Middle East make for an unstable mix, with a large and rapidly growing population of unemployed, uneducated and frustrated young men. By all indicators from the United Nations, the World Bank and other authorities, the Arab countries – in matters such as job creation, education, technology and productivity – lag even further behind the West.

'The comparative figures for the performance of Muslim countries, as reflected in the statistics, are devastating. In the listing of economies by (absolute) gross domestic product, the highest-ranking Muslim majority country is Turkey, with 64 million inhabitants, in twenty-third place, between Austria and Denmark, with about 5 million each. The next is Indonesia, with 212 million, in twenty-eighth place, following Norway with 4.5 million, and followed by Saudi Arabia with 21 million. In comparative purchasing power, the first Muslim state is Indonesia, in fifteenth place, followed by Turkey, in nineteenth place. The highest-ranking Arab country is Saudi Arabia, in twenty-ninth place, followed by Egypt. In living standards, as reflected by gross domestic product per head, the first Muslim state is Qatar, in twenty-third place, followed by the United Arab Emirates in twenty-fifth place and Kuwait in twenty-eighth. ... In a listing of life expectancy, the first Arab state is Kuwait, in thirty-second place ... following Denmark, and followed by Cuba.

'Book sales represent an even more dismal picture. A listing of twenty-seven countries, beginning with the United States and ending with Vietnam, does not include a single Muslim state. In a human-development index, Brunei is 32nd, Kuwait 36th, Bahrain 40th, Qatar 41st, the United Arab Emirates 44th, Libya 66th, Kazakhstan 67th and Saudi Arabia tied with Brazil at number 68.

Most devastating of all, 'a report on Arab human development in 2002, prepared by a committee of Arab intellectuals and published under the auspices of the United Nations, again reveals some striking contrasts. ... The Arab world translates about 330 books annually, one-fifth of the number that Greece translates. The cumulative total of translated books since the Caliph Maa'moun's (sic) time (the ninth century) is about 100,000, almost the average that Spain translates in one year.' The economic situation is no better: 'The GDP in all Arab countries combined stood at $531.2 billion in 1999 – less than that of a single European country, Spain ($595.5 billion).

'The general economic performance of the Arab, and more broadly, the Muslim world remains relatively poor. According to the World Bank, in 2000 the average annual income in Muslim countries from Morocco to Bangladesh was only half the world average, and in the 1990s the combined gross national product of Jordan, Syria and Lebanon – that is, three of Israel's Arab neighbours – was considerably smaller than that of Israel alone. The per capita figures are worse. According to UN statistics, Israel's GDP was three and a half times that of Lebanon and Syria, twelve times that of Jordan, and thirteen and a half times that of Egypt.

'The contrast with the West, and now also the Far East, is even more disconcerting. In earlier times, such discrepancies might have passed unnoticed by the vast mass of the population. Today, thanks to modern media and communications, even the poorest and most ignorant are painfully aware of the differences between themselves and others, alike at the personal, familial, local and societal levels.

'Modernisation in politics has fared no better. ... Many Islamic countries have experimented with democratic institutions of one kind or another. In some, as in Turkey and Iran, they were introduced by innovative native reformers; in others, as in several of the Arab countries, they were installed and then bequeathed by departing imperialists. *The record, with the exception of Turkey, is one of almost unrelieved failure.*

'The people of the Middle East are increasingly aware of the deep and widening gulf between the opportunities of the free world outside their borders and the appalling privation and repression within them. The resulting anger is naturally directed first against their rulers, and then against those whom they see as keeping those rulers in power for selfish reasons. It is surely significant that all the terrorists who have been identified in the September 11 attack on New York and Washington came from Saudi Arabia and Egypt – that is, countries whose rulers are friendly to the United States.

'One reason for this curious fact, advanced by an al-Qaeda operative, is that terrorists from friendly countries have less trouble getting US visas. A more basic reason is the deeper hostility in countries where the United States is held responsible for maintaining tyrannical regimes.'[25]

While some of these statistics are slightly out of date and some of the commentary perhaps overstated, the core failure is clear. Many from within the region and outside it have noted and commented on this.

Muslims widely understand the relative failure of their societies nowadays. They are also vividly aware of the great success of Islam in medieval times. 'In this – the huge contrast between medieval success and more recent tribulations – lies the trauma of modern Islam.'[39]

To summarise: the International Institute for Strategic Studies has noted that the United Nations Arab development report, prepared by Arab intellectuals, businessmen and NGOs (all people from the area, not outsiders), identified three major 'deficits' in the Middle East/Gulf area: freedom, knowledge and female empowerment.[46] As the author William Shawcross, quoting the same report, said: 'Labour productivity is declining, real wages have fallen, poverty has grown. ... The report found that out of the seven regions of the world, the Arab region has the least freedoms of all – fewer liberties, few political rights and less free media. Women were stifled more completely in the Arab states than anywhere else; one in two Arab women can neither read nor write.'[14]

Looking to the future, the prospects are even grimmer. 'Between 2001 and 2015, the population in the region (including Iran) is estimated to rise from 304 million to 400 million. The 2 to 5 percent population growth rates responsible for this enormous increase will keep the population relatively young, which correlates with political violence. High [population] growth rates also practically mandate low or negative GDP growth and, without substantial government intervention, would help perpetuate the low status of women, a low standard of living and low literacy rates. As some Middle Eastern governments try to placate Islamist pressure groups by permitting the continuation of restrictions on the role of women in their societies, these high birth rates will continue. At the same time, deteriorating educational systems will constrain literacy growth, and declining per capita GDP will be reflected in lower standards of living.

'Even as these ominous demographic changes are taking place, loading weak and increasingly poor states in competition for oil and water with a disproportionately large cohort of unemployable, frustrated young men, thanks to the advances in information technology and freer speech, political consciousness in the region will grow as options for ruling elites shrink.'[21]

The Islamic world can therefore be seen as a failure in many measurable, non-religious areas. This compares to a dazzling history of success and pre-eminence and a potentially grim future. The UN Arab development report mentioned above shows that the Arab world in particular is fully aware of this situation. This contrast between a terrible present, a potentially worse future and a collective belief in a hugely successful and glorious past is, I believe, the foundation stone for the ideology of al-Qaedaism, and particularly its rage against others.

The period of Islamic success and glory lasted from approximately the eighth century until the thirteenth and fourteenth centuries. Almost all commentators and all measurable information suggests that the decline of Islam started then. Many believe this was because of internal divisions within the widespread Muslim empire wordwide, while others cite either invasions of Muslim territories by mainly non-western imperialists or the corruption of Islamic leaders. As the decline of Islam from its period of glory and the resultant crisis is a key reason for support for al-Qaedaism, it is important to understand why this decline occurred.

Introducing Islam, co-authored by Ziauddin Sardar and Zafar Abbas Malik, clearly states: 'the decline of the Muslim civilisation has been attributed to a number of factors. Internal divisions and feuds within the Muslim empire, the corrupt and luxuriant lifestyles of the rulers, the fall of Baghdad and the loss of Spain are commonly cited reasons for the downfall of the Muslims. ... But the sack of Baghdad and the fall of Granada, though turning points in Muslim history, cannot really be considered as the main causes for Muslim decline. The force that placed Muslim civilisation in reverse gear was an internal and conceptual one.

'Towards the end of the fourteenth century, the *ulama* (religious scholars), who, thanks to Al-Ghazzali, were in a position of dominance, began to conceive of the written word as an independent realm of representation and truth apart from life. The proliferation of books had created a distance between authors and the words that carried their ideas across space and time. The text was open to every variety of interpretation, irrespective of real facts and truth.

'So what if the given text is open to a number of interpretations? The *ulama* had two concerns. First, there were concerns that the Koran was open to all kinds of wild interpretations, not just by untutored readers, but also by theologically unqualified professional writers. To some extent, this was a genuine concern given that a variety of irrational and exploitative behaviour was being justified on the basis of the Koran and tradition. But this was intimately linked to the second and more important worry: the proliferation of written texts had begun to undermine the authority and control that the *ulama* enjoyed over both the Muslim rulers and the masses.'

'The *ulama* over a period of a hundred years then restricted the gates of independent reasoning on matters of religion, and effectively removed the power of the consensus of the community and replaced it with the consensus of themselves – the religious scholars. This had a devastating effect on Muslim society. *Ijtihad* (independent reasoning on matters of religion) thus gave way to *Taqlid* (blind imitation); reasoning, speculation and innovation were replaced by imitation. The interpretation of the Koran was frozen in history. In the absence of new ideas, reflection and understanding of changing circumstances, Muslim thought ossified and became totally obscurantist. Consequently, Muslim culture lost its dynamism and degenerated, while the Muslim community was transformed from an open to a closed society.'[49]

On this decline, colonialism, and the need for regeneration, the authors say: 'It has been customary for Muslim thinkers to blame the present condition of Muslim societies solely on colonialism. But in the 1950s and 1960s the Algerian social philosopher Malek Bennabi knocked this suggestion for six. Bennabi introduced a theory of "colonizability." In essence, the theory holds that the real ills of the Muslim world do not spring from the fact of being colonized but from a state previous to this, which made it ripe for colonization. The real liberation of Muslim people, Bennabi argued, will come from addressing the injustices introduced into the thought and body-politic of Islam in the late thirteenth century. Bennabi forced Muslim society to look at itself and re-examine its history and sources. Other writers have written similar analyses of the Muslim predicament.'

'The overall consensus among Muslim scholars is that the Muslim world is in urgent need of new thought which:

1   liberates tradition from fossilized history and transforms it from a suffocating into a life-enhancing enterprise
2   formulates a new *fiqh* – that is, a new jurisprudence and law, focused on contemporary needs, requirements and issues facing Muslim society.
3   Reopens 'the gates of *Ijtihad*' and leads, through reasoned and sustained struggle, to a fresh understanding and a new comprehension of the teachings of the Koran and the life and traditions of the Prophet Muhammad.'[49]

[I should point out that this commentary is talking about Sunni Islam in the main, as *Ijtihad* did continue in the Shiite tradition.]

Other Islamic scholars also see the decline happening due to internal developments within Islam, but for slightly different reasons.

As Malise Ruthven explains: 'The Mu'tazilites, sometimes known as "rationalists", were a group of Muslim scholars who came under the influence of Greek philosophical thought. They achieved considerable power during the caliphate of al-Ma'mum (813–33) when they established a kind of inquisition, known as the *mihna*, according to which scholars at the caliphal court were obliged to proclaim their adherence to the doctrine that the Koran had been created in time. Emphasising references to an "Arabic Koran" that occur in the sacred test, they argued that the decrees embedded in such a text were evidently subject to time and place, and might possibly be overruled by an inspired imam or caliph. The attractions of this theory for al-Ma'mum were clear. Their opponents, who came to be known as the *ahl al-Hadith*, 'the People of Tradition', argued that, on the contrary, the Koran was "uncreated", being, as it were, an inseparable part of the Godhead. (This is part of the Sunni tradition.)

'Obviously the decrees of the "uncreated" Koran were eternally unchangeable: a doctrine that would make the caliph and other worldly rulers clearly subject to the decrees of 'What God sent down'. The Mu'tazilites were eventually overthrown by the *ahl al-Hadith*. They rallied around Ahmid Ibn Hanbal, whose refusal to accept the Mu'tazilite doctrine, despite torture and imprisonment, made him into an heroic figure for what could be called, anachronistically, the "Islamic religious Right". Islamic modernists [and the Shiites] tended to view the defeat of Mu'tazilism in the face of populist pressure as an underlying reason for Muslim intellectual decline, although it took centuries to take effect.'[24]

'This attitude of cultural intransigence is consistent with the traditional Sunni insistence on the primacy of revelation over reason. Although historically the Arabs took over, and advanced, the learning of the Greeks and other peoples of late antiquity, making the advances in mathematics, optics, medicine and other disciplines that are often seen as laying the foundations for the humanism of Renaissance Europe, the dogma that revealed knowledge supersedes or encompasses knowledge acquired by the exercise of reason has remained part of the Arab-Muslim cultural outlook into the twenty-first century. Its origins lie in the defeat of the Mu'tazila during the 'Abbasid period, a populist revolt against the intellectual elitism represented by the court of al-Ma'mun.

'The prodigious intellectual achievements of subsequent generations of Muslims always occurred in the face of populist pressure. The courts fostered talents that were placed at the disposal of ordinary Muslims in the magnificent public buildings we associate with the civilisations of Islam at their height. But despite the achievements of individual Muslim scientists, cultural attitudes as a whole remained hostile to borrowing, experimentation and innovation, which are fundamental to scientific method. Education remained a limited preserve, because of the systematic hostility to the introduction of printing on the part of the *ulama*. The high rates of illiteracy in countries such as Afghanistan and Pakistan have been major obstacles to development and to the introduction of reformist or modernist trends in the way Islam is interpreted. The supremacy of revelation over reason made philosophy the marginal pursuit of an intellectual elite which preached one truth to itself (founded on speculative inquiry) and another (based exclusively on revelation) to the people.'[24]

It is also very clear that political and religious differences within Islam have had a devastating effect over very many centuries. Such differences between the Sunni and Shiite traditions and many others started just after the death of the Prophet Muhammad and have continued to this day. These conflicts have frequently been extremely bloody – the Iran-Iraq war being a particularly vicious example.

Daniel Easterman makes an important point here: 'Much modern Muslim writing tries to play down the triumph of the West by emphasising the dark side of the European and North American experience, the inner angst of a bankrupt civilisation on the verge of collapse. The problem is that Islam itself is peculiarly vulnerable on this score. There is very little point in sneering at the material success of others if at the same time one measures one's own achievements by precisely the same criteria: the unprecedented triumph of Muslim arms, the glories of the Abbasid, Andalusian or Mughal empires, the scientific advances of the Islamic Middle Ages.'[50]

This Islamic analysis is confirmed by a Western view on this decline: 'The origins of the Muslim decline began in the thirteenth century, the point at which Muslim atrophy and Christendom's advances became discernable. Nevertheless for some five hundred years hence, Muslims remained largely oblivious to the extraordinary developments taking place in Europe.'[39]

So clearly the decline and current crisis occurred because of internal Islamic developments and issues – not because of external aggression or conquest or conspiracy. This is contrary to much popular perception – especially but not only in the Islamic world.

There are other, more common explanations for the decline and current crisis in the Muslim world.

THE ISRAELI-PALESTINE DISPUTE? THE UNITED STATES?

Many blame US support for the state of Israel for the growth of al-Qaedaism. This is a point I will deal with later. At this point we are considering generally accepted reasons for the current crisis within Islam, which as we have seen from the analysis above commenced in the 13th and 14th centuries and arose because of internal developments within Islam itself.

It is obviously impossible to blame the Israeli-Palestinian dispute, which commenced in 1948, on the declaration of independence for the state of Israel following the UN resolution dividing the disputed territories between Jews and Palestinians, for a decline which commenced more than five hundred years before the establishment of Israel. In addition, it is also clearly impossible to blame the United States, whose very active role in the Middle East/Gulf began around 1973, and which did not even exist when the decline of Islam began.

WESTERN IMPERIALISM?

Many people, including many in the West, blame Western imperialism for what happened to Islam. However, it is clear that the decline in Islam occurred long before imperialism from Europe got under way. In addition, many experts are very clear that the Western role vis-à-vis Islam was not that important an issue and that, in particular, the Mongols and Hindus were much more important in imperial terms, and much more devastating to Islam, as was inter-Islamic conflict in general. Moreover, the Western encounter with Islam, and in particular European imperialism, was very time-limited, for example, Aden from 1839 to 1967, Egypt from 1882 to 1954, and Sudan from 1890 to 1956, all long after the decline in Islam commenced.

We therefore cannot blame Western imperialism for the decline of Islam. Warfare with non-Western powers and within Islam was much more damaging to it throughout most of the period of its decline. Western imperialism certainly had a negative impact, particularly in the 19th and 20th Centuries, but was not the causal factor for the decline of Islam which had started much earlier.

THE MIDDLE-EASTERN CRUSADES?

Nor should we blame the Crusades to the Middle-East.

'The capture of Jerusalem by the Crusaders in 1099 was a triumph for Christendom and a disaster for the Muslims and also for the Jews in the city. To judge by the Arabic historiography of the period, it aroused very little interest in the region.

'Awareness of the Crusades as a distinctive historical phenomenon dates from the 19th Century, and the translation of European books on history. Since then, there is a new perception of the Crusades as an early prototype of the expansion of European imperialism into the Islamic world. A more accurate description would present them as a long-delayed, very limited, and finally ineffectual response to the jihad. The crusades ended in failure and defeat, and were soon forgotten in the lands of Islam, but later European efforts to resist and reverse the Muslim advance into Christendom [sometimes also called Crusades] were more successful, and initiated what became a series of painful defeats on the frontiers of the Islamic world'[25].

Edward Peters makes a number of crucial points here: 'The over-whelming European presence in the Middle East in the late 19th and early 20th Centuries implied to many Arab historians an equally formidable European presence in the 12th and 13th. Accordingly, they drew sharper identifications of the Crusades with the modern period. Such a view was strengthened by what [Emmanuel] Sivan terms the "topicality" of the Crusades in some 20th Century Arab thought: "The concept of the topicality of the Crusades stems, then, from a belief in a certain parallelism between the 12th to 13th Centuries and the last 100 years ... the Crusades as well as current developments are part and parcel of the same historical process – the age long struggle between East and West'.

'Because many Muslim thinkers did not regard Islamic expansion in the 7th and 8th Centuries as a conquest, but rather as a peaceful opening of the lands to the message of Muhammad, they assumed the Crusades to have been a Western initiative rather than a counter-offensive, just as Turkish and Arab writers and political leaders perceived the 19th and 20th Century European presence in the Middle East'.

'It is a short step from some Zionists' invoking the language of the Crusades that Europeans had used in the 19th and 20 th Centuries, to Arabs taking up the theme that had been incipient in Arabic historiography and political propaganda since at least 1865: modern Europeans were identical with the Crusaders, and European-exported Zionists were the next Crusaders, another chapter in the Ilm Al-Karitha ("the Science of the Catastrophe")'.

'Moreover the original French argument that the Crusades were Europe's first venture into colonisation [solely for inter-Europe propaganda purposes] was also used in the path-breaking scholarship of the great late 20th Century French historian of the Crusades, Jean Richard, and the French–trained Israeli historian Joshua Prawer, pioneer and patron of modern Israeli Crusade studies. Both, however, used the term in the context of contemporary theoretical debates about the nature and history of colonialism. This focus, as well as subsequent post-colonialist theory, have kept the subject of the Crusader states and modern Israel as colonies in the forefront of modern scholarly debate'.

'By 2003, when Tariq Aziz and Osama Bin Laden used the term "crusades" they were speaking in a conceptual language that had taken shape since the mid-nineteenth century in several very different cultural contexts'.

'Carole Hillenbrand rightly notes that "the psychological scars left by the Crusades (are) deeply etched into the modern Islamic consciousness". But etched scars and damaged psyches may be deliberately cultivated'[52]

'In 2003, when Saddam Hussein wished to emphasise the idea of a terrible foreign threat to Baghdad, he referred not to earlier Christian attacks on Islam ... but to the Mongols'. 'The Mongols were far more important to the history of the 13th Century Islamic world than the Crusades. Persia and Anatolia had already been overrun by the Mongols, and in 1260 Hulegu captured Damascus, as the Crusaders had failed to do in 1148.'[52]

So the Middle-Eastern Crusades, from having been a relatively innocuous counter-offensive on the part of Europe, which failed dismally, and was almost totally ignored by the Islamic world at the time, was converted by a whole series of misunderstandings and political manipulations, particularly on the part of French propagandists in the 18th and 19th Century, into a major expression of colonialism. That propaganda was then picked up by Arab and other thinkers, leading to the current completely unbalanced view of the importance, and the impact, of the Middle-Eastern Crusades on Islamic society. Their actual impact on Islamic society, particularly in the Middle East and Gulf, was minimal and was essentially ignored by Islam at the time.

In fact some historians are of the view that the impact of the Crusades on the Middle-East was broadly positive on Islamic life there as it led to greater unity within Islam, and eventually enabled that stronger Islam to defeat those Crusaders completely.

We therefore cannot blame the Middle-Eastern Crusades for the later decline of Islam.

Recent history proves this and the limited impact of Western imperialism: 'The early Crusading expeditions attracted very little attention from Muslim chroniclers and far less than the conflicts with Byzantium and the later Mongol invasions (which were what the Palestinian newspaper Al-Quds likened the US war on Iraq to, comparing the fall of Baghdad in April 2003 to its conquest by the Mongols in 1258)'.[52]

In summary it is clear that the lengthy decline in Islam starting in the 13th and 14th centuries, and its current crisis, did not occur because of Western imperialism, the Middle-Eastern Crusades, US actions, or the Israeli -

Palestinian dispute. The key and originating cause was within Islam itself probably from a number of causes, but particularly due to the religious scholars taking control starting in the late 14th Century. On top of that, inter-Islamic conflict (principally Sunni-Shiite) had a major negative impact down through each of the centuries of this decline.

Undoubtedly invasions of Islamic lands by Mongols, Hindus and Europeans did not help but such were not the key reasons for the Islamic decline and crisis.

Irrespective of its cause, we cannot ignore the fact that there is a significant rage in the Islamic world at present, with much of it directed at the West, particularly the United States. This rage appears widespread across Islam, and is constantly inflamed by certain Western (especially US) and Israeli actions. This has been the case particularly since 1973, when it is generally accepted that US involvement in the Middle East and Gulf region became the predominant Western influence there. Since then, generally uncritical support of Israel by the United States, particularly during a variety of crises and continued Israeli occupation of Palestinian territories and military actions, inflamed this negative reaction. The first Gulf war, although UN-approved and supported by a significant number of Arab states, produced an extraordinarily widespread negative reaction in the region, particularly with the stationing of US troops in the land of the two shrines, Saudi Arabia. The impact of globalisation, as we shall see, and the UN-mandated war in Afghanistan, as well as the invasion and war in Iraq, significantly worsened the views of public opinion in the region against the West, and particularly the United States. This has been worsened by anti-Western propaganda in many Islamic states, very poor or non-existent education in many of those states, and sermons by religious leaders. Particularly in the Middle East and the Gulf region, local despotic leaders have learned to distract their people from their own appalling tribulations by focusing all possible media attention on Israeli, US and Western inequities, and on the negative impact on their societies of globalisation.

As one commentator has said, many in Islam have 'no rights, no money, and no future'. How would most people react to such a situation? The West, and particularly the United States, with its massive cultural presence in the region, is the obvious and easy target to blame for the current problems in these societies.

5

Why This Hyper-
terrorist Threat to the
World Now?

'One only has to shed the tyranny of fashion in order to think of it.'
CARL VON CLAUSEWITZ[53]

The decline of Islam clearly has been occuring for centuries. Why then has al-Qaedaism only emerged as such a threat in the last decade?

NALYSING WHY AL-QAEDAISM has become the threat it is currently is crucial. It is only through understanding the core reasons for the problem that we can begin to identify the correct solutions to it.

Many reasons are given for the emergence of this threat now – some of which are partially or completely unfounded or unsubstantiated. Let us examine them one by one. Firstly, let us discard the explanations that do not stand up to detailed analysis.

Is poverty the problem?
No.

There is no doubt that the relative economic performance of many of the Islamic states is dismal. However, it is clear from a brief examination of the backgrounds of the 9/11 hijackers and other al-Qaedaist militants that they share in the main a middle-class background, a good education, and a considerable knowledge of the West, frequently gained in Europe.

As Daniel Pipes has put it: 'Like fascism and Marxism-Leninism in their heydays, militant Islam attracts highly competent, motivated and ambitious individuals. Far from being the laggards of society, they are its leaders. Brooks, a much-travelled journalist, found Islamists to be "the most gifted"of the youth encountered. Those "hearing the Islamic call included the students with the most options, not just the desperate cases. ... They were the elites of the next decade: the people who would shape their nation's future."'[39]

In addition, as Paul Berman put it, Osama bin Laden 'is a man from the Saudi plutocracy, instructed by some of the most brilliant and radical of the anti-Western Islamist radicals – yet, at the same time, a man whose relatives have studied in universities all over the Western world, and who have donated to some of the best of these universities, Harvard, Tufts and Oxford. He is a man whose family has functioned for many years within the elite of the Western world. The family has even gone into business with Bush the Elder in an enterprise called the Carlyle Group (a shocking fact in regard to Bush the Elder's sense of judgement – but let it pass). And who are [Osama] bin Laden's foot soldiers? The 9/11 terrorists, most of them, likewise turn out to have been people with claims on both the Arab past and the Western present.'[37]

So we are not exactly dealing with marginalized, poverty-stricken, downtrodden peasants here.

But what about the masses in Islamic countries – many of them at or below the poverty line?

There has been considerable research on the possible relationship between poverty and terrorism. As Professor Michael Mousseau of Koç University in Istanbul, Turkey, notes: 'The direct causal linkages between poverty and terror are more elusive than scholars suggest, however. Indeed, I am unaware of any comprehensive explanation in print for how poverty causes terror, nor has there been any demonstrated correlation between the two.'[54]

Similarly, research has been done on the type of individual who is prepared to engage in terrorist action. 'The profiles of captured or killed lower-level al-Qaeda operatives suggest an ideal type: young men of conservative religious and middle- or lower-middle-class backgrounds, caught between cultures and often living lives of alienation and anomie. The radical Islamist myth created by the ideologues gives shape and direction to these outsiders' anger, which is as likely to have a personal source as to derive from political grievances.'[38]

Very poor societies do not necessarily generate terrorism. Major increases in financial well-being, such as occurred in the Middle East and the Gulf region in the 1970s (when oil prices were raised dramatically) did not reduce terrorism: in fact, it was in this period that the roots of al-Qaedaism were put down.

As William Rosenau of Rand puts it: 'We don't know what the root causes [of terrorism] are. Poverty? If it were, Haiti would be the godhead of international terror, and upper-class Italians would never have joined the Brigate Rosse during the 1970s.'[4]

From a broader perspective , none of the four waves of terrorism – pressure for reform within autocratic states, anti-colonialism, left-wing revolutionary vanguards, and the current jihad era – were motivated primarily by poverty.

It is clear that poverty alone does not cause terrorism. In particular, poverty does not seem to be a key driving force for al-Qaedaists, but it may of course provide 'justification' in relative if not absolute terms for the support from substantial numbers of Muslims who blame the 'other' (the West generally, and the United States in particular) for the current failure of their societies and for supporting their despotic leaders.

So is Islam itself the problem?

No: not directly, anyway.

The history of Islam shows that, on certain occasions, Islam has adopted an expansionist mode, but this does not explain the current hyper-terrorism. All religions, including Christianity and Judaism, at some stage in their history or development have produced zealots who twisted core religious beliefs into something unrecognisable to the majority, usually for their own reasons. Islam is no different.

To quote one expert on the 9/11 atrocity: 'The callous destruction of thousands in the World Trade Centre, including many who were not American, some of them Muslims from Muslim countries, has no justification in Islamic doctrine or law and no precedent in Islamic history. Indeed, there are few acts of comparable deliberate and indiscriminative wickedness in human history. These are not just crimes against humanity and against civilisation; they are also acts – from a Muslim point of view – of blasphemy, as those who perpetrate such crimes claim to be doing so in the name of God, His Prophet, and His scriptures.'[25]

Many, blaming the rise of al-Qaeda and its associated groups on Islam, compare al-Qaedaists to the Assassins of ancient times – a group that targeted what they saw as corrupt leaders within Islam and assassinated a considerable number of them. The Assassins, however, were careful only to kill their direct target – usually unjust Islamic rulers. They did not kill innocent civilians and did not commit suicide, although they were prepared to die for their beliefs. They are thus not a precedent for al-Qaedaism.

Nonetheless, Osama bin Laden does refer endlessly – and deliberately – to Islam, and al-Qaedaists invariably describe themselves in Islamic terms.

The nature of al-Qaedaists' perversion of Islam, and the failure of much of Islam to confront them, was covered in an interview with the Kurdish intellectual and author Kanan Makiya on the PBS television program *Frontline* in winter 2002:

Connect it to the hijackers. What, if anything, have they brought to the discussion of evil? Do you see them as part of the banality of evil? Or something different?

No. The hijackers bring in a different element of evil. … They have invented a form of it. … Not fully invented it, but they'll say they've carried it to an extreme. … I would say it's this sort of perfection of the death instinct. It is the infatuation, rapture, in the event of killing oneself and others, of death, as many people as possible. That's what they bring that's so new – this ability to be at one with the desire to die and to inflict death on as many people as possible – not as an instrument, not as a means. … In order to get into this state of mind, all sorts of bizarre changes take place in the person's mind. But death is absolutely essential – an enormous act of destruction, apocalyptic in nature.

This is what September 11 is about, in that this was done in a new way. We don't know anything quite like it on this scale and with that kind of dedication of purpose, and with that kind of, let's say, greatness of execution. A planning of a spectacle that combines all these various qualities: numbers, death, greatness of spectacle, and absolute commitment to, desire to, kill oneself. ... I don't think politics, economics, sociology and certainly not pathology are what is truly the essence of this human phenomenon, evil. It's somewhere else. ...

We've had a number of people respond to the videotape of [Osama] bin Laden laughing, feeling that they had moved into a different zone of trying to understand evil – the disregard and the humour and the playfulness and the giggling. Did you have a response to looking at that [Osama] bin Laden tape? If so, what was it?

The tape that depicts Osama bin Laden joking around and sitting in a social situation with a sheik from Saudi Arabia and other visitors and talking about what happened at the World Trade Centre towers building is, I think, a good illustration of the phrase that Hannah Arendt uses, 'banality of evil,' because the social setting was utterly banal. This was a typical Gulf Arab congregation in the evening. ... What was evil was not the laughter and the various gestures and mannerisms that are part and parcel of that particular setting if you are a Gulf Arab.

What was so jarring was what the conversation was about, which was this act of apocalyptic destruction. So here are these men having a totally ordinary social conversation, perhaps around cups of coffee and teas and pastry. ... But what they're talking about is the death and destruction of 3,500 people, and they're praising it and so on. That is the jarring element.

It's exactly like Eichmann sitting behind his desk, turning out his paperwork, which results in hundreds of thousands of people being shipped off to the concentration camps. It's the coming together, the confluence of these two things that is, I think, so evil. The fact that these people have so internalised the act, so accepted it; not a single qualm is there. Nothing. They're very happy with it. They're talking about how many people are going to be converted to Islam because of it. ... The kind of demented quality of this speech and the expectations that was present in that tape, that is frightening. Frightening, and truly exceptional.

In the wake of September 11 . . . I think all of us . . . have had the most searing conversations about the role of religion, and not even one particular religion, which we'll get to, but just religion generally, and the darkness at the heart of religion. . . . One rabbi said to me off-camera and on-camera, 'Religion drove those planes in to the building', and developed his thinking about why that was the case. . . . What is your response to that very provocative phrase, 'Religion drove those planes into the building'?

At this point in time, in this place, at this conjuncture in our history, religion did drive those planes into those towers. In that sense, in some deep sense, some deep way, religion is responsible. ... Not any religion, but Islam in particular. But you just have to change the time and the circumstance, the moment. Move back fifty years, a hundred years, whatever, and you can have an entirely different circumstance. ...

I have always thought there were dark . . . corners in religion. I took that for granted. That's not the surprising thing for me. ... The frightening thing is rather that, in the Arab world, we have let the darkness of religion flourish. The forces that are dampening it at this moment in our history are weak, and that is frightening. ...

It was born out of conditions which I can follow and track and see. I think that's very important to understanding it, because there are all sorts of elements in Islamic tradition. For instance, you can take a word like 'jihad'. These young men saw themselves as committing an act of jihad – martyrdom for their faith.

But there is an entirely different notion of jihad, which is a self-questioning of the soul. They chose not to see jihad in that sense. ... They chose to pick a martial tradition. They chose to reference themselves to ten years of Muslim history. There's 1,400 years of Muslim history to pick and choose from. But these young men chose the years 622 to 632 exactly, because that is the period when the Prophet was essentially forced by Meccan society, which considered him a dangerous threat to them, to leave Mecca. After he left Mecca, he set up a city-state.

So [in] the first ten years of the Muslim city-state experiment, based in the city of Medina, the Prophet waged war against his enemies – defensive war at times, and offensive war at others – and unified the peninsula. This, for these young men, is chosen and singled out to be the paradigmatically perfect model society. They disregard what the Prophet said previously to that in Mecca, which are some of the most generous and sort of compassionate verses of the Koran. They choose a particular interpretation, and they argue that that interpretation excludes and supersedes all the others. ...

I say this to highlight what you can do with religion. You could have chosen those ten years, or you could choose another ten years. What's frightening is that so few people are repudiating their choice. ... The frightening thing about that choice is that it has touched a chord in large numbers of people. ... Obviously, [the chord] was there already. But they picked it ... and they have enormously strengthened it by what they've done. That's frightening. That's truly frightening. But it's not inevitable....

The rejection and repudiation of that, in the name of Islam, is still inadequate, too weak, to counter that. It doesn't yet have the force that is required – the moral force.

In other words, these young men have captured the moral high ground. Not the whole of Islam yet, but they are in danger of capturing the moral high ground of a great religious tradition. The great, great challenge that faces Muslims today is to repudiate that. Not just the act; it's not about saying, 'We're against an act of terrorism here or there.' It's a much more foundational act of rejection.

What specific parts of tradition did they [the September 11 hijackers] pick up and make their own? They didn't make them up of a whole cloth. ... Who did these kids speak for? How deep is the chord throughout the Muslim world?

Perhaps the most dangerous element that was picked out of the Muslim tradition and changed and transformed in the hands of these young men who perpetrated September 11 is this idea of committing suicide. They call it martyrdom, of course. Suicide is firmly rejected in Islam as an act of worship. In the tradition, generally, to die in battle for a larger purpose – that is, for the sake of the community at large – is a noble thing to do. Self-sacrifice yourself as you defend the community – that is a traditional thing, and that has a traditional meaning of 'jihad'. But what is non-traditional, what is new is this idea that jihad is almost like an act of private worship. You become closer to God by blowing yourself up in such a way. You, privately, irrespective of what effect it has on everyone else. ... For these young men, that is the new idea of jihad.

This idea of jihad allows you to lose all the old distinctions between combatants and non-combatants, between just and unjust wars, between the rules of engagement of different types. All of that is gone, because now the act of martyrdom is an act of worship . . . in and of itself. It's like going on the pilgrimage. It's like paying your alms, which every Muslim has to do. It's like praying in the direction of Mecca, and so on and so forth. It is an individual act of worship. That's terrifying, and that's new. That's an entirely new idea, which these young men have taken out, developed. . . .

The battle to rid Islam of that notion of jihad . . . is a terribly, terribly important one, which it does not seem to me we are up to yet. Moderate, that is, Muslim thinkers from within the tradition themselves, have not yet met the challenge.

Why not?

There is an intellectual failure. There is a lack of courage at the moment in the Middle East. And I should say it's very important to single out the Middle East here from the whole of Islam . . . because that's where all of this comes from. Even if [Afghanistan] has become involved and Pakistan has become involved, the origin of all of this unfortunately is in the Arab part of the Muslim world, which is less than 20 percent of the whole.

Why are we not up to it? . . . One reason is that my generation did not appropriate its own traditions. It considered this part of the past, and ignored it and pressed ahead with ideologies that came from the West. It did not try to reappropriate its own tradition and take it on board, thus leaving it to clerics and other elements. So there is a generational break. . . .

We have lost contact with our roots. That means that those roots were appropriated by the ignoramuses and the other clerics, so we don't even have a battle of ideas engaged. . . . So there is a battle over texts, over ideas, that needs to take place within Muslims, among Muslims. . . . So people like myself and my generation ought now to consider it necessary to engage, however liberal, socialist, nationalist they may be in other outlooks, in their general outlook on life. But [we] haven't.

Isn't there also a problem, too, which is theologically based, in that [the Koran], your bible so to speak, is not considered a human document? The scholarship around it hasn't been approached in the same as ours has been, for good or for ill. I mean, to raise questions about the Koran is to incur a kind of wrath or death threats or exclusion from academic circles. To ask the appropriate sort of textual questions is very difficult.

The Western societies have had hundreds of years of reformation behind them. Islam has never had its reformation, and that is part of the problem. If you look back to the sixteenth and seventeenth centuries, when men were killing one another in the name of religion throughout Europe, that's where we're at more or less, historically speaking, in terms of the level of debate and discourse. The Koran is considered an untouchable text, not a historical document. ... This is the literal word of God, and it is very dangerous to play with that in the Middle East today. ...

Modern scholarship has moved on different tracks. I mean, you get excellent works of sociology and political science and so on. ... But that secular intelligentsia, very interestingly, has not touched religion, has left it to others. That's what I meant about this bifurcation. So it operates on two planes. We are left with a medieval concept of religious texts and a modern life, in many other respects, with no lines, organic connection, between the two. That is another level of failure in the society.

Which also helps make a [Osama] bin Laden possible?

Yes, exactly. All he has to do is return to those texts, especially in a country like Saudi Arabia. What's so interesting is that all these people, so many of them, come from Saudi Arabia. ... It's so important to keep in mind that, of the nineteen hijackers, fifteen were Saudis. Of all the various men that are being held in the base by the United States, prisoners, at the moment, hundreds upon hundreds apparently are Saudis.

Saudi Arabia is not a country that produced a single interesting political thought or political idea in the last thirty, forty years of Arab politics. But all of a sudden, it's a moving force. It's shaping. Bin Laden is emerging. Young Saudis are coming up with these ideas. It's not coincidence, because my generation, the modern ideas – the Palestinian resistance movement – all of these were ideas associated with the Fertile Crescent, with countries like Palestine, Lebanon, Iraq, et cetera. All of a sudden, the countries that had remained in the backwaters are now appropriating the religion to themselves.

And, by the way, they started doing that much earlier. The Saudi government has been pumping money in a quiet kind of revolution to shape Islam in its own images since 1973, [with] oil-price rises. It wasn't a noisy revolution like the Iranian revolution was. It didn't have so much hubbub and noise associated with it and all. But it was quietly done [with] Saudi influence, using money, and the building of [madrassas] – that is, religious schools and mosques all across the world. ...

The very particular kind of Islam associated with Saudi Arabia . . . is an upstart. It was created in the eighteenth century. It was constrained and confined entirely to the Arabian Peninsula right through to the late 1960s. All of a sudden, this [Wahhabi] Islam – which is espoused by these young men, which considers even a Muslim like myself, because of my Shiite background, to be dirty or not a real Muslim – [is] probably the dominant form [of Islam] in the United States. It spreads from one end of the world to the next. It's been a quiet, silent revolution that's been happening, and suddenly exploded on the scene with September 11. ...

What kind of reflections has September 11 sort of provoked in you about [Islam]?

The defensiveness of Islam is its crucial feature today. It's what, by the way, is in such contrast to the most interesting period of Islamic history, when Islam was an open, absorbing religion, constantly taking in outside influences, as opposed to its current hedgehog-like posture, prickly to the outside . . . always looking backward. This is not how it was in the creative moment, in the first four, six, eight centuries of Islam, where it was constantly seeking out and absorbing.

So the existential question for Muslims today is, Can they construct such a dynamic sense of their own religion that is open to the world? Accepting of it? Of 'otherness', of people and religions and so on? . . . That takes on these guys, this alternative 'jihadic' strain of Islam . . . [and] defeats it intellectually . . . pulls the rug under it, by undermining the pillars and pointing out the inhuman and ungodly, if you like, qualities and characters it has taken on. ...

If you could talk about evil as we are seeing – Americans are seeing – from that perspective, and how those nineteen hijackers came to believe that we are the very embodiment of evil. ...

I have no doubt whatsoever that [Osama] bin Laden and his cohorts, the broader trend that he represents, think of the United States as evil. But I don't think they come there because they are defeated internally. ... There's something very different going on here. For these people, Islam is a resurgent force. That resurgence is expressed in their actions, and I think even in their conception of the evilness of the United States.

Now, on one level, evil for them is anyone who is not a true Muslim. That's quite clear. An infidel, or a better word for it in this particular case is a non-believer. But they're certainly not out to convert the population of the United States. ... This is not an act – the language, the symbols... the martyrdom, all of this – designed to address Americans or attract them to anything. So there's a kind of a wall here. In a way, it's addressing somebody else first.

Bin Laden's real audience is the Middle East, his other Muslims. I think he thought that, by this act, he would win large numbers of converts to his cause . . . [to] bring Arab regimes down. He would perhaps even take power in this or that country, preferably Saudi Arabia. That is where he is looking to; that is who is the audience. That is who his symbols are directed towards.

So this is unlike anything else in the history of Islam. Early Muslims, when they left the Arabian Peninsula and entered the [Fertile Crescent], were conquerors. They converted peoples, and they gave them time to convert. So they didn't force them sometimes, and they were perfectly happy ruling over them. They were setting up a state, and then people converted over time. Syria remained Christian for hundreds of years after the Muslim conquest. So something different is going on here.

The obvious sense in which the United States is evil is in the cultural icons that are seen everywhere. They are seemingly trivial things, the influence of the America culture, which is everywhere: TV, how women dress, the lack of importance of religion. So these are the senses in which they are rejecting the United States. But you're right; they don't see Americans as people. ... They block that out. They only see as people the Muslims they want to convert to their side, and that's terrifying. ...

But what drives [Osama bin Laden] really is then an ancient, spiritual, religious idea – whether you like it or not – which drives so many of the religions, which is the 'pure' and the 'impure'.

Yes. It's that simple. That is very true. ... The world is . . . divided into these good and bad, very simple categories. He is out to restore justice in the absolute sense, and good against evil. ...

As Andrew Sullivan said, 'Yes, this is a religious war.'

Yes. I mean, his [Osama bin Laden's] part of it is a religious war, with this curious twist that he is not demented enough to think that he can actually take on the power of the United States and destroy it. But he is hoping to win over Muslims to him. So the battle has a kind of a long strategy with various stages to it. The attack on the United States was, I think, primarily intended to win over recruits to his cause, bring about disruption in the Arab world and lead to his type of person coming into power in the Arab world, and then sort of gradually would expand his post.

Earlier you were saying to me, it's a story in the end that, when all the fancy interpretations are over with, it puts cruelty first. How do you create a religion out of a story that . . . puts cruelty first?

I find it very significant that no religious traditions, Islam included, is ever in a position, I think almost by definition, to put cruelty first in the order of its priorities of the terrible things that human beings can do. That is perfectly illustrated in the story of Abraham's sacrifice with his son. Because, of course, what the story's all about is faith, the importance and the primacy of faith. ...

What is the essence of faith in the story is Abraham's willingness (a) not to question God about his command to sacrifice his son, and (b) to proceed slowly, deliberately, over a period of time – three days, I think it was – [and] march up the mountain, prepare the sacrifice, unquestioning, resolute. [It was] the perfect, as Kierkegaard put it, 'night of faith' model, exemplar of faith. And [Abraham] is, in the Muslim tradition, exactly that – an exemplar of faith. That is the importance of Abraham to Muslims. ...

Had he faltered, his faith would have been less, a degree or so less. He didn't falter. God immediately stops it at the absolute last moment and, of course, the act is ended. But what the story is all about is how faith in God comes first, before anything else, and then follow various virtues, of which harm to other human beings surely has to be below faith. It seemed to me that that is something that the hijackers certainly took to heart.

In the . . . manual that they seemed to have discussed before the event, that was setting them up psychologically to proceed with their mission, various circumstances are laid out in this document. One of them is, what happens if one of the [passengers] resists? The manual very clearly tells the hijacker to stiffen his resolve and make him able to do the deed he is about to do. Consider if one of the [passengers] does, in fact, rise up and stop you, consider that this is an offering that God has given you. ... It is a gift – not an offering, a gift – that has been bestowed, which you can give as an offering to your mother and father as you slaughter the passenger.

The language used is exactly the same as the language in the Abraham story. The word [means] .... 'to slaughter', not 'to kill.' It is a sense that the killing of the passenger ... is an act of slaughter emulating the great sacrifice that stands at the foundations of religious faith, namely that of Abraham sacrificing his son.

That's probably one of the most chilling moments. Here you see a story, a great foundational story of faith in God and a definitional story of what is faith, turned on its head. ...

Is it fair to say that submission to the rule of Allah is a core belief in Islam, and to a greater degree even than in any other great monotheistic traditions? Or has it come to be submission? Does that make it particularly vulnerable for people like the hijackers?

That's a good question. Certainly submission is a key; that's the meaning of the word 'Islam', to surrender, to submit to the will of God. The Muslim idea of God is, in many ways, more abstract, more remote and less human, certainly, than the Christian and the God of the Old Testament, who has passions and has angers and often behaves very much like a human being in the various stories. The Muslim [God] is more remote, aloof, distant, and has to be obeyed. He has many, many different facets. ...

There are stories in the Old Testament, for instance, where Abraham questions God. I mean, Abraham, in the story of ... Sodom and Gomorrah, I think, he turns around and he's not sure; he has a discussion with God over something. That doesn't happen in the Muslim account of things. I think that perhaps contributes to a more apocalyptic sort of notion of identification with something that's more remote, therefore less human. ...

Submission has had different meanings over the ages. Submission can mean [what] my grandmother used to mean by it, namely fatalism. A fatality. You believed in God. ... It was a surrender to the will of God. ... But in these men's hands, it's not submission so much as it's acting. ... It's acting, rather than submitting. It's being. It's moving. It's about action. So it's a different notion. ...

It's more like the unflinching Abraham. When you've got it fixed in your mind, you don't flinch, you don't question. You know what to do because that is what God wants. That is God's will. ...

What allows men like that to feel so confident that they are on a 1-800 line to God? What is it about the times they live in, their own needs, or the religion itself, that makes that possible – that kind of confidence that they are on some ecstatic connection with God and can speak for him with such fluency?

What makes people enter into cults? I think that kind of certainty about something is not necessarily just religious. It was seen in secular organizations, secular ideologues, ideological organizations of one kind or another. I've experienced it among people I used to know in the 1960s and 1970s. It's a terrifying thing when you see it at work.

And in the end of the day, it can always have these deadly consequences: betrayal of your friends and comrades with the greatest of ease. ... All of a sudden, you can betray left, right and centre, and people will die as a consequence. It's been there in communist traditions. It's been there all the time.

Clearly, then, it is not the nature of Islam per se that produced the threat from al-Qaedaism now. A perverted view of certain parts of Muslim tradition, however, and an extraordinarily selective interpretation of Muslim history and of the Koran gives some people, such as al-Qaedaists, 'justification' for their actions.

The serious issue for Islam and the West in this regard is the apparently muted response within Islam to the appalling acts carried out by al-Qaedaists in the name of Islam, even against fellow Muslims. The future of Islam itself is now at stake in this regard.

Is Arab culture to blame?
No.

There is absolutely no evidence to support such a racist view of this problem. There is, however, potentially a reason why underlying aspects of certain Arab countries may lead people to draw the wrong conclusions here.

A number of writers have pointed out that the nature of national income, and therefore the way income is distributed, in certain countries may have a bearing in this area. Referring to oil and the type of relationship it generates between a country and its citizens, Galal Amin points out that 'there may be a strong relationship between the growth of incomes that have the nature of economic rent and the growth of religious fanaticism.'[55]

Oil is a form of income that has the nature of economic rent, in both Arab and non-Arab countries. It is now very widely accepted that the blessing of oil is a decidedly mixed one. The drawbacks of the possession of oil resources are becoming quite well known and include a significant tendency to endemic corruption, unless very carefully managed; skewed economic development, with its benefits frequently directed at 'insiders' or rulers and their family, friends and associates; exaggerated boom-and-bust cycles that move with the price of oil; and an apparent tendency towards despotic or populist governments who can for a period 'buy off' opposition, leading to weak democratic norms. Such negative features seem to be particularly strong in societies with weak market norms or weak or corrupt governments and bureaucracies, or both. Such negative features clearly have nothing to do, *per se*, with Arab culture, but are nonetheless very evident in some Arab states.

In this regard, Michael Mousseau, associate professor of international relations at Koç University in Istanbul, Turkey, says that 'mineral wealth in a developing economy with weak market norms probably works to reinforce the influence of traditional clientalist (non-market) in-groups, as patrons spread their riches in return for pledges of loyalty.'[54]

In addition, with regard to Arab culture, Mousseau points out that the growth of terrorism can hardly be seen as an issue to attach to any particular traditional culture because this does not explain why it did not arise in the past in that particular culture.[54]

One aspect of Arab society must however be noted as a possible contributory factor to the support for and acceptance of hyper-terrorism now: cruelty in certain Arab societies and the widespread failure to condemn or oppose it within some of those societies.

This has been well documented by Kanan Makiya in his book *Cruelty and Silence: War, Tyranny, Uprising and the Arab World*. He is quite clear: 'Since 1975, and the beginning of the Lebanese civil war, the Arab world east of Egypt has become an exceptionally nasty place. The forerunners for Lebanon were the glorification of violence, armed struggle, and ideas of revolution, all born decades earlier in Iraq and Syria. The result is that Arab human-rights sensibilities today lag behind other parts of the developing world like India and Latin America. Powerful despotisms and populist lawlessness are accompanied by an intelligentsia with no liberal or "rights-centred" critique of either. Meanwhile, wealth on an unprecedented scale has been flowing into the Middle East, even as Arabs themselves have been running away from the region in ever-growing numbers. They run away not because there are no economic opportunities but because cruelty has everywhere become the rule. This cruelty is a highly specific phenomenon of the 1970s and 1980s, with no general implications for the "Arabs" or "Islam".

Makiya goes on to say: 'In the end, the contention of this book is very simple: the politics of keeping silent over escalating cruelties inside the Arab world, cruelties inflicted for the most part by one Arab on another, is principally responsible for an Arab moral collapse which has today reached epidemic proportions. Leaders like Saddam Hussein thrive on the silence of the Arab intelligentsia towards cruelty. They are also created by that silence. Intellectuals created the discourse of silence.'

He concludes: 'The first step out of the morass is the ruthless and radical one of uprooting, from deep within our own sensibilities, the intellectual and moral authority that blaming someone else still carries today among us Arabs. If I have bent that stick as far as I know how in the opposite direction, it is because I firmly believe that only upon its demise can a healthy multi-dimensional and pluralist meaning to Arabness be born.

'The second step is to "put cruelty first". This wonderfully simple aphorism has the great quality of being deeply anti-ideological in its disregard for the idea of sin, whether in its religious form (transgression of divine rules) or in its modern form of "historical blame". The two forms are interlinked and go to the roots of modern Arab malaise'[56]

Unfortunately, Makiya's advice has not been taken, as was seen from the reaction of the Arab League to the developing catastrophe in Darfur in the

Sudan in 2004 and 2005. The Arab League spent considerable time trying to convince the world that there was no problem in Darfur whatsoever, despite significant evidence to the contrary, even before 2004. Its response when the problem could no longer be denied became quite defensive and focused overwhelmingly on keeping external help out rather than the key issue of helping end the killings, displacement and malnutrition.

Still, the acceptance of cruelty, while it may predispose some, especially in certain countries in the Arab world, to tolerate appalling terrorist actions does not of itself explain the emergence of the al-Qaedaist hyper-terrorism threat now.

Is it directly due to the Arab-Israeli dispute?
No.

This is is a common assumption that needs to be put in context. As Bernard Lewis notes: 'The collapse of the Soviet Union, followed by the defeat of Saddam Hussein in the Gulf war of 1991, was a devastating blow to secular nationalist movements, notably that of the Palestinians, who once again, as in 1945, found themselves bereft of a great power patron and helper in their cause. Their Soviet protector was gone. Even their Arab financial backers in Kuwait and Saudi Arabia, angered by enthusiastic Palestinian support for Saddam Hussein, for a while stopped their subsidies, leaving the Palestinians isolated, impoverished and enfeebled. It was this situation that forced them to think the unthinkable and enter into a peace process with Israel. The PLO was rescued, in fundamentalist eyes ignominiously, by the Americans and the Israelis, and induced to enter into a demeaning dialogue with Israel.'[25]

As the anonymous author of *Through Our Enemies' Eyes: Osama bin Laden, Radical Islam and the Future of America* puts it: 'In the eyes of al-Qaeda, the PLO are hardly much better than the Jews, and although al-Qaeda make reference to the Palestinian cause, it is to the Islamic resistance (Hamas in particular) that they really direct their support. They detest the secular and Shiite Palestinians almost as much as the Jews, and consider them "hypocrites, apostates or pagans". Al-Qaeda refer to "the so-called Palestinian authority" or "Arafat regime", which they say is run by "those who sympathize with the infidels."[57] In addition, it is now known that the planning for 9/11 started many years before the attack itself and was at its peak when the Oslo peace process between the Israelis and Palestinians was also at its peak.

Jason Burke agrees with this interpretation. As he puts it: 'Televised images of Israeli troops violently repressing Palestinian protestors in the occupied territories certainly reinforce the militants' key message that the lands of Islam are under attack and that all Muslims must rise up and fight. However, although a resolution to the Israeli-Palestinian conflict would help alleviate political tensions in the region, it would not end the threat of militant Islam.

'The roots of contemporary Sunni Islamic militancy cannot be reduced to any single, albeit thorny, problem. Militants feel the *umma* is under attack. In their view, Israel is merely the West's most obvious outpost – as it was when it became a Crusader kingdom in the twelfth century. If the Jewish state disappeared, the Islamists would still fight in Chechnya, Kashmir, Egypt, Uzbekistan, Indonesia and Algeria.

'Moreover considerable support for the Islamic cause stems from Muslims' sense of humiliation. A two-state solution to the Israeli-Palestinian conflict, which would still leave the "Zionist entity" intact, would therefore offer little succour to the wounded pride of any committed militant or, more crucially, to the pride of those in the wider community who support and legitimise extremism and violence'.[1]

So the Arab-Israeli dispute, although it does not explain the rise of al-Qaedaism, has clearly inflamed the wider Islamic community and indirectly provides support to the al-Qaedaists.

Is the growth of al-Qaedaism a reaction to Great Power activities?
No.

Some observers believe that at least some terrorism is a reaction to the activities of Great Powers. Some interesting examples are quoted in this regard, including Jewish terrorism in the Ukraine during World War II and Irish terrorism used against British forces in Ireland in the early twentieth century.

There are, however, also some interesting examples of the non-use of terrorism against Great Power activities; including the mainly passive resistance to the Chinese in Tibet and the absence of significant terrorism by those invaded during the Japanese war in the Pacific.

The key issue is the extent to which the actions of the West, particularly the United States, are used as justification for terrorist actions and the support for them. The United States is blamed for a whole range of issues, including globalisation, the Arab-Israeli dispute, the first Gulf war, the war in Afghanistan and the invasion of Iraq. Each of these issues on their own or taken together probably would not generate the extreme hatred directed at the West in general, and the United States in particular, that is so evident now in the Islamic world.

Logic also seems not to apply here. The first Gulf war was a UN-approved action supported by most Arab states, with many actively involved in the fighting, while the war in Afghanistan was also UN-approved. In addition, US pressure to rescue the Islamic community in Bosnia was never fully appreciated other than by the Bosnians themselves. Similarly, the effort in Kosovo was ignored or even attacked in the Islamic world as part of a supposed Judaeo-Christian conspiracy against Islam.

The issue seems to be a much broader one therefore than great-power activities. Perhaps, more accurately, the reaction to great-power activities is determined by something other than the facts surrounding these activities themselves. In short, in the light of the unclear historical lessons or direct causal links, the connection here should be treated as 'case not proven' for the moment.

Is the growth of al-Qaedaism due to the Saudi Arabian fundamentalist Wahhabi influence?
No, not directly.

As fifteen of the nineteen 9/11 hijackers were from Saudi Arabia, it is tempting to blame the al-Qaeda threat on the Saudi Arabian fundamentalist Wahhabi influence, and many commentators do so. (For a full discussion of Wahhabism, see Chapter 2 above.)

The term 'Wahhabism' is subject to many meanings and is frequently deliberately used to tarnish legitimate local Islamic opposition to an unsatisfactory status quo. In its religious essence and original true meaning, it is part of the Sunni tradition: Wahhabism is conservative, ultra-traditional, literalist, puritanical and violent only in the way in which its social tenets are enforced on less puritanical Muslims. It can, however, provide a foundation for the development of thinking that eventually becomes so exclusivist and rigid that it constitutes a strategic threat to both Islam itself and the world. Wahhabism has strengthened the Sunni identity vis-à-vis all others, and especially Shiites, Jews and Christians, and, as I set out below, has indirectly led to the growth of al-Qaedaism through the impact of globalisation, the rage within the Islamic community and the Sunni Shiite struggle. So, Wahhabism, while not in itself creating al-Qaedaism and its terrorist impulses, has provided a fertile ground for the type of thinking that in some circumstances, and after considerable 'revisionism', can produce such a terrorist threat. The irony is that this unforeseen and unwanted offspring has now turned violently against the house of Saud in Saudi Arabia itself.

In summary, poverty, Islam, Arab culture, the Arab-Israeli dispute, Great Power activities and Wahhabism have not in themselves directly caused the recent rise of al-Qaedaism. Some of these issues may indirectly provide support or fertile ground for the development of this ideology in certain circumstances, but we must look elsewhere to understand where this threat directly came from.

Is globalisation to blame?
Yes.

Many people blame the growth in al-Qaedaist terrorism on globalisation, without advancing any evidence for this belief. I initially approached this 'explanation' with considerable misgivings but as I continued my research I become convinced that this explanation has significant credibility and may also help tell us how we can solve the al-Qaedaism problem by addressing the correct underlying issues.

There has been, and continues to be, considerable comment about the impact of globalisation on the growth of terrorism, although much of it without much analytical depth. One helpful contribution to this issue, however, was a long article in the journal *International Security* by Professor Michael Mousseau on 'Market Civilisation and Its Clash with Terror'. This article, and the subsequent debate on it, is a very good reference point for a broader explanation of the recent rise in hyper-terrorism in certain parts of the world.

In his article, Professor Mousseau focuses on the values and beliefs of the wider population that lead them to support the usage of terror and mass murder against other groups or peoples. While his thinking is still to some extent 'a work in progress', it is helpful to consider it in some detail, as it appears to me to be a very good explanation for the current wave of al-Qaedaist terrorism.

He summarises his views thus: 'I drew on several generations of research in anthropology, economics, political science and sociology to show how the values and beliefs that support terror – a lack of empathy for out-groups, an emphasis on community over the individual, and an incomprehension for objective truth and individual innocence – arise from the clientalist economic linkages (linkages based on reciprocity or gift-giving) that are commonplace in many developing countries. In contrast, values that work against terror – individualism, tolerance, equity and the rule of common law – arise with a market (or contract) economy. Because all market economies in the contemporary period have been developed economies, there appears to be a link between underdevelopment and terror. As I have argued, however, the real culprit is social anarchy produced by globalisation and the difficulties attending the transition to a market economy. Just as millions in the last century turned to anti-market and sectarian values during the rise of market economies in Europe, today millions in the developing world support anti-market and sectarian values reflected in support for ethno-facism, sectarian murder and fundamentalist religions – anything that offers psychic comfort (or even physical and economic protection) in the face of volatile social anarchy.'[54]

To explain some key concepts there, feudal Europe was an example of a clientalist economy based on reciprocity or gift giving rather than contracting, but such also exists currently, *particularly in the developing world*. In such economies the obligations of co-operating parties are implied rather than explicit and are rarely set out in any form of contract. Economic exchanges occur through the giving of gifts which reinforces a sense of trust and obligation amongst the parties. Over time patrons tend to emerge, and they rather than states regulate economic co-operation and it is to them that ultimate loyalty is owed. Such economies are frequently based on social linkages such as kinship and ethnicity. Such linkages make in-groups much more important than out-groups, making such economies much more inward looking than market economies in terms of identity, values and beliefs. Unfortunately for us in the developed world in such economies with their prevailing collectivism and excessive in-group loyalty (of necessity, as there is no other 'safety net') there is a strong lack of empathy for the members of out-groups who are frequently viewed with suspicion and/or contempt.[54]

'A society with clientalist values and beliefs but with fading protections from in-groups (due to the impact of the dislocation caused by economic change or globalisation) is extremely vulnerable to any in-group system that promises to put an end to its deep sense of insecurity. This explains the allure of alternative value systems in developing countries that support ethnic sectarianism, extreme nationalism, or various types of religious fundamentalism.'[54]

'Cultures change slowly; so when endogenous factors (such as economic development) cause a rise in contractual exchange, in a clientalist society economic norms divert from prevailing cultural values and beliefs. When this happens, individuals with deeply embedded clientalist values have difficulty grasping new market norms; they perceive that those who are driven by self-interest not only lack social ties but have no values at all. … During this period of social anarchy, a zero-sum culture may emerge in which strangers pursue their interests without any regard for shared values – market or clientalist. This explains the circumstances in many developing-world societies today: that is, widespread disrespect for the rule of law (everyone wants the law to apply to someone else); social chaos, as many act without regard for others (e.g. unwillingness to wait in line or obey rules); and the apparent lack of empathy for anyone outside one's in-groups (family, friends and co-workers).'

He then pulls this together to explain why the resort to terror has occurred: 'Those with the most to lose, however, are patrons and their lieutenants who hold privileged positions in the old clientalist hierarchies. This is why leaders of terrorist organisations frequently come from privileged backgrounds [including of course Osama bin Laden and other al-Qaedaist leaders]. To maintain the clientalist structure that carries with it higher social status, these leaders seek to rally their client base by appealing to some anti-market ideology. Because it is in a client's interest to have a powerful patron [to offer them protection in a time of significant and unpleasant change], leaders attract and maintain followers by demonstrations of strength. In this way, the mass murder of Westerners serves two purposes: it reflects the leaders' power, and it taps into widespread anti-market fury.'[54]

Having commented on 'the social origin of the presumption of individual innocence in market societies' he says 'from the clientalist perspective, in contrast, no one is innocent; individuals share a responsibility for the actions of others within the in-group; if followers do not support their leaders, then they are betraying the entire in-group. From their clientalist perspective, all in-group members are privileged and all out-group members are enemies, or at best, outsiders unworthy of empathy. A paucity of empathy is necessary for doing harm to, and tolerating the suffering of all out-group members'. He states 'in cultures where the individual is less important than the group and the absence of science increases devotion to insular beliefs, suicide – under conditions of extreme socio-economic disruption – may emerge as a socially approved way of expressing ultimately loyalty to the in-group. In this way, cultural insularism, characterised by the absence of a market economy, is a necessary condition for the social approval of suicidal mass murder and sectarian violence'. ... 'Cultural insularism combined with a particular grievance – such as the negative consequences associated with globalisation – can create a deadly mix for Americans and other Westerners.'

'Although latent anti-Americanism and anti-Westernism exists throughout much of the developing world, these are most likely to rise to the surface during economic crises – when nascent middle classes lose their status and turn against emerging liberal values'.[54]

To narrow the frame of our reference to terrorism, it is clear that terrorist action requires a diverging set of values. Professor Mousseau points out that the use of terror is not just the use of violence, it is the use of that violence in a way that does not discriminate between combatants and civilian non-combatants. He makes the point that an act of terror is thus similar to genocide, as both involve the killing of innocents. (In terror, the motive is political and the act largely symbolic; in genocide, the killing is the end itself.)

Professor Mousseau also set out the various ways in which globalisation has contributed to increased tension between the West and developing countries. Firstly, free trade resulted in the arrival of Western businesses and the related mass advertising of their products. As many of these products can only be afforded by the new rich and the middle class, these people are frequently seen as having betrayed their in-group values, which renders their status illegitimate in those societies and identifies them with the West – particularly when they are seen driving around in Western cars, wearing Western clothes and so on.

Secondly, many foreign corporations build 'haughty towers' in the centre of cities in the developing world which are often visible from poorer neighbourhoods. 'Babylonian Towers' have become a powerful symbol of the negative impact of globalisation to many in the developing world. This partly explains the attacks on the World Trade Centre and also the negative view of the World Bank, the IMF and similar institutions among al-Qaedaists and many others.

Thirdly, the United States and other countries in the West, and some Western financial institutions, have encouraged deregulation and less state involvement in many developing economies. This has led to a reduction, in some Islamic countries, of state subsidies to the urban poor and also, in some cases, to an increase in joblessness. This has clearly led to a rise in anti-modern and anti-Western feeling in many such countries.

Fourthly, the classical economic theory of the English School of International Political Economy assumes that the propensity to barter is universal – so free trade benefits everyone. This assumption may not be fully correct: some states and societies need help, and of course time, to develop the norms of contracting. Absent such time and help, in some less developed countries (LDCs) free trade can unfairly and almost permanently benefit the corporations of the more developed countries (MDCs). This has an adverse impact on the local economy and worsens the conditions of the urban poor and jobless – and thereby increases their dependency on frequently extremist in-groups.

It is a deep irony that the people of the West are now playing a similar role for many in the developing world as the Jews did in the developing economies of central Europe two generations ago. It is not necessarily Western actions or Western beliefs that are detested; rather, it is Western values – at least as they are perceived – that are detested and rejected and which make Westerners guilty in the eyes of some. The 'war on terror' is, in the final analysis, not a clash of civilisations (although al-Qaedaism wishes to provoke such) but a clash of cultures at different stages of economic development, and therefore at its core a clash between the values generated by economic development and those that existed prior to this economic development. The West is hated because many people in particular LDCs view Western out-group members (to them) as untrustworthy, and perceive Western values as selfish and antagonistic.

Professor Mousseau's ideas are helpful in explaining the increase in international Islamic identity and the feeling that Islam is under attack which is now clearly pervasive in much of the Muslim world. They also explain why many in Islamic states blame their problems on the West. It is a short step then to an increase in support for terrorism, an unwillingness to stand up to or confront those in their societies who carry out such actions and eventually to terrorism itself.

But do these ideas stand up in practical terms?

I think they do, having considered the impact of globalisation on al-Qaedaism from a completely different perspective.

To do this I return to a lengthy article I referred to above. It is: 'Behind the Curve: Globalisation and International Terrorism'. It was written by Audrey Kurth Cronin, who is a specialist in international terrorism at the US Congressional Research Service at the Library of Congress. The article was written for the journal *International Security*. [5]

'Whether deliberately intending to or not, the United States is projecting un-coordinated economic, social and political power even more sweepingly than it is in military terms.' She continues: 'Globalisation, in forms including Westernerisation, secularisation, democratisation, consumerism and the growth of market capitalism, represents an onslaught to less privileged people in conservative cultures repelled by the fundamental changes that these forces are bringing – or angered by the distortions and uneven distributions of benefits that result. This is especially true of the Arab world.' [I would extend that also to much of the remainder of the Islamic world].

'Yet the current US approach to this growing repulsion is coloured by a kind of cultural naiveté and an unwillingness to recognise – let alone appreciate or take responsibility for – the influence of US power except in its military dimensions. Even doing nothing in the economic, social and political policy realms is still doing something, because the United States is blamed by disadvantaged and alienated populations for the powerful

Western-led forces of globalisation that are proceeding apace, despite the absence of a focused, coordinated US policy. And those penetrating mechanisms of globalisation, such as the Internet, the media, and the increasing flows of goods and peoples, are exploited in return. The means and ends of terrorism are being reformulated in the current environment.

'The objectives of international terrorism have also changed as a result of globalisation. Foreign intrusions and growing awareness of shrinking global space have created incentives to use the ideal asymmetrical weapon, terrorism, for more ambitious purposes.

'The political incentives to attack major targets such as the United States with powerful weapons have greatly increased. The perceived corruption of indigenous customs, religions, languages, economies and so on are blamed on an international system often unconsciously moulded by American behaviour. The accompanying distortions in local communities as a result of exposure to the global marketplace of goods and ideas are increasingly blamed on US-sponsored modernisation and those who support it. The advancement of technology, however, is not the driving force behind the terrorist threat to the United States and its allies, despite what some have assumed. Instead, at the heart of this threat are frustrated populations and international movements that are increasingly inclined to lash out against US-led globalisation.

'As Christopher Coker observes, globalisation is reducing tendencies toward instrumental violence (i.e. violence between states and even between communities), but it is enhancing incentives for expressive violence (or violence that is ritualistic, symbolic and communicative). The new international terrorism is increasingly engendered by a need to assert identity or meaning against forces of homogeneity, especially on the part of cultures that are threatened by, or left behind by, the secular future that Western-led globalisation brings.'[83]

'According to a report recently published by the UN Development Programme, the region of greatest deficit in measures of human development – the Arab world – is also the heart of the most threatening religiously inspired terrorism. Much more work needs to be done on the significance of this correlation, but increasingly sources of political discontent are arising from disenfranchised areas in the Arab world that feel left behind by the promise of globalisation and its assurances of broader freedom, prosperity and access to knowledge. The results are dashed expectations, heightened resentment of the perceived US-led hegemonic system, and a shift of focus away from more proximate targets within the region.

'Of course, the motivations behind this threat should not be oversimplified: anti-American terrorism is spurred in part by a desire to change US policy in the Middle East and Persian Gulf regions as well as by growing antipathy in the developing world vis-à-vis the forces of globalisation. It is also crucial to distinguish between the motivations of leaders such as Osama bin Laden and their followers. The former seem to be more driven by calculated strategic decisions to shift the locus of attack away from the repressive indigenous governments to the more attractive and media-rich target of the United States. The latter appear to be more driven by religious concepts cleverly distorted to arouse anger and passion in societies full of pent-up frustration. To some degree, terrorism is directed against the United States because of its engagement and policies in various regions. Anti-Americanism is closely related to antiglobalisation, because (intentionally or not) the primary driver of the powerful forces resulting in globalisation is the United States.

'Analysing terrorism as something separate from globalisation is misleading and potentially dangerous. Indeed globalisation and terrorism are intricately intertwined forces characterising international security in the twenty-first century. The main question is whether terrorism will succeed in disrupting the promise of improved livelihoods for millions of people on Earth. Globalisation is not an inevitable, linear development, and it can be disrupted by such unconventional means as international terrorism. Conversely, modern international terrorism is especially dangerous because of the power that it potentially derives from globalisation – whether through access to CBNR [chemical, biological, nuclear and radiological] weapons, global media outreach, or a diverse network of financial and information resources'.

'Long after the focus on Osama bin Laden has receded and US troops have quit their mission in Afghanistan, terrorism will be a serious threat to the world community and especially to the United States. The relative preponderance of US military power virtually guarantees an impulse to respond asymmetrically. The lagging of the Arab region behind the rest of the world is impelling a violent redirection of antiglobalisation and anti-modernization forces toward available targets, particularly the United

States, whose scope and policies are engendering rage. Al-Qaeda will eventually be replaced or redefined, but its successors' reach may continue to grow via the same globalised channels and to direct their attacks against US and Western targets. The current trajectory is discouraging, because as things currently stand, the wellspring of terrorism's means and ends is likely to be renewed: Arab governments will probably not reform peacefully, and existing Western governments and their supporting academic and professional institutions are disinclined to understand or analyse in depth the sources, patterns and history of terrorism.

'Terrorism is a by-product of broader historical shifts in the international distribution of power in all of its forms – political, economic, military, ideological and cultural. These are the same forms of power that characterize the forces of Western-led globalisation. At times of dramatic international change, human beings (especially those not benefiting from the change – or not benefiting as much or as rapidly from the change) grasp for alternative means to control and understand their environments. If current trends continue, widening global disparities, coupled with burgeoning information and connectivity, are likely to accelerate – unless the terrorist backlash, which is increasingly taking its inspiration from misoneistic religious or pseudoreligious concepts, successfully counters these trends. Because of globalisation, terrorists have access to more powerful technologies, more targets, more territory, more means of recruitment, and more exploitable sources of rage than ever before. The West's twentieth-century approach to terrorism is highly unlikely to mitigate any of these long-term trends.

'From a Manichean perspective, the ad hoc and purportedly benign intentions of the preponderant, secular West do not seem benign at all to those ill served by globalisation. To frustrated people in the Arab and Muslim world, adherence to radical religious philosophies and practices may seem a rational response to the perceived assault, especially when no feasible alternative for progress is offered by their own governments. This is not to suggest that terrorists should be excused because of environmental factors or conditions. Instead, Western governments must recognize that the tiny proportion of the population that ends up in terrorist cells cannot exist without the availability of broader sources of active or passive sympathy, resources and support. Those avenues of sustenance are where the centre of gravity for an effective response to the terrorist threat must reside.

The response to transnational terrorism must deal with the question of whether the broader enabling environment will increase or decrease over time, and the answer will be strongly influenced by the policy choices that the United States and its allies make in the near future.'[5]

She makes three other important points in conclusion: 'Even though the newest international terrorist threat, emanating largely from Muslim countries, has more than a modicum of religious inspiration, it is more accurate to see it as part of a larger phenomenon of antiglobalisation and tension between the haves and have-not nations, as well as between the elite and underprivileged within those nations. In an era where reforms occur at a pace which is much slower than is desired, terrorists today, like those before them, aim to exploit the frustrations of the common people (especially in the Arab world).

'The jihad era is animated by widespread alienation combined with elements of religious identity and doctrine – a dangerous mix of forces that resonate deep in the human psyche'.

Finally: 'There is significant evidence that the global links and activities that al-Qaeda and its associated groups perpetuated are not short-term or anomalous. Indeed they are changing the nature of the terrorist threat as we move further into the twenty-first century. The resulting intersection between the United States, globalisation and international terrorism will define the major challenges to international security.'[5]

These views, I believe, provide a very practical confirmation of the broad accuracy of Professor Mousseau's theories in this area.

I have no hesitation in concluding that globalisation in its many forms is a key and continuing reason for the growth in al-Qaedaism we are experiencing at present. However, as all states and societies do not respond to the impact of globalisation in this fashion or resort to terrorist violence, it is clearly only part of the answer we are seeking – not the full picture. We need to consider other possible explanations to complete the picture.

Is al-Qaedaism just another in the long line of attacks on liberal society?

Yes, but . . .

There have been many attacks on liberal society or liberal democracy in the last hundred years. Some see al-Qaedaism as just another in a long line of such attacks. This point has been made by a number of commentators, including Paul Berman[37] and Avishai Margalit and Ian Buruma.[42]

Margalit and Buruma believe that liberal society, usually represented by the West, includes materialism, liberalism, capitalism, individualism, humanism, rationalism, socialism, decadence and moral laxity. Some of these traits can be seen as non-heroic and boring to certain enemies of liberal society.

Occidentalism, which the authors believe played a large part in the 9/11 attack, 'is a cluster of images and ideas of the West in the minds of its haters. Four features of Occidentalism can be seen in most versions of it; we can call them the City, the Bourgeois, Reason and Feminism. Each contains a set of attributes, such as arrogance, feebleness, greed, depravity and decadence, which are invoked as typical Western, or even American, characteristics.

'Anti-liberal revolts almost invariably contain a deep hatred of the City, that is to say, everything represented by urban civilisation, commerce, mixed populations, artistic freedom, sexual licence, scientific pursuits, leisure, personal safety, wealth and its usual concomitant, power. Mao Zedong, Pol Pot, Hitler, Japanese agrarian fascists, and of course Islamists all extolled the simple life of the pious peasant, pure at heart, uncorrupted by city pleasures, used to hard work and self-denial, tied to the soil, and obedient to authority. Behind this idyll of rural simplicity lies the desire to control masses of people, but also an old religious rage, which goes back at least as far as the ancient superpower Babylon.'

They go on to say: 'But the Taliban, like other purists, are much concerned with the private domain too. In big, anonymous cities, separation between the private and the public makes hypocrisy possible. Indeed in Occidentalist eyes, the image of the West, populated by city-dwellers, is marked by artificiality and hypocrisy, in contrast to the honesty and purity of the Bedouin shepherd's life. ... When purity must be restored and foreign blood removed from the native soil, it is these people who must be purged: the Chinese from Pol Pot's Phnom Penh, the Indians from Rangoon or Kampala, and the Jews from everywhere.'

Margalit and Buruma point out that the enemies of the West usually aspire to be heroes – whether it is Islamism, Nazism, fascism or communism: 'The common enemy of revolutionary heroes is the settled

Bourgeois. ... The hero courts death. The Bourgeois is addicted to personal safety. The hero counts death tolls, the Bourgeois counts money.'

The attack on the third feature of Occidentalism, Reason, has taken many forms, including Hitler's reference to 'Jewish science', Chairman Mao's slogan 'science is simply acting daringly', and the views of Japanese professors that 'Japanese victory over Anglo-American materialism was assured because the former embodied 'the spiritual culture of the East'. 'Occidentalists extol soul or spirit but despise intellectuals and intellectual life. They regard the intellectual life as fragmented, indeed as a higher form of idiocy, with no sense of "totality", the "absolute", and what is truly important in life.'

With respect to the fourth feature of Occidentalism, Feminism: 'Aurel Kolnai argued in 1938 in his *War Against the West* that "the trend towards the emancipation of women [is] keenly distinctive of the West". This somewhat sweeping claim seems to be borne out by the sentiments of Kolnai's enemies. Here is Alfred Rosenberg, the Nazi propagandist: "Emancipation of woman from the women's emancipation movement is the first demand of a generation of women which would like to save the Volk and the race, the Eternal-Unconscious, the foundation of all culture, from decline and fall".

'[Osama] Bin Laden is equally obsessed with manliness and women. It is indeed one of his most cherished Occidentalist creeds. "The rulers of that region (the Gulf states) have been deprived of their manhood," he said in 1998. "And they think the people are women. By God, Muslim women refuse to be defended by these American and Jewish prostitutes." The West, in his account, is determined to "deprive us of our manhood. We believe we are men."'

Margalit and Buruma continue: 'Few modern societies were as dominated by males as wartime Japan, and the brutal policy of forcing Korean, Chinese and Filipina, as well as Japanese, girls to serve in military brothels was a sign of the low status of women in the Japanese empire.

'To all those who see military discipline, self-sacrifice, austerity, and worship of the Leader as the highest social ideals, the power of female sexuality will be seen as a dire threat. From ancient times women are the givers and the guardians of life. Women's freedom is incompatible with a death cult. Indeed, open displays of female sexuality are a provocation, not only to holy men, but to all repressed people whose only way to exaltation is death for a higher cause.'

They conclude: 'There is no clash of civilisations. Most religions, especially monotheistic ones, have the capacity to harbour the anti-Western poison. And varieties of secular fascism can occur in all cultures. The current conflict, therefore, is not between East and West, Anglo-America and the rest, or Judeo-Christianity and Islam. The death cult is a deadly virus which now thrives, for all manner of historical and political reasons, in extreme forms of Islam.'[42]

It is also worth noting what Margalit and Buruma have to say about some intellectuals: 'Intellectuals, themselves only rarely heroic, have often displayed a hatred of the Bourgeois and an infatuation with heroism – heroic leaders, heroic creeds.'[42] In support of this thesis, they point to certain artists in Mussolini's Italy, some German social scientists before World War II and some episodes in World War I, especially the Battle of Langemarck, where '145,000 men died in a sequence of utterly futile attacks'. 'The famous words of Theodor Körner, written a century before, were often evoked in remembrance: "Happiness lies only in sacrificial death."'[42]

In his book *The Reckless Mind: Intellectuals In Politics*, Mark Lilla develops this point: 'As continental Europe gave birth to two great tyrannical systems in the twentieth century, communism and fascism, it also gave birth to a new social type, for which we need a new name: the philotyrannical intellectual. A few major thinkers of that period whose work is still meaningful for us today dared to serve the modern Dionysus (tyrannical leader) openly in word and deed, and their names are infamous: Martin Heidegger and Carl Schmitt in Nazi Germany, Gurg Lukács in Hungary, perhaps a few others. A great many joined Fascist and Communist parties on both sides of the Iron Curtain, whether out of elective affinities or professional ambition, without taking great risks; a few played soldier for a time in the jungles and deserts of the Third World. A surprising number were pilgrims to the new Syracuses being built in Moscow, Berlin, Hanoi and Havana. These were the political voyeurs who made carefully choreographed tours of the tyrants' domains with return tickets in hand, admiring the collective farms, the tractor factories, the sugarcane groves, the schools, but somehow never visiting the prisons.

'Mainly, though, European intellectuals stayed at their desks, visiting Syracuse only in their imaginations, developing interesting, sometimes brilliant ideas to explain away the sufferings of people whose eyes they will never meet. Distinguished professors, gifted poets and influential journalists summoned their talents to convince all that would listen that modern tyrants were liberators and that their unconscionable crimes were noble, when seen in the proper perspective. Whoever takes it upon himself to write an honest intellectual history of twentieth-century Europe will need a strong stomach.'[58]

To conclude on the broader anti-liberal issue, many writers have pointed out the historical continuity between Nazism, communism and the type of thinking that has energised al-Qaedaism. This anti-liberalism has been found in many cultures and in many countries over time. What all these anti-liberal attackers, be they Japanese, Nazi, Communist, or al-Qaedaist, have in common, is their own individual vision of purity that aggressively seeks either to convert or to eradicate enemies who are deemed to be hypocritical, polluting and corrupting the 'true believers'. In these circumstances, Jews, Zionists, 'Crusaders', Christians, 'infidels', Americans or simply Christians or Westerners in general are seen as less than human, more like vermin, and thus to be destroyed.

This is where the prejudice against Christianity, Judaism or atheism or an aversion to Western culture, or a criticism of American or Israeli policies, very quickly turns into mass murder. As Ian Buruma has said: 'When people are in this state of mind, there is no room for negotiation, nor will a change of foreign policy – making the Israelis concede to all Palestinian demands, say – make the problem go away. To see it as an inevitable clash of civilisations is to deny that Islamist revolutionaries are the enemies not only of the liberal West, but of most Muslims too. The only antidote to Occidentalism is a political transformation in the Arab world. More political freedom, achieved by Muslims, will take the sting out of holy war.'[59]

Liberal society itself is therefore both a target for and a provocation to al-Qaedaism. The citizens of such countries, irrespective of their beliefs, are 'guilty' in this type of thinking and so may be killed without compunction by al-Qaedaists, as we have seen.

There is clearly considerable validity to the view that a key part of the al-Qaedaist campaign is targeted against Western liberal society. I believe, however, that the best explanation for *why* this is occurring now is the impact on Muslim societies in general and Muslims in particular of globalisation, as set out above.

Has the Sunni/Shiite struggle had a role in the development of al-Qaedaism?
Yes, I suspect so.

Many know of the Sunni/Shiite struggle and in particular the impact it had in provoking the Iran/Iraq war, the longest conventional war of the last century and the only one that involved the repeated use of WMD (by Iraq). It is also obvious that many commentators either do not want to discuss this issue at all or are blind to the possibility that the struggle might have had any impact on the rise in al-Qaedaism through 'provoking' Sunni militancy. Indeed, very little research has been carried out in this area.

As far as I am aware, only one commentator has analysed this issue from a contemporary perspective. He is Vali Nasr, professor of Middle Eastern and South Asian politics in the Department of National Security Affairs at the Naval Postgraduate School in Monterey, California.[40] In a paper entitled 'Regional Implications of Shiite Revival in Iraq', Professor Nasr makes some relevant comments on the struggle between the Sunni and Shiite traditions.

He notes that: 'The competition for power between the Shiite and Sunnis is neither a new development nor one limited to Iraq. In fact, it has shaped alliances and determined how various actors have defined and pursued their interests in the region for the past three decades. Often overlooked in political analyses of greater Middle Eastern politics, this competition is key to grasping how current developments in Iraq will shape this region in years to come. Sectarianism during this time period has also been closely tied to the development of militant Islamist ideology and activism among Sunnis. Sunni identity is part and parcel of the ideology and politics of jihadi groups associated with al-Qaeda; the Taliban, militant Wahhabis, a puritanical sectarian movement that emerged in the eighteenth century in modern Saudi Arabia; and the various branches of the Muslim Brotherhood, a Sunni Islamist organization that appeared in Egypt in the 1920s and is associated with the rise of political Islam, especially in the Arab world. Anti-Shiite violence is not just a strategic ploy used by al-Qaeda operatives, such as Abu Musab al-Zarqawi, to create instability in Iraq and undermine Washington's plans for that country's future; it is a constituent part of the ideology of Sunni militancy.

'The anti-Shiite violence that plagues Iraq today was first born in South Asia and Afghanistan in the 1990s by militant groups with ties to the Taliban and al-Qaeda. In the past nine months, bombings in Baghdad, Iskandariya,

Karbala, Najaf and other Shiite strongholds in Iraq have claimed many lives. These attacks closely resemble acts in Mashad [Iran], Karachi [Pakistan], Quetta [Pakistan], and Mazar-i Sharif [Afghanistan] since the early 1990s. The current sectarian threat in Iraq is therefore more the product of a deeply rooted rivalry in the region than the direct result of recent developments in Iraq. In other words, the Shiite revival and the decline in Sunni power in Iraq has not created Sunni militancy; it has invigorated and emboldened it. The ascendance of Sunni militancy is at the forefront of anti-Americanism in Iraq today and, as such, is likely to spread anti-Americanism in tandem with sectarian tensions throughout the greater Middle East region. On the day of the early March Ashura [holiest day in Shiite calendar] bombings, a Kuwaiti Wahhabi cleric condemned the Shiite rite on his website as "the biggest display of idolatry" and accused the Shiites of forming an "evil axis linking Washington, Tel Aviv and the Shiite holy city of Najaf" to grab Persian Gulf oil and disenfranchise Sunnis.'

Nasr continues: [After the Iranian Revolution in 1979], 'in the 1980s many [Shiites] joined the ranks of distinctly Shiite political movements. Groups such as Amal in Lebanon, Al-Da'waa al-Islamiya ('the Islamic Call') in Iraq, Hizb-i Wahdat ('Party of Unity') in Afghanistan and Tahrik-i Jafaria ('Shiite Movement') in Pakistan received financial and political support from Tehran to push for specifically Shiite agendas.

'The rise of Sunni consciousness and its sectarian posturing after the Iranian revolution [in 1979] was central to containing [Ayatollah Ruhullah] Khomeini's threat in the greater Middle East and beyond. Sunni identity served as the bulwark against the Islamist challenge that was then associated with Shiite Iran and imbued ruling regimes with religious legitimacy. Since the 1980s, governments from Nigeria to Indonesia and Malaysia have relied on Sunni identity to draw a clear wedge between Sunni and Shiite Islam, equating the former with 'true' Islam – and their governments as its defenders – and branding the latter as obscurantist extremism.

'The Shiite-Sunni struggles for the soul of Islam that had punctuated Islamic history since the advent of the faith were thus re-enacted in the late-twentieth century, with the Saudi monarchy assuming the role once played by Sunni caliphs ruling from Damascus and Baghdad. In Pakistan, Bahrain, Kuwait, Saudi Arabia and Iraq, where emboldened Shiite communities threatened Sunni regimes, the response was both swifter and more violent.

Rulers ranging from [General] Zia ul-Haq in Pakistan to Saddam [Hussein] in Iraq not only emphasised the Sunni identity of their countries and regimes as a bulwark against Khomeini's appeal but also sanctioned the use of sectarian violence to put local Shiite communities back in their place. To this effect, Saddam in 1980 began purges of government agencies, the military, and the Baath Party, which, combined with executions, assassinations, and mass killings, in 1991 alone took the lives of some 30,000 subdued Iraqi Shiites.

'In Pakistan, the cycle of bombings and assassinations that resulted from Sunni-Shiite clashes throughout the 1980s and the 1990s scarred both communities. Some nine hundred incidents of street clashes and sectarian riots since 1989 have claimed more than two thousand lives. Over five days in northwest Pakistan in 1996, sectarian combatants used mortars, rocket launchers, and anti-aircraft missiles, killing about two hundred people. Between January and May 1997, Sunni militant groups assassinated seventy-five Shiite community leaders in an attempt to remove the Shiites systematically from positions of authority.

'Anti-Shiite sectarianism is an important dimension of the Taliban's and al-Qaeda's political objective, one that their war on the West has largely overshadowed. Pakistani Sunni, Taliban and al-Qaeda combatants fought together in military campaigns in Afghanistan, most notably in the capture of Mazar-i Sharif and Bamiyan [in Afghanistan] in 1997 [and 1998], which involved the wide-scale massacre of the Shiites. Pakistani Sipah-i Sahabah ['Army of Companions of the Prophet'] fighters did most of the killing, nearly precipitating a war with Iran when they captured the Iranian consulate and killed eleven Iranian diplomats. Sectarian Sunni fighters in Iraq will draw on the ideological and organizational resources of the broader network of Sunni militancy that developed over the past decade and has been ensconced in society and politics in the greater Middle East, impacting sectarian relations where those resources originate, in Afghanistan and South Asia.

'Throughout the 1980s and the 1990s, Wahhabi *ulama* issued fatwas declaring the Shiite as *rafidis* (those who reject the truth of Islam), or infidels. Muslim Brotherhood activists in the Arab world and Deobandi *ulama* in India and Pakistan who are close to Wahhabi groups in Saudi Arabia have reiterated these opinions, justifying violence against the Shiites. The Taliban too echoed the same opinions, characterizing their massacre of the Shiites in Mazar-i Sharif in 1997 as the "revenge of Truth".

'Although it took the attacks of September 11, 2001, and the prolific use of suicide bombing by Hamas and Islamic Jihad in Israel to alert the West to the threat posed by Sunni militancy, it has in fact been on the rise throughout the region for the past two decades, at least partially if not primarily as a response to the Shiite activism that followed the Iranian Revolution. At that time, Sunni militancy emerged to maintain the balance of power in favor of Sunnis in the region, but Saddam's fall has now radically changed that balance. The occupation of Iraq went hand in hand with a Shiite cultural revival in that country. The celebration of Arbaeen (the commemoration of the 40th day after martyrdom of the Shiite Imam Husayn (d. 680)) in Karbala in May 2003 by some two million Shiites early on attested to the fact that Iraq was now a Shiite country. The growing prominence of the Shiites in Iraq, visible in the composition of the Iraqi Governing Council and later confirmed by the veto power that Ayatollah Ali al-Sistani has attained over its proceedings, has only further underscored this sea change.

'Iraq will be the first Arab country to become openly Shiite. Of all Arab countries, Iraq is one of the most important – a claimant to the mantle of Arab leadership and the seat of the Abbasid Empire (750-1258), which established and embodied Sunni supremacy and brutally suppressed the Shiites (many of whose main figures were killed by the Abbasids in and around Baghdad and are now buried in the shrines of Iraq). To pass from Sunni to Shiite domination under the aegis of the United States has immense symbolic significance.

'The Shiite cultural revival in Iraq has broad implications not only for the future political development of Iraq but also for future sectarian developments in the greater Middle East, tipping the balance of power in favor of the Shiites. The cultural and religious ties that bind Shiite populations from Lebanon to Pakistan are once again of political significance; after two decades of suppression at the hands of Sunni regimes, the Shiites are again demanding greater rights and their place in the political arena. In Saudi Arabia, Shiite political activism, brutally suppressed since 1979, is on the rise; and organizations such as the Saudi Hizballah, the Tajammu' al-Ulama al-Hijaz (The Hijazi Ulama Group), and al-Haraka al-Islahiyah (the Reform Movement) are demanding political and religious rights for the Shiites from the monarchy.'

Crucially: 'In militant Sunni circles, the Shiite revival in Iraq is proof of sinister US intentions towards Islam after the events of September 11, 2001 – the grand conspiracy to weaken and subjugate the faith. To these circles, Washington has snatched Iraq from the hands of true Islam and delivered it to Shiite rafidis. Sectarian feelings constitute an important dimension, and one to which the United States has not paid adequate attention, of the reaction in the Arab world and beyond to the US occupation of Iraq, especially among the burgeoning militant Sunni forces that are growing in prominence as the expression of Sunni frustration with the decline in Sunni power.

'Moreover, sectarianism's anti- Shiite and anti-US rhetoric is central to perceptions of US policy in the Muslim world, especially in Arab countries where the impact of the US presence in Iraq is more clearly felt. The Middle East historian, Michael Scott Doran, writes that Wahhabi ulama in Saudi Arabia continue to issue fatwas or give sermons denouncing Shiite beliefs and practices as heresy but now tie the opprobrium for Shiism to anti-Americanism. The Shiites are portrayed as a "fifth column for the enemies of true Islam ... The danger of the [Shiite] heretics to the region ... is not less than the danger of the Jews and Christians." The war in Iraq has been viewed as proof of the "strength of the bond between America and the Shiite heretics." The language of Wahhabi ulama in Saudi Arabia echoes the anti-Shiite vitriol of the Taliban in Afghanistan and militant Sunni forces in Pakistan, as do threats to annihiliate the Shiite minority in the Saudi kingdom.

Finally: 'Today, Sunni militancy is an ascendant, violent, ideological force that is not only anti-Shiite but also violently anti-American. From Bali to Baghdad, it is producing networks of activists that sustain the most dangerous forms of terrorism. Al-Qaeda captures the ideological and political essence of Sunni militancy, but this movement extends far beyond al-Qaeda. Shiite revolutionary activism, on the other hand, is essentially a spent force. Iran is currently a tired dictatorship teetering on the verge of collapse. The ideas emerging from modern-day Iran, similar to those that characterized the end of the Soviet era, do not support revolutionary fervor but rather demand liberal change.

'Sunni militancy has since inception been anti-American and has produced the most violent expressions of this position in the form of al-Qaeda. Today, as evidenced by the rhetoric of the Wahhabi ulama and militants such as al-Zarqawi, Sunni militancy is a two-pronged effort: to extricate US influence from the greater Middle East and to restore Sunni dominance to it. These aims are interrelated, for, just as the United States facilitated the empowerment of the Shiites by dismantling the Sunni dictatorship in Iraq, only defeating the United States in Iraq can reverse the gains made by the Shiites in that country and the region more broadly. In his letter, al-Zarqawi referred to the Shiites as "the insurmountable obstacle, the lurking snake, the crafty and malicious scorpion, the spying enemy and the penetrating venom." He added that: "We here (in Iraq) are entering a battle on two levels. One, evident and open, is with an attacking enemy and patent infidelity." In his audiotape, released during US operations in Falluja and against the Army of the Mahdi, al-Zarqawi reiterated his vitriol against Shiism with threats against US forces. The bombings in Karbala, Najaf and other Shiite holy sites make clear that Sunni militancy is designed both to combat the Shiite revival and provoke a sectarian civil war in Iraq to confound US plans for the country.'[40]

It is impossible to be fully certain of the direct impact of the Shiite revival after the 1979 Iranian Revolution on the rise of al-Qaedaism: it is an area that requires further study. The points set out above, however, and the timing of the Shiite activism seems to suggest a very clear link between the Shiite revival and the growth in Sunni militancy which is now reflected in al-Qaedaism.

Is US support for the rebels who fought the Soviet occupation of Afghanistan to blame?
No, but Afghanistan is undoubtedly a major issue.

Many blame US support for rebels fighting the Soviet occupation of Afghanistan for the subsequent rise of – and current threat posed by – al-Qaedaism. This ignores the historical context in Afghanistan itself, however.

As *The Black Book of Communism* puts it: 'The communist coup d'état and the subsequent intervention by the Soviet army [in 1979] had tragic consequences for Afghanistan. In the 1960s, the country was on the road to prosperity, modernisation and democracy; [Muhammad] Daoud's coup, which was supported by the communists, ended economic development and plunged Afghanistan deep into civil war. The country was forced to make do with a war economy, which was oriented heavily in favour of the Soviet Union. Smuggling (of drugs, guns and other goods) became common, and the economy rapidly fell into ruin. The scale of the disaster is still hard to measure today. Out of a population of approximately 15.5 million, more than 5 million inhabitants have left for Pakistan and Iran, where they now live in miserable conditions. The number of dead is extremely hard to determine but most observers agree that the war took between 1.5 million and 2 million lives, 90 percent of whom were civilians. Between 2 million and 4 million were wounded. The direct and indirect role played by communism in the growth of extremist Islamic movements, and in the reawakening of tensions between different ethnic groups, is undeniable, although it may be hard to quantify. Afghanistan was once on the path to modernity, but it has become a country in which war and violence seem to have become the central reference points in society.'[60]

When one also takes account of the displacement of approximately 2 million internal refugees, the scale of the disaster the communist period constituted for Afghanistan is clear. More than 75 percent of the population were killed, wounded or forced to leave their homes as refugees during this period.

In a review of the development of al-Qaeda, the IISS summarised the Afghan connection in these circumstances: 'The rise of [Osama] bin Laden and his al-Qaeda organisation was deeply connected with the radicalisation of Afghanistan. In the early 1980s, bin Laden began visiting Pakistan to deliver funds raised from Saudi Arabia to support fundamentalist groups in the Afghan resistance. By 1986, he had moved to Peshawar to operate a programme to train and deploy Arab "volunteers" who wished to fight in the anti-Soviet jihad. During this period, he made connections with radical Islamists from around the world and forged close ties with his future lieutenants from Islamic Jihad in Egypt. In 1989, he formed al-Qaeda as a vehicle to maintain contacts and coordinate actions among the radical Islamists who had fought in Afghanistan and then returned to their native countries. At the same time, [Osama] bin Laden had trained a sufficient numbers of fighters to deploy units in Eastern Paktia province [of Afghanistan], though they fared poorly in combat against the Soviets. From 1989 to 1996, [Osama] bin Laden relocated his operation to Sudan and started to launch terrorist attacks around the world. When Sudan forced him to leave in 1996, he returned to Afghanistan, where the ISI (Pakistani intelligence) introduced him to Mullah Omar, the leader of the Taliban. The two men forged a strong alliance between the two movements. In ensuing years, al-Qaeda provided trained fighters to battle against the Northern Alliance, while the Taliban gave al-Qaeda sanctuary to train terrorists and plan operations.

'From this base, al-Qaeda escalated its terrorist operations. During the Clinton administration, the United States initiated covert action, and in retaliation for the August 1998 bombings of US embassies in Nairobi, Kenya, and Dar es Salaam, Tanzania, carried out cruise-missile strikes against al-Qaeda. None of these operations substantially undercut al-Qaeda's effectiveness. By 2001, when the Bush administration took office, al-Qaeda had dozens of training camps in Afghanistan, which accepted recruits from Islamic religious schools (*Madrassas*) and radical groups worldwide. At several facilities, it had programmes to research and develop weapons of mass destruction. Moreover, al-Qaeda had established cells in about fifty countries.'

In summary, the IISS said: 'Afghanistan permitted Osama bin Laden and his organisation al-Qaeda to establish twenty-eight training camps and headquarters for an international terrorist network of unprecedented scope and sophistication. Though the roots of this terrorist movement extended to the Islamist clerical circles in Saudi Arabia and the anti-Soviet war in Afghanistan, the proximate cause of its rise as a global threat was the sanctuary and support received from the Taliban government in Afghanistan, as well as support from other states and wealthy individuals in the Persian Gulf. From this base of operations in Afghanistan, the preparations for the attacks of 9/11 were under way for at least two years before they occurred.'[61]

Clearly, US actions in Afghanistan did not create al-Qaedaism or the hyper-terrorist threat that it now represents to the world. It is also very clear that three separate developments in Afghanistan played a significant part in creating the problem the world now faces with regard to al-Qaedaism.

Firstly, the communist period in Afghanistan, through the extraordinary level of death and destruction it caused, helped radicalise and internationalise Islam in general and the international jihadists who fought there in particular. Victory over the Soviet Union and the subsequent collapse of communism led to the belief that they could also be successful in other conflicts.

Secondly, as set out in Chapter 2, the free-booting Afghan jihadists who had nothing else to do after the victory against the Soviet Union, and in many cases with nowhere they could safely go, naturally came up with a justification for what they were expert in: fighting, killing and destruction. Appropriating the concept of the vanguard from a number of Islamic ideologists, the early history of Islam, and the extreme left and right in Europe, they became extraordinarily influential militants instead of unwanted and unwelcome 'has-beens'.

The United States, Pakistan and Saudi Arabia must accept some responsibility for not ensuring that this international cadre of jihadists remaining in Afghanistan after the Soviet pullout was properly demobilised and absorbed back into society (to the extent that this was possible) and that Afghanistan was fully stabilised with militant groups disarmed. The international community also failed in this respect.

It is now well known that dealing properly with militants when conflict is terminated is crucial to ensuring future peace. This did not occur in Afghanistan. The international jihadists were left to justify their existence through continued conflict and by developing an ideology of militant Islamic jihadism to bless their actions.

Thirdly and finally, the subsequent relationship with the Taliban regime in Afghanistan, as we have seen, allowed al-Qaedaism to dramatically grow and flourish and become the threat it is today. A number of experts from Rand, in a symposium with the US political magazine *Frontpage*, summarised this latter relationship well:

William Rosenau: Al-Qaeda's relationship with the Taliban was unique – the Afghan 'state', such as it was, became a wholly owned subsidiary of Osama bin Laden and his hard-core inner circle. As Jason Burke observes in his excellent new study *Al-Qaeda: Casting a Shadow of Terror,* by late 2001, '[Osama] bin Laden and the men around him had access to huge resources, both symbolic and material, which they could use to project their power and influence internationally. They even had a country they could virtually call their own. They were thus able to offer everything a state could offer to a militant group by way of support.'

John Parachini: Taliban-led Afghanistan was a weak state that became beholden to al-Qaeda, a strong terrorist group. Al-Qaeda operatives bankrolled several of the Taliban's government ministries and provided the most formidable fighting force for its military. Thus, al-Qaeda operated in the sanctuary of Afghanistan with the benefits states enjoy in the international system, but without assuming any of the expected responsibilities.

Brian Jenkins: Al-Qaeda was the guest who ate the host. By providing the Taliban with resources, manpower, money and technical support, al-Qaeda evolved from helpful to essential to dominant. It suggests a pattern. Groups affiliated with al-Qaeda initially may be independent, but gradually al-Qaeda will use its resources and training to improve local effectiveness while increasing its own control.

Bruce Hoffman: The situation and constellation of factors that gave rise to a terrorist group (al-Qaeda) in essence sponsoring a state (the Taliban-ruled Afghanistan) were arguably idiosyncratic. This reflects the entire mujahedin struggle against the Soviet occupation since the early 1980s, the chaos that followed the Red Army's withdrawal a decade later, and the damage wrought to Afghanistan's infrastructure from the war with the Soviets, the civil war and intense fighting that followed, the lack of international concern, the rise of radical Islamist influence in Pakistan, etc.

Gregory Treverton: The term 'wholly owned subsidiary' is right. In that sense, the Bush administration is exactly right in pinning responsibility on such states. Unfortunately, that means we will have to intervene in some of them, or engage in nation-building, lest they become failures that might be wholly owned. We will also need to increase the price states pay for using terrorism as an instrument of statecraft.[4]

These three factors, the international Islamic radicalisation produced by the communist period in Afghanistan, followed by allowing a large group of international jihadi veterans complete freedom of action when that period ended in chaos, and the extraordinary and unique relationship between al-Qaedaism and the Taliban-controlled state of Afghanistan, inexorably led to the dramatic development of al-Qaedaism.

There is clearly no single explanation for the recent growth in al-Qaedaism and the wide support for it. Instead, I believe that a combination of factors has contributed to its growth and the support for it, as I show on the chart on the facing page: The Tree of Destruction.

The most significant factor, the foundation of the problem, is the current failure of Islam, the appalling vista of its likely continued failure in the future, both compared to its great success in the past. This has led to a rage by many in the Islamic world, who blame 'others' for this failure, which they incorrectly attribute to the Crusades, Western imperialism, Great-Power actions, the Jews etc. This leads to a belief in conspiracy theories, and in particular that the West in general, and Jews and Christians in particular, wish to destroy Islam.

On its own such rage might never have led to the growth in al-Qaedaism without the existence of other causal factors.

It is when you add to that rage the impact of market civilisation and the dislocation that is bringing, through globalisation to many in the developing world, that you can see why al-Qaedaism has such support now, and why terrorism is frequently not opposed but in fact seen as justified, especially against what in their eyes are 'guilty' civilians. (This also explains why such terrorism has not been provoked in other societies and cultures impacted upon by globalisation.)

The growth in al-Qaedaist terror and the support for same has clearly built upon this rage (from two separate sources – relative Islamic failure and globalisation) and was then ignited by the parallel growth in Sunni militancy and radicalisation as a reaction to Shiite activism following the 1979 Iranian Revolution and the radicalisation of thousands of Islamic fighters from many countries around the world, during the various struggles in Afghanistan. All this gives an ideology and a movement of very dangerous potential, fully committed to their objectives and willing to die and take many with them while doing so.

In conclusion, with al-Qaedaism we are now dealing with an ideology and movement that has a complete hatred for all but its own tiny vanguard, and a strong belief that the United States will be destroyed by them very easily – much more easily than the Soviet Union was. For Europe, al-Qaedaism holds only contempt, believing that it is utterly corrupt and ready to collapse. It can be 'easily rolled up' once the US 'paper tiger' has been destroyed. In the meantime, as I have shown above, globalisation is used by

THE TREE OF DESTRUCTION

Al-Qaedaism

**Afghanistan
"creates" militant
International jihadists**

**Sunni militancy as a
reaction to Shiite activism**

**The impact of globalisation on
certain societies**

Rage against the west

Failure of Islam   **Illustrious Past**

al-Qaedaism to strengthen its terrorist capability and to enable it to strike at the world.

Kumar Ramakrishna summarises this dilemma well: 'Not only has globalisation significantly increased the capacity of terrorists to wreak havoc, it has also enhanced the vulnerability of modern societies to the new terrorism.'[6]

But even given all of this, why does al-Qaedaism see the United States as a 'paper tiger'? There are a number of reasons for this: perceived economic weaknesses (Osama bin Laden is an economist), the defeat of the United States in Vietnam, the withdrawal of US troops from Somalia by President Clinton after eighteen US soldiers were killed by militants supported by al-Qaedaists there (as noted above), and the withdrawal of US troops from Lebanon after a terrorist attack on a military base there. United States withdrawals from Somalia and Lebanon are repeatedly referred to by al-Qaedaists who believe that the US cannot take casualties because of the presumed volatile nature of US public opinion in this area and the general presumed weakness of Westerners and therefore can be defeated by guerrilla warfare relatively easily.

A statement posted on al-Qaeda's phantom website, 'Al-Neda', on 9 April 2003 explains the situation clearly: 'With guerrilla warfare, the Americans were defeated in Vietnam and the Soviets were defeated in Afghanistan. This is the method that expelled the direct Crusader colonialism from most of the Muslim lands, with Algeria the most well known. We still see how this method stopped Jewish immigration to Palestine and caused reverse immigration of Jews from Palestine. The successful attempts of dealing defeat to invaders using guerrilla warfare were many, and we will not expound on them. However, these attempts have proven that the most effective method for the materially weak against the strong is guerrilla warfare.'[19]

I explained in Chapter 1 how al-Qaeda's guerrilla war would target US civilians, possibly using WMD or MMD, with the sole objective of breaking the will of the American people. We have also seen the propaganda impact of al-Qaedaist strikes, particularly 9/11, on the United States and other Western countries.

Undoubtedly part of the intent on the part of al-Qaeda in relation to 9/11 was to cause major economic dislocation. Articles posted on the 'Al-Neda' website after September 11 drew attention to the impact of the attacks on the US economy in considerable detail and drew parallels with the decline and demise of the Soviet Union, which was precipitated by the jihad in Afghanistan. This has been a consistent theme of al-Qaedaists for a substantial period of time.

In Osama bin Laden's address to his fighters in December 2001, he stated: 'America is in retreat by the grace of God Almighty, and economic attrition is continuing up to today. But it needs further blows. The young men need to seek out the nodes of the American economy and strike the enemies' nodes.'[19]

This economic theme continues: in the tape broadcast on Al-Jazeera TV on 4 January 2004, Osama Bin Laden was very clear that the al-Qaedaist campaign 'is a religious/economic war. ... There can be no dialogue with the occupiers except through arms.'

A key question then is: will al-Qaedaism stay the course? I fear that the answer may be yes, for at least a decade or two. As Brian Michael Jenkins of Rand points out: 'Religious conviction gives them strength, but the armed struggle is what holds them together. Violence is their *raison d'être*. The enterprise of terrorism provides status, power and psychological satisfaction. It attracts new recruits. It demonstrates their devotion and gives them a historical importance. Without terrorism, al-Qaeda would collapse into just another exotic sect.

'Terrorists understand when they suffer setbacks, but they operate in a clandestine world, a closed universe cut off from normal discourse and competing views. They measure success differently: they define death and destruction as achievements in themselves. Terrorists do not feel that it is necessary to translate these into political progress, and they have a high tolerance for cognitive dissonance. Adversity is seen as a test of their commitment. Compromise equals apostasy, so leaders counselling restraint risk accusations of betrayal. In an association of extremists, it is perilous to be less than the most extreme. Successes are seen to derive from violence, and setbacks thus call for greater violence. Individual terrorists may become disillusioned, but there is no easy way for them to leave the organisation. A few groups have officially suspended their campaigns of violence, but their leaders were denounced, while splinter and rival groups vowed to fight on.'[10]

The commitment of al-Qaedaism must not be underestimated. Particularly if they obtain WMD or can use MMD effectively, their destructive capacity would be enormous and potentially very destabilising for the Western world, both socially and economically. The 'war on terror' could be far more difficult – and much more dangerous – than the cold war. During the cold war, WMD were not seen by any of those states possessing them as something they could use; each nuclear-weapons state went to great lengths to ensure such weapons were in fact not used. With al-Qaedaists, the position is the exact opposite: core al-Qaedaists seek WMD not to deter but to actually use as soon as obtained to cause mass casualties. That is the core concern and the reason why, in 2004, the UN passed Resolution 1540 with respect to the terrorist threat of WMD. In short, we are dealing with a very significant threat which we may have to live with for decades. We must therefore face up to this threat and deal with it fully.

So, what does the West need to do to deal with this potentially decades-long hyper-terrorist threat? The response to it must deal directly and comprehensively with the underlying factors that created the threat, as well as defending ourselves while these issues are being resolved.

6

How to Defeat al-Qaedaism

'In the current war . . . the centre of gravity remains the hearts
and minds of the transnational Muslim *umma.*'

KUMAR RAMAKRISHNA[6]

THE IMPLICATIONS OF THIS totalitarian ideological threat for
the rest of the world beyond the tiny vanguard of al-Qaedaists,
are, unfortunately, deadly. Al-Qaedaists' willingness to entertain
the mass murder of 4 million Americans and their desire to re-establish the
Sunni Islamic Caliphate are appalling and unattainable objectives. The
replacement of all existing Islamic governments or regimes by Taliban-like
al-Qaedaists would be a disaster for both Islam and the rest of the world.
Similarly, their desire to eliminate the separation of church and state, and
liberal democracy itself, and to roll back most civil, religious and human
rights, and women's rights, leaves no room for compromise.

The nature of the regime that would be instituted in any Islamic state
after such a change, or in a new Sunni Islamic Caliphate, is well known from
the actions of al-Qaeda's allies, the Taliban, in Afghanistan. John L. Esposito
explains: 'Many Muslim religious leaders around the world denounced the
Taliban "Islamic" policies as aberrant. Muslim governments as diverse as

Iran and Egypt, along with Western governments and international human-rights organisations, condemned Taliban violations of human rights. Despite their control of most of Afghanistan, by the fall of 1998, neither the United Nations nor most of the global community acknowledged their legitimacy. The Taliban government was recognised by only three nations: Saudi Arabia, Pakistan and the United Arab Emirates.'[23]

The IISS, in a review of al-Qaeda, made some key points in this regard: 'Measures to draw down America's military deployments in the Middle East/Gulf region and constructive US intervention in the Israeli-Palestinian conflict would not defuse al-Qaeda's overriding intention to debilitate the United States as a superpower. Unlike "old" ethno-nationalistic or ideological terrorist groups, al-Qaeda cannot be tamed or controlled through political compromise or conflict resolution. ... Al-Qaeda is a resilient organisation with a religious turbocharged absolutist agenda; it will not go quietly. ... Long-term political and economic diplomacy would be key to defeating al-Qaeda, but because its agenda is not negotiable these instruments must aim to outflank rather than directly tame al-Qaeda. The United States and its partners will need to adopt proactive and coordinated policies to set the Israelis and the Palestinians on the path to accommodation, thus vitiating one of [Osama] bin Laden's central political pretexts. More broadly, through economic diplomacy and discreet pressure to democratise, [the United States and its partners] will need to convince untrusting and systematically misled Muslim populations that they can prosper without either destroying the West or relinquishing their traditions to Western cultural influences.'[13]

There are no easy answers to the threat posed by al-Qaedaism. Having an understanding of what has created the threat tells us what issues to address in order to deal with it fully, however. The chart on the following page summarises the necessary response to the underlying four issues, identified in Chapter 5, that have led to the rise in al-Qaedaism.

The West needs to be realistic about the nature of the threat it faces. That includes acceptance that it will take decades at least to deal with this issue. Crucially, the West needs to defend itself in the meantime. The history of terrorism shows clearly that many far smaller groups than those now embracing al-Qaedaism fought on for two or three decades in much less favourable circumstances. We should assume nothing less with the

TREE OF RESPONSE TO AL-QAEDAISM

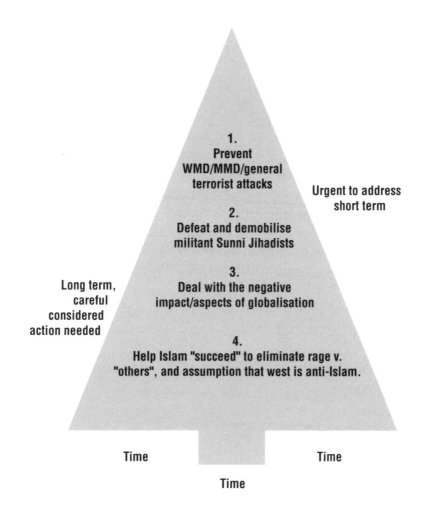

1.
Prevent
WMD/MMD/general
terrorist attacks

Urgent to address
short term

2.
Defeat and demobilise
militant Sunni Jihadists

Long term,
careful
considered
action needed

3.
Deal with the negative
impact/aspects of globalisation

4.
Help Islam "succeed" to eliminate rage v.
"others", and assumption that west is anti-Islam.

Time   Time

Time

totalitarian ideological terrorist threat we are now facing. Due to the nature of al-Qaedaism, we should accept that it is, and will be, a formidable challenge for some time to come. As two experts on terrorism, Stephen Simon and Daniel Benjamin, have put it: 'Deployed assets have proved to be technologically savvy, confident about operating in enemy territory, resourceful, highly motivated and able to act on their own initiative.

'The looseness of these networks, and the way in which the cells within them coalesce, makes identification, penetration and disruption of the groups extremely difficult, particularly for Western intelligence agencies with expertise mainly in recruiting foreign government officials as sources.'[62]

In addition, the fact that al-Qaedaist terrorist networks are spread over many countries and many groups, embracing informal alliances in many cases, with minimal or no hi-tech communications, makes tracking down al-Qaedaists extremely difficult. Finally, with respect to the threat of al-Qaedaists using WMD, as has been mentioned already, this has been a major concern in the strategic-studies community for almost two decades. The absence of any such attack has led some to consider that defences against such attacks are adequate and that the possibility of such an attack occurring is lower than was originally thought.

For the reasons that have been set out earlier, in particular the clear declaration by al-Qaedaists of their intention to obtain WMD, religious 'clearance' to use WMD, together with the failure by the world's major powers to deal with all known stocks of fissile material, and the growing understanding that biological weapons cannot be 'kept in the box', the possibility of a WMD attack is a significant strategic threat that must be addressed immediately.

With this in mind, the following steps should be taken by the world's major powers:

RESPONSE I: PREVENT WMD, MMD AND OTHER TERRORIST
ATTACKS

Operationally, to minimise the impact of al-Qaedaist terrorist attacks, with or without NRBC WMD or whether using MMD or otherwise, as the IISS has put it, 'European security organisations – which are generally geared to act on emergent threats on the basis of current intelligence – may now have to move closer to the United States' vulnerability-based conception of homeland security, under which law-enforcement and intelligence agencies seek, through preventative measures, to minimise unspecified threats by denying terrorists access to territory and opportunities to act.'[63] This change, which draws on historic experiences in Europe and elsewhere, may have to become the norm worldwide, as al-Qaedaists tend to seek softer targets when defensive measures prevent them from hitting their preferred targets.

To deal with the potentially devastating impact of al-Qaedaist NRBC WMD or MMD attacks, Europe and the rest of the world will have to engage in a much stronger effort to control the diffusion of NRBC WMD, reduce the demand-side incentives for seeking WMD and increase significantly the protection of all targets that could be used as MMD. This latter approach will require divergent, proactive thinking and significant ongoing police, paramilitary and military protection of sensitive targets.

The possibility of what Thomas Homer-Dixon calls 'complex terrorism' (attacks on highly complex hi-tech systems, particularly in energy and communications) may, in addition to such protection, require decentralisation, large-scale 'circuit breakers', built-in redundancy, and possibly some form of control of media reporting should such an attack occur.[64] Controls on radiological, chemical, and particularly nuclear WMD will need to be further tightened. Much work is being done in this area now, but much more needs to be done, especially in the nuclear area.

As set out above, expert opinion now sees the threat of radiological and chemical WMD as less critical than that of nuclear and biological WMD, as the casualties from the former two will likely be much lower than from the usage of nuclear and biological WMD. I therefore now focus on the latter two forms of WMD.

PREVENT A NUCLEAR TERRORIST ATTACK

As a nuclear terrorist attack has not yet occurred, many have grown blasé about the threat, while others simply assume such an attack is inevitable. Both are dangerously wrong.

Dr Graham Allison summarises the current position here very well: 'The potential sources of a terrorist nuclear bomb span the globe. Many assume that nuclear weapons or materials are either too well guarded for a thief to obtain or too dangerous for an insider to consider selling. But, as we have already seen, both insiders and intruders are far less constrained than common sense would suggest. From Pakistani nuclear scientists meeting with al-Qaeda, to A. Q. Khan's nuclear import-export business, to impoverished Russian scientists' schemes for making an extra rouble – the list of insider activity is disturbingly long. For intruders, a nuclear heist at many Russian facilities would be easier than robbing a bank.

'Nuclear material and weapons are poorly guarded in much of the former Soviet Union and in the developing world, and proliferators like Pakistan and North Korea are making this bad situation worse. If terrorists do get their hands on a nuclear device or on highly enriched uranium or plutonium, they could easily make a bomb operational within a year. And once they have a nuclear weapon in hand, America's poor border controls will offer little resistance as they seek to deliver the bomb to its target. Whether the question asked begins with who, what, where, when or how, the answer comes back the same. If we continue along our present course, nuclear terrorism is inevitable. But this is not a counsel of fatalism. Unlike the many intractable problems facing humankind, nuclear terrorism is preventable if we act now to make it so.'[8]

In his book *Nuclear Terrorism: The Ultimate Preventable Catastrophe*, Allison gives many examples of inertia, incompetence and simple bureaucratic politics and stupidity which have exposed the world to this awful threat. In one telling example, he quotes former US Senator Sam Nunn, who co-sponsored the Nunn-Lugar program to secure fissile material in the former Soviet Union: 'There are a hundred nuclear research reactors and other facilities in forty countries using highly enriched uranium (HEU) – the raw material of nuclear terrorism. Some of it is secured by nothing more than an underpaid guard sitting inside a chain-link fence. Some of this HEU is sitting in research reactors in Iran, Pakistan, Israel and South Africa in sufficient quantities for at least one bomb.'[8]

The incompetence that has allowed this situation to develop is mind-boggling. For instance, the United States supplied HEU to Iran during the days of the Shah; this material could now be used by Iran to construct a nuclear bomb for use against the United States or others.

The impact of a nuclear attack by al-Qaedaists would be much wider than the direct and indirect impact on the people and the country targeted. In an article entitled 'The Day After', the American political scientist Stephen Krasner, Director of the Center on Democracy, Development and the Rule of Law at Stanford University (and recently appointed Head of the Policy Planning Staff of the US State Department) states that 'the lethality and scope of future terrorist attacks will determine whether or not we are at a fulcrum of history, a turning point analogous to the transition from the medieval to the modern world.' In his opinion, the political fallout from such an attack would include the rollback of certain civil liberties, fundamental changes to conventional rules of international sovereignty, wider acceptance of preventative strikes against specific targets, more preventative strikes such as that on Iraq, changes in UN membership rules, and policing activities without the consent of certain states. [65]

Clearly, whatever one's opinion of such a scenario, the key is to prevent any nuclear attack. Successful prevention will require action on both the supply side – to limit the availability of nuclear weapons and materials – and the demand side, which addresses the balance of factors that states and individuals take into consideration when deciding on nuclear-weapons policies.

The best and most complete programme to prevent a nuclear terrorist attack in the open unclassified sources I have come across is set out in Allison's book. Firstly, he puts the need for a comprehensive strategy in context: 'While the Bush administration has correctly identified the threat of nuclear terrorism, it has not formulated a comprehensive strategy to address it. Without such a strategy, Americans will be no safer from a nuclear terrorist attack next year or the year following than they were on September 10, 2001.

'Waging war on nuclear terrorism will require strategic focus in mobilising a concert of the great powers based on a shared assessment of the threat, a vision of a world beyond nuclear terror, and a joint effort to persuade international publics of the urgency and legitimacy of the actions required to defeat this common danger. The move beyond the current war on terrorism to a serious war on nuclear terrorism would be ambitious. But the stretch involved would be no greater than the distance already travelled since September 11.'

He then presents a summary of his proposals: 'For all the dangers enumerated ... a simple fact remains: nuclear terrorism is, in fact, preventable. Only a fission chain reaction releases the vast blast of energy that is the hallmark of a nuclear bomb. No fissile material, no nuclear explosion, no nuclear terrorism. It is that simple.

'All that the United States and its allies have to do to prevent nuclear terrorism is to prevent terrorists from acquiring highly enriched uranium or weapons-grade plutonium. This "all", of course, will require a huge undertaking. But large as it is, this is a finite challenge, subject to a finite solution.

'The world's stockpiles of nuclear weapons and weapons-usable materials are vast but not unlimited. Technologies for locking up super-dangerous or valuable items are well developed. The United States does not lose gold from Fort Knox, nor does Russia lose treasures from the Kremlin Armoury. Producing additional fissile material requires large, complex, expensive and visible facilities, leaving such enterprises vulnerable to interruption by a watchful, determined international community. Keeping nuclear weapons and materials out of the hands of the world's most dangerous people is thus a challenge to international will and determination, not to our technical capabilities.

'The centrepiece of a strategy to prevent nuclear terrorism must be to deny terrorists access to nuclear weapons or materials. To do this, we must shape a new international security order according to a doctrine of "Three No's":

- No Loose Nukes
- No New Nascent Nukes
- No New Nuclear Weapons States

'The first strand of this strategy – "No Loose Nukes" – begins with the recognition that insecure nuclear weapons or materials anywhere pose a grave threat to all nations everywhere. The international community can thus rightly insist that all weapons and materials – wherever they are – be protected to a standard sufficient to ensure the safety of citizens around the world. Russia, which holds the largest stockpile of actual and potential nuclear weapons, has been the principal focus of concern for the past decade, but in recent years a new, urgent test of this principle has come from Pakistan, where the developer of its nuclear establishment has been exposed as the kingpin in black-market sales of nuclear-weapons technology.

'Application of the second principle – "No New Nascent Nukes" – would prevent the construction of any national production facilities for enriching uranium or reprocessing plutonium. The head of the International Atomic Energy Agency, Mohamed ElBaradei, now recognises that the existing system under the Nuclear Nonproliferation Treaty (NPT) erred in allowing nonnuclear states to build uranium-enrichment and plutonium-production plants. In his words, "This is a different ball game, and we have to change the rules." Closing this loophole will require deft diplomacy, imaginative inducements and demonstrable readiness to employ sanctions, including use of military capabilities, to establish a new bright line. Iran is currently testing this line. The international community's response will demonstrate the feasibility – or, alternatively, forfeit the possibility – of a world in which this principle holds.

The third element of this strategy draws a line under the current eight nuclear powers – the United States, Russia, Great Britain, France, China, India, Pakistan and Israel – and declares unambiguously "No more". North Korea poses a decisive challenge for the "No New Nuclear Weapons States" policy. Unless its current plans are aborted, North Korea will soon have something like eight nuclear weapons and facilities for producing a dozen more each year. If North Korea becomes a nuclear-weapons state, South Korea and Japan will almost certainly go nuclear in the decade thereafter, making Northeast Asia a far more dangerous place than it is today. More important, if North Korea successfully completes its nuclear-weapons production line, it might well sell weapons to others, including terrorists. In that future, the prospects for preventing nuclear terrorism would plummet.

'Some critics disparage the call for a world of Three No's as little more than a nuclear version of "I have a dream". They maintain that the nuclear genie is out of the bottle, that nuclear proliferation is therefore unstoppable, and nuclear terrorism inevitable. They say that no matter how much we try to stop terrorists from attacking us with nuclear weapons, there is no such thing as enough.

'It is realistic to recognise that the actions required are ambitious. But realism does not require fatalism or defeatism. In fact, most of the world is already signed up to the third no, could live with the second no, and supports the first. The "Three No's" framework stretches beyond current realities, but not further than we have stretched before. For courage as well as clues, it is instructive to recall the prevailing expectations of the early 1960s, when President John F. Kennedy predicted that "by 1970 there may be ten nuclear powers instead of four, and by 1975, fifteen or twenty". Had those nations with the technical capacity to build nuclear weapons gone ahead and created their own arsenals, Kennedy's prediction would have been correct. But his warning helped awaken the world to the unacceptable dangers of unconstrained nuclear proliferation. The United States and other nations refused to accept these projections, instead negotiating international constraints, providing security guarantees, offering incentives and posing credible threats. As a result, today 183 nations, including scores that have the technical capacity to build arsenals, have renounced nuclear weapons and have committed themselves, in the NPT, to eschew the nuclear option. Forty years after Kennedy's prediction, there are only eight nuclear weapons states, not twenty. Today's leaders can achieve similar success in combating nuclear terrorism.'[8]

Allison and many others stress the importance of preventing Iranian and North Korean nuclear-weapons developments. Why? Although ignored or downplayed by many, the key danger here is the impact this would have on nuclear proliferation and the then much-increased danger of nuclear weapons or materials getting into the wrong hands, or actually being used.

If North Korea is conclusively known to have nuclear weapons, there is a significant risk that South Korea, Japan and possibly others (including Taiwan) will eventually feel the need to follow suit. The impact of this on China in particular and Asia in general would be very destabilising, while the possibility of nuclear 'leakage' from North Korea to terrorist groups, either directly or indirectly, would increase, in view of known and suspected North Korean activities to date.[8]

If Iran acquires nuclear weapons, it is feared that Iraq, Egypt and Saudi Arabia principally, and possibly Syria, Algeria, the UAE and others, would feel the need to respond, creating significant instability, increased uncertainty, further financial and economic hardship and greater tension in an already volatile region. In such circumstances, the possibility of nuclear weapons or materials being acquired by al-Qaedaists, directly or indirectly, increases dramatically. For all these reasons, the world needs to seriously focus on the nuclear crises in North Korea and Iran now.

Part of this effort would involve the United States in a 'Grand Bargain' with both these states. Most experts now see the United States as effectively having no clear policy for dealing with nuclear issues in Iran and North Korea and many agree on the need to give incentives to both regimes to accept the elimination of their nuclear-weapons capabilities, either actual or planned. The US administration needs to come up with such policies urgently after years of drift, and agree a basis for finally solving these issues with the EU and the other major powers.

The EU needs to acknowledge with respect to Iran that the diplomatic approach of the trio of the UK, France and Germany has so far failed to achieve its objectives – and time is running out. In addition, with respect to North Korea, a comprehensive policy needs to be developed by the EU: it is not good enough to leave it to the six-party talks, led by the United States, which have effectively run into the ground.

The EU, together with the United States, China, Russia, South Korea and Japan, then needs to agree on the broad parameters of a policy for these two countries to deal with the significant nuclear proliferation threat they now represent. In the long run, the United States is the only nation which can give Iran and North Korea what they need: assurances that there will be no forced regime change. Without this, both will eventually seek to develop nuclear weapons. With both states time is running out, however. Former Iranian president Ayatollah Rafsanjani recently stated that '[The assertion] that we are on the verge of nuclear breakout is true.'[66]

To quote Ray Takeyh, whose article 'Iran Builds the Arms' is the best analysis of Iranian thinking and pressures in this area I have read: 'Iran today stands at a crossroads. In the near future, it needs to make fundamental choices regarding the direction of its nuclear programmes. When assessing a state's nuclear path, it is important to note that its motivations cannot be exclusively examined within the context of national interests and security considerations. Whatever strategic benefits such weapons offer a state, they are certainly a source of national prestige and parochial benefits to various bureaucracies and politicians. As such constituencies emerge, a state can potentially cross the nuclear threshold even if the initial strategic factors that provoked the programme are no longer salient. The emergence of bureaucratic and nationalist pressures in Iran is generating its own proliferation momentum, empowering those seeking a nuclear breakout. As time passes, the pragmatic voices calling for hedging are likely to be marginalized and lose their influence within the regime. The notion that the United States has the luxury of time is belied by Iran's internal domestic alignments on the nuclear issue.

'As Iran's nuclear programme matures and becomes subject of international scrutiny, another dynamic is entering the debate: [Iranian] public opinion. Far from being a source of restraint, the emerging popular sentiment is that, as a great civilisation with a long history, Iran has a right to acquire a nuclear capability. The recent disclosures of the sophisticated nature of Iran's nuclear programme have been a source of national pride for a citizenry accustomed to the revolution's failures and setbacks. Rafsanjani, one of the Islamic Republic's most astute politicians, noted this trend when he said, "No official would dare allow himself to defy the people on such an issue."'[67]

Nor does the issue divide neatly between reformers and conservatives. Many in Iran, including many students (frequently seen as a barometer of opinion), support nuclear power and oppose agreement with the EU trio. So regime change would, in most circumstances, not defuse this issue. In addition, in one of life's many ironies, Iranian acquisition of nuclear weapons would more than likely lead to whatever regime was in power then in Iraq following suit. ... With respect to the Iraqi nuclear program, we now have the *Duelfer Report*, based on the debriefing of Iraqi-regime loyalists, which concluded: 'Iran was the pre-eminent motivator of this policy. All senior-level Iraqi officials considered Iran to be Iraq's principal enemy in the region. The wish to balance Israel and acquire status and influence in the Arab world were also considerations, but secondary.'[68]

CIA Director George Tenet has said: 'No Iranian government, regardless of its ideological leaning, is likely to willingly abandon WMD programmes that are seen as guaranteeing Iran's security.'[69]

The impact on Iranian thinking in this area of the deepening Sunni/Shiite struggle is an unquantifiable factor that should not be ignored.

Further, as one expert on deterrence, Robert S. Litwak, puts it: 'Regime intention, rather than regime type, is the telling proliferation indicator. Regime change or evolution will not necessarily lead to the altering of intentions and nuclear restraint if the underlying motivations for proliferation, which are unrelated to regime character, remain unaddressed.'[70]

A US Grand Bargain with both Iran and North Korea, supported by the UN and the other Great Powers, with respect to Iran, and by its neighbours and the UN in the case of North Korea, is the only long-term solution. It involves an effective US guarantee of non-aggression and no forced regime change, and economic and political support, in return for adherence to the 'Three No's', either fully or as far as is possible at this time.

With respect to North Korea, using a multilateral forum, approval by the UN and policing of the agreement by the IAEA and its neighbours increases the odds of success compared to a bilateral US-North Korea deal. (This bilateral approach was one of the reasons for the failure of the earlier US-North Korean deal.) This approach would also give time for a slow evolution of the North Korean state, which is the preferred option for South Korea.

With respect to Iran, a US-China-Russia-EU deal is needed due to the current interests of each of these powers in Iran. Such a deal could also help improve relations between the United States and Iran, who are in the long term natural allies in the battle against the Sunni al-Qaedaists. This approach would also help improve the US image in the Islamic world in general. If such a Grand Bargain fails, and the United States is seen as having made a genuine effort to reach agreement, there would be some increased 'justification' for any subsequent preventative attacks on illegal nuclear sites.

The concept of a Grand Bargain with Iran is not a fanciful one. Iran tried to initiate such a deal relatively recently, as the IISS has pointed out: 'In the spring of 2003, in the aftermath of the Iraq war, Tehran approached Washington in secret with an offer to begin negotiations aimed at resolving concerns about its fuel-cycle programme, the existence of which had first come to light in August 2002. Washington spurned Tehran's advances, however, following the May 2003 bombings in Riyadh, which the United States traced to senior al-Qaeda officials residing in Iran. Concerned that it was next on Washington's target list, and faced with the threat of referral to the UN Security Council for past violations of its Safeguards Agreement with the IAEA, Iran turned to Europe for a diplomatic solution. In October 2003, the French, German and British foreign ministers reached agreement with Hassan Rowhani, secretary of the powerful Supreme National Security Council, whereby Iran pledged full cooperation with the IAEA to address and resolve outstanding issues; to allow more intrusive IAEA inspections under the Additional Protocol; and to voluntarily suspend all uranium-enrichment and reprocessing activities, pending efforts to negotiate a permanent resolution of the nuclear issue. In return, the EU-3 agreed to block American efforts to refer Iran to the UN Security Council for past violations of its safeguards agreement. By early 2004, however, as America's predicament in Iraq deepened, an emboldened Iran began to renege on the October 2003 deal.'[71]

The programme of action set out above is a daunting but not impossible one. Regrettably, there must be some possibility that it will only be implemented after the event – a nuclear 9/11. World leaders need to urgently address this challenge now.[72]

DEFEND AGAINST BIOLOGICAL ATTACK

Unfortunately, as I show below, the proliferation of biological weapons is now a certainty – the only question is when. The latest thinking in this area is that, with developments in civilian research, such weapons will become more widely available, and therefore the efforts of major powers need to be directed at defence against such weapons rather than solely at preventing their proliferation.

In an article entitled "Biotechnology and Bioterrorism: An Unprecedented World" in *Survival*, the IISS Quarterly, in Summer 2004, Christopher Chyba and Alex Greninger made some crucial comments with respect to this threat:

'Biotechnological capacity is increasing and spreading rapidly. This trend seems unstoppable, since the economic, medical and food-security benefits of genetic manipulation appear so great. As a consequence, thresholds for the artificial enhancement or creation of dangerous pathogens – disease-causing organisms – will steadily drop. The revolution in biotechnology will therefore almost inevitably place greater destructive power in the hands of smaller groups of the technically competent: those with skills sufficient to make use of the advances of the international scientific community. This future is being driven not primarily by military programmes, but rather by open, legitimate private and academic research.

Lessons from the past half-century of relative success in blocking nuclear proliferation cannot be easily applied to the twenty-first century challenge of biological proliferation. Neither cold-war bilateral arms control nor multilateral nonproliferation provide good models for how we are to manage this new challenge. Much more than in the nuclear case, civilisation will have to cope with, rather than shape, its biological future.

'In the biological realm, we are entering an unprecedented world.'[11]

Four developments in the 1990s have led to this serious challenge to the world – an increase in the number of new infectious diseases (one per year on average for the previous two decades), the rise of mass-casualty terrorism, violations of the 1972 Biological and Toxic Weapons Convention (BWC) and dramatic advances in biotechnology.

It is notable that in July 2001 the US government withdrew from the negotiations on an international protocol for compliance with the BWC, declaring it to be 'inherently unverifiable' due to past violations by Iraq, the Soviet Union and others – which violations they considered impossible to detect by 'normal' means.

The threat is therefore now seen in public heath defensive terms rather than in inappropriate analogies to other WMD. Dealing with this threat will require a broad range of measures to make biological terrorism more difficult, including disease surveillance and response, anti-proliferation measures, security over dangerous stocks, development of and stockpiling vaccines, developing and implementing last-move defences (dealing with drug resistance on an organism-by-organism basis), etc.[11]

In addition and at a wider level: 'Broad-based and publicly acknowledged bio-defence research would aim to globalise dissuasion, convincing non-state terrorist groups that they cannot hope to counter the entire array of defences that the world's legitimate bio-defence research community has arrayed against them. With research on de facto "last-move" defences, the bio-defence community should thereby endeavour to circumvent, or at least mitigate, an otherwise endless biological (offence-defence) arms race.'[11]

Other more mundane action can be taken in this area to restrict the diffusion of all NRBC WMD, including enticing scientists who have worked in such areas in the Soviet Union, Africa and the Middle East into appropriate civilian employment. This will require the provision of funding by Western powers to the relevant state and can be effected through existing programmes to encourage ex-Soviet scientists to take up 'safer' civilian employment.

In addition, Europe and the rest of the world will have to invest in civil defence, disaster-recovery techniques, immunisation, and vaccine research and development in order to mitigate the impact of any such WMD or MMD attacks. Much of the expertise to implement such programmes is available from cold-war studies and programmes, and from medical-contingency planning. We can no longer assume that proliferation efforts will be completely successful, especially in the biological area. The ad hoc programmes already in train in certain EU countries need to be formally extended EU-wide as a matter of urgency.

There is one ray of hope in this dark picture. Most experts had assumed for some time that, in dealing with al-Qaedaists, the traditional strategy of deterrence does not apply. This is not entirely correct, however: there are some circumstances where the strategy of deterrence still has utility.

Brian Michael Jenkins, a noted expert on deterence, has this to say: 'The very nature of the terrorist enterprise makes the traditional strategy of deterrence difficult to apply to terrorist groups. In traditional deterrence, the adversaries do not exceed mutually understood limits and will not employ certain weapons, although their continued existence is accepted. Deterrence worked in the cold war, where central decision-makers were in charge and in control on both sides. The limits and the consequences [of action by either side] were mutually understood. Coexistence was acceptable. Deterrence regulated the conflict; it did not end the struggle.

'Deterring terrorism is an entirely different matter. Here, there are diverse foes rather than a single enemy with different goals and values. Terrorist leaders are not always in complete control, and they often have difficulty constraining their own followers. Coexistence is not a goal, on either side. Would the United States accept the existence of al-Qaeda and any form of freedom for its current leaders, even with credible promises that they will suspend operations against this country? As individual 'repentants' ready to cooperate in the destruction of the organization, perhaps; as leaders of al-Qaeda, never.

'The United States … may prefer to demonstrate that large-scale attacks will bring unrelenting pursuit and ultimate destruction in order to deter future terrorist groups.

'Deterrence might also be employed in targeting terrorists' support systems. Economic sanctions, although blunt instruments, have had some effect in modifying state behaviour. The fate of the Taliban serves as a warning to state supporters of terrorism.

'Financial contributors to terrorist fronts may also be deterred by threats of negative publicity, blocked investments, asset seizures, exposure to lawsuits, or merely increased scrutiny of their financial activities. Institutions that assist or tolerate terrorist recruiting may be deterred by the prospect of all members or participants coming under close surveillance.

Communities supporting terrorists might be deterred by the threat of expulsions, deportations, selective suspensions of immigration and visa applications, or increased controls on remittances.

Stings may also be used as a deterrent to terrorists seeking WMD. Bogus offers of materials or expertise can be set up to identify and eliminate would-be buyers or middlemen, divert terrorists' financial resources, and provoke uncertainty in terrorists' acquisition efforts.

'Even if attacks involving unconventional weapons [i.e. WMD or MMD] do not result in mass casualties, their use could still cause widespread panic, with enormous social and economic disruption. This would be true of radiological attacks and almost any deliberate release of a contagious disease. It is, therefore, appropriate to speak of weapons of mass effect as well as weapons of mass destruction. For purposes of response, the United States may decide to treat them as the same.

'Another possible deterrent, perhaps more compelling to the terrorist's supporters and sympathizers than to the terrorists themselves, would be to widely publicize the fact that a major bioterrorism attack involving a highly contagious disease such as smallpox would almost certainly result in a pandemic that would spread beyond US borders. Despite some weaknesses in its public-health system, the United States, with its vast medical resources, would be able to cope with an outbreak, as would Europe. But with weak public-health institutions and limited medical capabilities, the world's poorer nations would suffer enormously, perhaps losing significant portions of their populations. And if terrorists were to unleash some diabolically designed bug that even the United States could not cope with, the world would be doomed. This grim realization may not stop the most determined fanatic, but it may cause populations that currently find comfort in the illusion that only arrogant Americans will suffer from bio-terrorism to come to the view that taboos against certain weapons are necessary to protect all.'[10]

In a recent Adelphi paper published by the IISS, Jonathan Stevenson points out that US analysts have started to consider how to apply deterrence theory to meet the WMD terrorist threat. Starting by quoting Brian Jenkins, he says: 'Al-Qaeda and its affiliates are not monolithic institutions; they are complex institutions depending on tolerance and support. Deterrence in its traditional form may not work very well against the committed core or the wild-eyed recruits of enterprises like al-Qaeda, but other parts of the system may be amenable to influence.

'There may be useful distinctions to make even within the hard-core category. For example, some Muslim terrorists regard WMD as indispensable instruments of eschatology. Others, however, seem to see them merely as prime war-fighting assets, useful in compensating for the conventional military disparity between Western militaries and terrorists with no state apparatus. Terrorists in the first group are liable to use WMD as soon as they have them, those in the second are more inclined to weigh the political and tactical trade-offs crossing that threshold would entail. The latter can probably be deterred – at least from using WMD.

'The larger point is that, in spite of the religiously absolute imperatives laid down by al-Qaeda's leadership, the highly dispersed and pragmatic character of the transnational Islamic terrorist network means that terrorists' religious and political intensity and tactical mindsets are highly variable. Like more manageable 'old' terrorist groups, al-Qaeda too encompasses professional terrorists and wavering 'fellow travellers' as well as maniacal true believers. It would be an obvious mistake to cast them as impervious to political, social and tactical influence. In their confessions and statements, for instance, captured members of Turkish Hizbullah placed immense importance on perceived divine approval for their actions. They assumed that their leaders were not so much giving them orders as transmitting divine commands, and apprehended the success of their operations as proof of divine approval. But several militants said that when their leader – a man named Huseyin Velioglu – was killed, the organisation's archives captured and its cell network rolled up, they 'realised that God was not on their side after all.' Velioglu's death functioned as deterrence by denial of political objectives. It is possible that the killing of a highly charismatic individual like Osama bin Laden would actually enhance his iconic power through martyrdom and increase recruitment to militant organisations. The demonstrable failure of violent Islam to achieve its stated goals over a certain period of time, however, would probably erode assumptions of divine approval. The Turkish Hizbullah prisoners suggest that for many, such a period would be relatively short. Violent Islam would not disappear. But a large number of potential or actual perpetrators of violence would simply conclude: 'God isn't supporting this.' There is a precedent in the life of Muhammad for initial setbacks (i.e. the exile to Medina), but in the end he triumphed. So, in the medium term, from a theological perspective, al-Qaeda's leadership still needs to be able to demonstrate both the validity of their assumptions about the predation of the West and progress in opposing it to sustain the momentum of the global jihad.

'Fashioning a comprehensive counter-terrorism policy, then, will require experts on Islam to identify who falls into what category in terms of amenability to influence, and operational analysts in the mould of the great nuclear strategists of the 1950s and 1960s to formulate non-proliferation and deterrence strategies for handling different brands of terrorists. More broadly, Thomas C. Schelling's conviction that "most conflict situations are essentially bargaining situations" is not irrelevant to counter-terrorism. Although al-Qaeda's *shura* [consultation body] – unlike, say, the IRA Army Council – is not interested in sitting down at a table and expressly negotiating with its adversaries, it is worth investigating what combinations of hard and soft counter-terrorism measures might strike what in the cold-war context Schelling dubbed "tacit bargains" or "coordination games" between the counter-terrorism coalition and the terrorists. Looking even farther out, Lawrence Freedman has contemplated a norms-based deterrence-by-denial strategy. It would be established by persuading not the jihadists but the rest of the international community, especially wider Islam, to accept principles and relationships that comprehensively reject terrorism. Freedman observes that "all political groups, however apparently fanatical in their ideology, adjust to shifting power relationships and act with some thought to the consequences." Thus, if the West and non-radical Islam can eventually find common ground on civil and political norms, Muslim terrorists could be deterred – indeed, defeated – by the adverse weight of Muslim opinion, backed only remotely by the threat of force'[21]

RESPONSE 2: DEFEAT AND DEMOBILISE MILITANT SUNNI JIHADISTS

In order to defeat al-Qaedaism it is essential to divide al-Qaedaists into three distinct groups. The first, the core extremists, cannot be negotiated with. The second, the militants outside the core, can be negotiated with as their grievances are frequently national or local and are best addressed at that level. The third, the 'walk-ins' and others who support al-Qaedaism by conviction rather than action, can be dealt with only by broader action, targeted at the impact of globalisation and the relative failure of Islam. Hard power has utility only with the first, hard power and soft power has utility with the second, and comprehensive soft power only is required to deal with the much larger third group.

HELP AFGHANISTAN AND IRAQ

The key to defeating and demobilising significant numbers of militant jihadists is military victory with broadly acceptable political structures and then demobilisation and stabilisation in both Afghanistan and Iraq.

In relation to Afghanistan, Europe is taking primary responsibility for security in that country. Unfortunately, the effort to date, while broadly going in the right direction, is too little too late. There is a widespread perception amongst the Islamic community that Afghanistan was abandoned by the United States and the international community in the early 1990s after the Soviet withdrawal. This, as we have seen, led to the growth of militant international jihadists who, as much as anyone or anything else, created al-Qaedaism to justify their continued existence.

The international community must not fail Afghanistan again. This requires intellectual input, military resources and financial support. The fallout from failure in Afghanistan again would be dramatic and long-lasting.

That country is broadly going in the right direction now, albeit very slowly, and perceptive experts agree that the Taliban are a regional threat to parts of Afghanistan rather than a threat to the country overall. Europe, the United States and the international community through the UN must work together to assist the new government there to provide proper security, to fully defeat the Taliban and al-Qaedaists, and to generate economic development. A significant and key first step must be made to encourage foreign investment in Afghanistan and to expedite post-war reconstruction. It will be a long, hard road, but it will be worth it in the end.

After many disagreements on Iraq, most observers now at least seem to agree on the importance of its problems being solved. Some, however, especially in Europe, seem to be more concerned with giving the United States the cold shoulder or scoring debating points than helping the long-oppressed Iraqi people. What Larry Diamond, a liberal described by *Foreign Affairs* as a 'leading theorist of democratisation and an outstanding proponent of putting human rights and democracy promotion high on the US foreign-policy agenda', has to say on this subject is interesting.

He opposed the war in Iraq, but when asked to go there in late 2003 to advise on the transition, agreed to do so. He notes: 'I was taken aback by the partisan tone of these objections (to him doing such), and by the failure of some (but not most) liberals to distinguish between the war and the post-war.

'If the war was a strategic mistake, it still opens the possibility for historic political progress in Iraq. And if the Bush administration bungled the post-war planning and management, as I believe it did, this did not preclude significant improvements and a more positive outcome down the road.'

He continues: 'After twenty-five years of weighing the evidence and studying democratic development in more than two dozen countries, I have concluded that there in fact are no preconditions for democracy other than a commitment by political elites to implement it (and, one hopes, broad popular support as well). Yes, richer countries fare better. But today, almost one-third of the countries with "low human development" (according to the UN Development Programme) are democracies. Yes, oil dependence is a curse, and deep ethnic divisions make democracy even more difficult to sustain. But Nigeria and Indonesia both have this volatile mix, and with all their problems and corruption, they are sustaining democracy in the popular belief that it is better than any other form of government.

'Most intellectuals and commentators who dismiss Iraq as a hopeless prospect for democracy have failed to consult the Iraqi people. They did not see what many of us in the Coalition Provisional Authority, the UN and other international groups saw: a people fed up with tyranny, who strongly aspire to live in freedom and to choose their own leaders.

'If large numbers of people in a country are willing to risk their lives and fortunes to build a democracy, don't we all have some obligation to help them? Even if the outcome is not an instant Costa Rica but a struggling and conflicted semi-democracy, that is still better for the Iraqi people than some new form of tyranny, or the anarchy that would result if the world simply threw up its hands and withdrew.

'Despite all its mistakes, I do not regard that post-war endeavour as a "pact with the devil". Let Smith [Tony Smith of Tufts University, who challenged him] and other critics visit Iraq and talk to Iraqis who are organising for democracy, development and human rights. Let them talk to the families that lived in constant, humiliating fear under Baathist rule. Let them see some of the roughly three hundred mass graves of opponents of the regime who were brutally slaughtered in the hundreds of thousands. Then they will find out who the devil really was.'[73]

The Iraqi people have since been consulted and almost 60 percent of them braved death to vote, whatever the imperfections in that election.

Key assumptions I have made in commenting here are that a majority of Iraqis want democracy and that this gives them the best chance of a reasonable future. I also assume that it is incumbent on all democracies to help them in such an effort – in the manner determined by the new Iraqi government itself. As UN Secretary General Kofi Annan said: 'We all share a common agenda, to move Iraq from the starting point – its successfully completed elections – to a peaceful, prosperous, democratic future.' ... 'I believe that with international help such a society can use democratic institutions to give itself a stable and prosperous future. That hope and that vision offers us in the outside world a real opportunity to start again together and support the Iraqi people in their great experiment.'[74]

We have to deal with this reality of Iraq now, not how it might have been or should be. To help in this regard it is worthwhile considering what most people in the world (both pro- and anti-war) would want for Iraq now. I believe such would involve a fully sovereign Iraq, at peace internally and with its neighbours, threatening neither generally and most especially not with WMD, with a moderate Islamic ethos and moving forward in a broadly democratic fashion with a gradually expanding economy. The key to this is to re-establish a sovereign Iraq urgently with as much democratic accountability as possible.

A core issue then is how sovereign Iraq is now and what would it take to get it to a reasonably sovereign position? To help in this analysis, the

American political scientist Stephen Krasner has developed a good defini-tion of sovereignty by dividing it into its various elements.[75] The first and most straightforward element is international legal sovereignty, which, after much uncertainty, was granted to the transitional government of Iraq by UN Security Council Resolution 1546.

The second element of sovereignty is what Krasner calls 'Westphalian sovereignty' and is based on the ability of the state to exclude external actors from interfering in its domestic activities or its ability to exercise its authority over its own people. This will be impacted upon for some time by the need for external security and economic assistance to Iraq by the Coalition or others, or both. It can also obviously be impacted upon by the actions of its neighbours. Many in Iraq are concerned about the activities of Iran and Syria. Other neighbours have also impacted on this element of sovereignty. But in essence, success in achieving the third element of sov-ereignty effectively deals with this second element, with the passing of time.

It is Krasner's third element of sovereignty, domestic sovereignty, that will determine for the Iraqi people and the rest of the world the legitimacy and therefore the success or otherwise of the new government in that coun-try. Domestic sovereignty, according to Krasner, is 'the organisation and effectiveness of political authority' across the whole country: 'It is the abil-ity of the new government to impose order and gain acceptance that will be the test of Resolution 1546.'[75]

Domestic sovereignty in essence consists of two elements. Firstly, 'It [the Iraqi government] will have to convince a sizeable proportion of the Iraq population that is is ruling in their interests, furthering their collective ideas of what Iraq is and what it is to become.'[75] The second element 'is the state's capacity to impose order on its population – to monopolise the means of collective violence across the whole of its territory. ... The most pressing short-term issue, the one that dominates the lives of ordinary Iraqis, is lack of order and the high level of political and criminal vio-lence.'[75]

Following the elections, it is clear that the Kurds and the Shiites will most likely accept that the new government is ruling in their interests. It is obvious that many in the Sunni community may not feel this way, although Sunni representation in the 275-person assembly, at 49 members, is in fact not out of line with its reputed percentage of the population.[76] The Shiites and the Kurds – the latter who are Sunni in the main – appear to plan to bring the Sunni community into the consultative process for the new constitution, a key issue for a peaceful, democratic future. That effort, the high election turnout, and the obvious point that the Sunni community has no natural right to rule or to prevent the march to democracy, suggests that the key to domestic sovereignty in Iraq is the second element: defeating the insurgency so the government has a monopoly on violence and can provide security for its people.

It is, therefore, in the interests of all who want to see a fully sovereign Iraq to help defeat the insurgency as soon as possible. That should now be the key focus. When such occurs, there will be no need for foreign troops and no 'excuse' for any insurgency or terrorist actions.

There is a 'catch 22' in this area: the insurgency gets some, but not all, of its lifeblood from the presence of Coalition troops in the country. Without such troops, until Iraqi forces are strong enough, the insurgents could take control of Iraq again or at least precipitate a disastrous loss of sovereignty and a security meltdown. So the key question is how the occupation should be effected to help Iraq achieve domestic and therefore full sovereignty through defeating the insurgency.

There have been a number of studies over the last two years on nation-building and military occupations which help suggest how the occupation in Iraq should now be operated and eventually terminated to achieve these objectives. The first was a Rand study which examined the role of the United States in previous efforts at nation-building in Germany, Japan, Somalia, Haiti, Bosnia, Kosovo and Afghanistan.

The results were summarised by one of the authors, James Dobbins, the Clinton administration's special envoy for Somalia, Haiti, Bosnia and Kosovo, and subsequently the Bush administration's special envoy for Afghanistan: 'The first lesson is that democratic nation-building can work given sufficient inputs of resources. These inputs, however, can be very high. The second lesson for Iraq is that short departure deadlines are incompatable with nation-building. The United States will succeed only if it makes a long-term commitment to establishing strong democratic institutions and does not beat a hasty retreat tied to an artificial deadline. Third, important hindrances to nation-building include both internal fragmentation (along political, ethnic or sectarian lines) and a lack of external support from neighboring states. Fourth, building a democracy, a strong country and long-term legitimacy depends in each case on striking the balance between international burden-sharing and unit of command.'[77]

The results of some US efforts at nation-building have been mixed. To put such efforts in context, a year later Dobbins listed the results of a subsequent Rand study on the UN's role in nation-building in the Congo, Namibia, El Salvador, Cambodia, Mozambique, Eastern Slovenia, East Timor and Sierra Leone. He records the study's conclusions: 'Despite the United Nations' significant achievements in the field of nation-building, the organisation continues to exhibit weaknesses that decades of experience have yet to overcome. Most UN missions are undermanned and underfunded. UN-led military forces are often sized and deployed on the basis of unrealistic best-case assumptions. Troop quality is uneven, and has even worsened as many rich Western nations have followed US practice and become less willing to commit their armed forces to UN operations. Police and civil personnel are always of mixed competence. All components of the mission arrive late; police and civil administrators arrive even more slowly than soldiers.

'These same weaknesses have been exhibited most recently in the US-led operation in Iraq. There it was an American-led stabilisation force that was deployed on the basis of unrealistic, best-case assumptions and American troops that arrived in inadequate numbers and had to be progressively reinforced as new, unanticipated challenges emerged. There it was the quality of a US-led coalition's military contingents that proved distinctly variable, as has been their willingness to take orders, risks and casualties. There it was that American civil administrators were late to arrive, of mixed competence, and never available in adequate numbers. These weaknesses thus appear endemic to nation-building, rather than unique to the United Nations.'[78]

Finally, David Edelstein published a study entitled 'Occupational Hazards: Why Military Occupations Succeed or Fail' in summer 2004 in the journal *International Security*.[79] After a detailed analysis, he concludes: 'The crux of my argument is that military occupations usually succeed only if they are lengthy, but lengthy occupations elicit nationalist reactions that impede success. Further, lengthy occupation produces anxiety in impatient occupying powers that would rather withdraw than stay. To succeed, therefore, occupiers must both maintain their own interest in a long occupation and convince an occupied population to accept extended control by a foreign power. More often than not, occupiers either fail to achieve these goals, or they achieve them only at a high cost.

'Three factors, however, can make a successful occupation possible. The first factor is a recognition by the occupied population of the need for occupation. Thus, occupation is more likely to succeed in societies that have been decimated by war and require help in rebuilding. The second factor is the perception by the occupying power and the occupied population of a common threat to the occupied territory. If the survival of the occupied country is threatened, then the occupying power will want to protect a country that it has already invested resources in and considers geopolitically significant, and the occupied population will value the protection offered to it. The third factor involves credibility. Occupation is likely to generate less opposition when the occupying power makes a credible guarantee that it will withdraw and return control to an indigenous government in a timely manner. When these three conditions are present, occupying powers will face less resistance both in the occupied territory and at home; they will be given more time to accomplish their occupation goals, and, therefore, will be more likely to succeed. Absent these three conditions, occupying powers will face the dilemma of either evacuating prematurely and increasing the probability that later intervention will be necessary or sustaining the occupation at an unacceptable cost.

'My conclusions with regard to the temporary occupation of Iraq are not sanguine. Whereas war-weary Germans and Japanese recognized the need for an occupation to help them rebuild, a significant portion of the Iraqi people have never welcomed US-led occupation as necessary. Further, the common analogy between the occupations of Germany and Japan and the occupation of Iraq usually undervalues the central role that the Soviet threat played in allowing those occupations to succeed. Whereas Germans, Japanese and Americans mostly agreed on the compelling nature of the Soviet threat, there is no similar threat that will enable Iraqis and the US-led coalition to coalesce around common occupation goals. Finally, the Bush administration has had difficulty convincing significant segments of the Iraqi population that it intends to return control to a truly independent, indigenous government that will represent their interests, not those of the United States.'

'If the argument presented in this article is correct, then it is difficult to reach optimistic conclusions about the continuing US-led occupation of Iraq. Based on all three critical variables, the occupation appears headed towards failure. After decades of Saddam Hussein's authoritarian rule, nationalist Iraqis have been understandably reluctant to welcome a US-led occupation. Further, the coalition victory over Iraq left much of the Baathist foundation in place and loyalists to the Hussein regime remain active. As for an agreed upon threat, while Iraq may indeed face some external threat from Iran, the most significant threats to Iraqi security are internal. The disparate ethnic and religious groups that make up Iraq are resisting efforts at central-ization. Finally, Iraqis are suspicious of US pledges to return their country to an indigenous and independent government. While movement towards more multilateralism may eventually lend some credibility to US guarantees to withdraw, it may also adversely affect the prospects for ultimate occupa-tion success by giving more countries a say in occupation policy.

'Washington faces few good options in Iraq. Comprehensive recon-struction of Iraq cannot be achieved quickly or cheaply, but nationalist Iraqis have become only more impatient with the occupation as it contin-ues. The United States faces the unwelcome choice between prolonging a failing occupation or withdrawing before US interests in the Gulf region have been secured. Already, the Bush administration has rethought and reduced its initial ambitious occupation goals. Ultimately, however, the US might be better advised to stay the course of comprehensive occupation. Premature withdrawal from Iraq promises greater costs in the future if civil war breaks out or a regime unfriendly to the United States emerges. Washington faces a difficult trade-off: it may be able to achieve its goals in Iraq eventually, but the costs are likely to be high.'[79]

In the light of subsequent events, some tentative conclusions can be drawn in relation to Iraq:

1   More resources are needed to achieve success. The United States or the Coalition cannot provide these on their own.

2   The United States should commit itself to stay the course until the insurgency is defeated or reduced to a level Iraqi forces can deal with, but no longer, and make that fact crystal-clear.

3   Help in the broadest sense from neighbouring states is essential, while not forgetting that all of them have very different agendas.

4   The UN is no guarantor of the success of a transition to democracy in Iraq, particularly in view of Iraqi views on it and al-Qaedaist actions against it, but is an essential factor in helping provide legitimacy and support for the new government there.

5   Liaising with the Shiite, Kurdish and Sunni elected representatives, the Coalition needs to agree on a strategy on the ground to reduce negative nationalist reactions to their occupation and draw as many of the insurgents as possible into mainstream politics, while isolating Baath, Shiite and al-Qaedaist extremists who wish to destroy democracy. The new government then needs to set out clearly to its people that the remaining insurgents, of whatever hue, are threatening Iraqi freedom and sovereignty, and that this is the only remaining reason for the presence of foreign military forces on Iraqi soil. The United States, in particular, should commit itself to remove all its troops on the request of the Iraqi government when the insurgency has been terminated or sufficiently reduced (and so domestic and full sovereignty achieved).

Two recent articles made interesting contributions to the debate on the US withdrawal strategy in Iraq. First, James Dobbins in 'Iraq: Winning the Unwinnable War', gives his view on a possible exit strategy: 'Extricating the United States from the costly conflict in Iraq, ending the insurgency, and leaving behind a representative Iraqi regime capable of securing its territory and protecting its population cannot be achieved without the support of the Iraqi people and the cooperation of their neighbors. To win that support, Washington will have to redefine its goals in Iraq in terms that the populations and governments of the region can identify with. The US-led campaigns against terrorism and for democracy are tainted in local eyes by their association with the doctrine of pre-emption and their application in occupied Iraq and occupied Palestine. Whatever their considerable objective merits and potential long-term appeal to Arab audiences, the war on terrorism and regional democratisation are not themes around which Iraqis and their neighbors will unite, as they must if the current insurgency is to be defeated.

'As the new Bush administration reaffirms its support for the current Iraqi government and for the electoral process, it should begin to reemphasize the importance it places on peace, stability, sovereignty and territorial integrity. It should commit the United States to a complete military withdrawal from Iraq as soon as the Iraqi government can safely be left in charge. It should conduct a counterinsurgency campaign focused on enhancing public security and should support the Iraqi government's efforts to co-opt elements of the resistance into the political mainstream. Once again, it should take the lead in brokering an Israeli-Palestinian peace agreement. And it should develop new consultative arrangements to engage all of Iraq's neighbors, as well as its allies across the Atlantic, and secure their active cooperation in stabilizing Iraq, thereby creating the conditions for an early draw-down and, eventually, for a complete withdrawal of United States forces.'[80]

On a premature withdrawal of its forces, he says: 'Yet if keeping US troops in Iraq provokes further resistance, withdrawing them prematurely could provoke much worse: a civil war and a regional crisis of unpredictable dimensions. A middle course is the best option. Wielding the promise of withdrawal, for example, could give Washington valuable leverage, compelling Iraqis, Iraq's neighbors, and much of the international community to look beyond their desire to see the United States chastened and toward their shared interest in Iraq's long-term stability. Thus the Bush administration should carefully modulate two simultaneous messages: a clear desire to leave Iraq and an equally clear willingness to stay until the Iraqi government, with the support of its neighbors and the international community, proves capable of securing its territory and protecting its citizens. Washington should establish that its ultimate goal is the complete withdrawal of all US forces as soon as circumstances permit and that it has no intention of seeking a permanent military presence in the country.'[80]

Secondly, Edward Luttwak, in a classic realpolitik article entitled 'Iraq: The Logic of Disengagement', has this to say: 'Given all that has happened in Iraq to date, the best strategy for the United States is disengagement. This would call for the careful planning and scheduling of the withdrawal of the US forces from much of the country – while making due provisions for sharp punitive strikes against any attempt to harass the withdrawing forces. But it would primarily require an intense diplomatic effort, to prepare and conduct parallel negotiations with several parties inside Iraq and out. All have much to lose or gain depending on exactly how the US withdrawal is carried out, and this would give Washington a great deal of leverage that could be used to advance US interests.

'The United States cannot threaten to unleash anarchy in Iraq in order to obtain concessions from others, nor can it make transparently conflicting promises about the country's future to different parties. For once it has declared its firm commitment to withdraw – or perhaps, given the widespread conviction that the United States entered Iraq to exploit its resources, once visible physical preparations for an evacuation have begun – the calculus of other parties will change. In a reversal of the usual sequence, the US hand will be strengthened by withdrawal, and Washington may well be able to lay the groundwork for a reasonably stable Iraq. Nevertheless, if key Iraqi factions or Iraq's neighbors are too short-sighted or blinded by resentment to cooperate in their own best interests, the withdrawal should still proceed, with the United States making such favourable or unfavourable arrangements for each party as will most enhance the future credibility of US diplomacy.

'The United States has now abridged its vastly ambitious project of creating a veritable Iraqi democracy to pursue the much more realistic aim of conducting some sort of general election. In the meantime, however, it has persisted in futile combat against factions that should be confronting one another instead. A strategy of disengagement would require bold, risk-taking statecraft of a high order, and much diplomatic competence in its execution. But it would be soundly based on the most fundamental of realities: geography that alone ensures all other parties are far more exposed to the dangers of an anarchical Iraq than is the United States itself.'[81]

While Luttwak is I think unduly pessimistic regarding the possibility of democracy succeeding in Iraq, he makes good points on how all Iraq's neighbours are seriously pressured by a US withdrawal, and how such can be used to maximise the financial and other support for Iraq by its neighbours.

I am anxious to see the new Iraqi elected representatives decide their own future – and am hopeful in this regard. Many negative or pessimistic

HOW TO DEFEAT AL-QAEDAISM

comments in this area do seem to be almost imperial or racist in dismissing the possibility of Iraqi democracy out of hand. I also believe, contrary to what many implicitly or explicity assume, that Islamic influence on the new Iraqi government is neither bad nor necessarily anti-democractic.

Almost all commentators agree that the alternatives to the development of a successful sovereign Iraq are all disastrous, being either civil war, massive internal repression again, or the establishment of a safe haven for al-Qaedaists – or, quite possibly all three. Most experts agree that the transition in Iraq will need a huge amount of international assistance – political, economic and military – for some time. Such help can only be provided multilaterally. The United States simply does not have enough 'deployable' troops available – a much-ignored fact in the debate. In addition, following the invasion of Iraq and a variety of other developments, it is clear that using US troops in active combat in Islamic lands, whether justified or not, or under UN approval or not, adds to the rage in the Muslim *umma*.

As the IISS has put it: 'The United States is under pressure to depart as quickly as possible from Iraq, but without appearing to "cut and run". Bush has laid out sweeping objectives for Iraq: US troops will not withdraw until Iraq becomes "a country that is democratic, representative of all its people, at peace with its neighbors and able to defend itself. ... You don't want the enemy to say, 'We'll just wait them out.' There will not be an "artificial timetable" for withdrawal, although the United States would "leave if asked."

'So far, there is no sign of such a request. The Sunni Association of Muslim Clerics has demanded a timetable for withdrawal, but not withdrawal per se. Muqtada al-Sadr holds a similar position, while Grand Ayatollah Ali al-Sistani, the country's most influential (Shiite) religious leader, has counselled patience and cooperation with the United States. None of the key leaders who have emerged since Iraq's January election favour early withdrawal either.

'Yet it seems likely that politics will reshape these positions over time. When the Shiites determine that the US presence has served its purpose in helping to consolidate their position, and their Sunni and Kurdish rivals assess that they are strong enough to defend their respective interests, demands for US withdrawal are likely to become loud and clear. In America, mid-term elections for Congress are scheduled to take place in

2006. These will be interpreted as a referendum on the US intervention in Iraq and as a bellwether for Republican national prospects in the presidential elections of 2008. At that point, demands for withdrawal might be as insistent within the Republican Party as they are in Baghdad.'[82]

We must not repeat history and do in Iraq what the international community did in Afghanistan, especially as it would give free rein to al-Qaedaists to significantly accelerate their activities with at least part of the infrastructure of a state behind them. The impetus such a situation in Afghanistan gave to al-Qaedaism must not be repeated.

In the final analysis, Europe – and the world – needs to look to its core beliefs. Does it believe in helping the long-oppressed people of Iraq or in standing idly by and letting those who launch appalling terrorist attacks on the UN, the International Red Cross, Shiites attending mosques, innocent foreign workers, and Iraqis who wish to see a better future for their country, effectively win?

HELP OTHER ISLAMIC STATES IN THEIR ENDEAVOUR TO
DEFEAT AND DEMOBILISE MILITANT JIHADISTS

Without getting directly involved in military operations, the EU and the United States should help other states in the world that are being attacked by militant jihadists or where militant jihadists are sheltering. These states include Pakistan, Indonesia, Saudi Arabia, Kashmir, Chechnya, Algeria and some other North African states.

In each case, the existing state structure may be able to deal with the issue – the one possible exception being Saudi Arabia. Even there, many underrate the strength and staying power of the house of Saud.

Helping to defeat militant jihadists is particularly important in Pakistan and Indonesia.

Pakistan is home to the top leadership in the core al-Qaeda group and also to a nuclear industry which has leaked nuclear access and secrets to a number of state and non-state actors, including al-Qaeda. Helping Pakistan defeat the militant jihadists on its territory is therefore vital to defeating al-Qaedaism and preventing nuclear proliferation.

As the largest Muslim country in the world, and one of its largest democracies, Indonesia is vital to the war against al-Qaedaism, and yet is frequently overlooked. Over the last six years, the country has gone through major political changes which have strengthened forces working for moderation and tolerance in that country. Of a total population of 220 million, approximately 190 million are Muslim – the vast majority of whom vote for parties that are moderate and tolerant. The key now is for Indonesian democracy to deliver to its people. The fastest-growing Islamic party, the Prosperous Justice Party, has seen its appeal grow when it reduced its emphasis on religion and instead stressed honesty and clean government. The West needs to aid Indonesia, particularly in helping it to deliver on the promise of democracy to its people. This will do more than anything else to defeat the small minority of militant jihadists in that country.

Overall, the West should adopt the approach of providing intelligence, and technical and other support, to each state that requests assistance. In many ways, the approach here is to wait al-Qaedaism out while patiently working to improve governance, the rule of law, economic development and levels of freedom in all these countries over the next few decades. If the West does not deal with the negative aspects of globalisation and reduce the rage in the Islamic world it is wasting its time on military and other forms of assistance.

IN EUROPE, STOP 'CREATING' FURTHER MILITANT INTERNATIONAL JIHADISTS

Europe now has prime responsibility for promoting political and economic reconstruction and development in Bosnia and Kosovo. It is well within Europe's ability to do so – but it needs continued focus, military, police, and financial input, and the political will to ensure we succeed in both. Success would ensure that neither becomes a major breeding ground for militant jihadists in future.

Equally if not more important, is ensuring that Europe does not continue to be a breeding ground for militant international jihadists within the EU itself. There is an issue here that many in Europe are not even aware of: 'the increasing importance of elements drawn from the North African diaspora in international jihadi activism. A large number of Muslims arrested across Europe and in North America on terrorism charges since 9/11 have been of North African, and especially Maghrebi, origin. In many if not most cases, they have been first- or even second-generation immigrants, and thus products of the North Africa diaspora rather than firmly rooted in their (or their parents') countries of origin. Detached from their original national backgrounds, they have generally been influenced by the transnational forms of Islamic activism, especially the Salafiyya movement, which give them a stable, if rather abstract, Islamic identity, as members of the international *umma*, wherever they find themselves. As such, their outlook is a direct product of the process of globalisation, and includes a strong disposition to identify with embattled Muslims elsewhere. With the proliferation of theatres of conflict involving Muslim populations (Afghanistan, Bosnia, Chechnya, Iraq and, of course, Palestine), the militantly activist minority within the North African diaspora is increasingly inclined to be drawn into the form of international Islamic activism developed by al-Qaeda, irrespective of developments in their countries of origin.'[28]

There are now large Muslim minorities in many European cities, particularly in France, Germany, Holland, the UK and Austria. Many live in poor conditions and have poor economic prospects. Most have not integrated fully – and indeed have not been welcomed.

These issues now need to be addressed as a matter of urgency. The assumption that militant international jihadists are all 'grown' in Afghanistan, Iraq, Saudi Arabia, Egypt and other Muslim countries is no longer accurate or sustainable. In addition, if Europe cannot treat its Muslim minority properly, thereby creating militant international jihadists who will eventually attack it, it has little chance of being successful in its efforts to prevent jihads abroad.

There is a huge issue to be dealt with here in Europe – what Jonathan Stevenson calls 'the absence of attitudinal integration.'[21] This is going to require considerably 'greater jihad' (self-examination, self-criticism and a willingness to change) by Europeans themselves – both within and outside the Muslim community.

Working with Turkey, hopefully during accession negotiations over the next decade, will help inform the EU of a more appropriate structure for its relationship with its Muslim citizens. The EU should also be much more careful about the way it speaks about Turkey. Some of the comments on Turkey made by senior EU politicians and others sounded quite racist and in effect seemed to say to the EU's existing Muslim citizens: 'We want no more of your type here'. This is not a very inspiring or intelligent way to talk to people who are disenchanted with the EU already in many cases. The EU needs to focus on its Muslim community much more, stop ignoring them, and deal with them in an open manner that respects their own and the EU's traditions fully, and to do so with confidence in European cultures and traditions.

ACKNOWLEDGE THE SUNNI/SHIITE STRUGGLE AND ITS ROLE IN THE RISE OF AL-QAEDAISM

Shiite activism after the Iranian Revolution in 1979 created a Sunni counter-reaction which, together with a conflict in Afghanistan, led to a growth in Sunni militancy, which in turn resulted in the growth in al-Qaedaism.

Policy choices or action by the West in general and the United States in particular could be very counterproductive in this area. Whatever is done needs to be handled with great care and sensitivity.

A number of actions are important:

(i)   *Helping Iraq to a democratic future*
      Whether planned or unplanned by the United States, helping democracy in Iraq and thereby potentially allowing the Shiite majority there to exercise its power within a democratic framework, after decades of Sunni Baath minority domination, is a positive development and helps counterbalance Sunni militancy. I say 'potentially' here as I believe that there is much greater national consciousness in Iraq and in the Sunni, Shiite and Kurdish communities than many think, and so, in the long run, a Shiite majority may not necessarily elect Shiite representatives, and hopefully not sectarian ones.

      Particularly if the Shiite community continues to reach out to the Sunni Arab community (as well as the Kurdish community, which also is mainly Sunni) and shares power fairly, then together they have the power to defeat al-Qaedaism in Iraq. This would be a major blow to al-Qaedaism and would present an attractive alternative to the Sunni community worldwide. The stakes here are therefore very high.

      This reinforces the strong conclusion above about the need for the United States and the rest of the world to help democracy succeed in

Iraq and help to restore its sovereignty through defeating (Al-Qaedaists) or co-opting (national Sunni militants) the insurgents.

(ii) *A grand bargain with Iran makes strategic sense now.*

There is now a major opportunity for the United States, the EU, China and Russia to come together to complete such a bargain with Iran. Each of these countries and the EU are threatened by al-Qaedaism, and in the broadest sense each has interests in Iran. A grand bargain will, however, never happen if an attempt is made to cover all possible issues.

If it focuses on Iranian nuclear developments, non-interference in and help in stabilising Iraq, economic and financial aid and support to Iran, pledges of non-interference, and action against terrorism, then it can succeed and is in the long-term interests of *all* parties. Democracy in Iran needs time to evolve and cannot be imposed by the United States: it simply does not have adequate deployable troops to do so, even if it wished. Iran as a Shiite power is in the long run potentially a natural ally of the world in its battle against al-Qaedaism. However, such must be effected carefully so as not to produce a Sunni reaction that actually worsens the struggle. As bureaucratic pressure from the military-industrial national complex in Iran is building up to 'go nuclear' and may soon pass the point of no return, this grand bargain is now a matter of extreme urgency.

(iii) *Iran and Iraq can be, in part, bulwarks against despotism in the Middle East/Gulf area*

To the extent that Iran and Iraq can be encouraged in a democratic direction (crucially, including fair treatment of minorities), such can then over time be encouraged in the rest of the Middle East/Gulf. Fair treatment of Sunni minorities in Iran and Iraq can then be presented as the only appropriate way for Sunni-majority countries to treat their Shiite minorities. Such over time, appropriately encouraged and helped by the West, will lead to greater tolerance, and acceptable norms in the human, civil and women's rights areas, and significantly challenges al-Qaedaism at its core.

(iv)   Encourage Shit'ite and Sunni moderation and self-questioning and 'greater jihad'

Over the years, many have seen the Shiite tradition as being somewhat more liberal, more open to democracy, and more willing to practise *Ijtihad* (self-questioning) – and therefore potential allies of the democratic West. Various developments in Iran have dashed many of these hopes. In addition, a formal Western/Shiite alliance could produce a Sunni counteraction, 'proving' a conspiracy theory and making matters much worse.

It is much safer, in the fashion set out earlier, to encourage Islam in general in a more moderate, less dogmatic direction. If, in addition, Iran and Iraq can be turned into attractive democratic states that respect minority rights (however imperfect they may be in Western eyes), then that would be a major blow to al-Qaedaism.

Finally the world in general and the West in particular should bear the Sunni/Shiite struggle in mind in all its decision-making and in all its dealings with Islamic states and in the war against al-Qaedaism.

RESPONSE 3: DEAL WITH THE NEGATIVE IMPACT AND
NEGATIVE ASPECTS OF GLOBALISATION

We have already seen the negative impact globalisation has had in creating an environment where 'others' or 'out-groups' are looked on with suspicion if not hatred and are assumed to be 'guilty' with respect to many Islamic issues. Part of the solution the International Crisis Group (ICG) suggests is to help strengthen nationalism in countries going through the process of globalisation. Professor Mousseau's theory on globalisation's impact also suggests that strengthening national identity might reduce the virulence of 'in-group' identity and thus help reduce anti-Western rage. While I have some concerns about this from our experience in Ireland, generally it makes sense and would help strengthen the resources of the relevant states in confronting militant opposition. In addition, structural adjustment and similar international programmes need to be amended to strengthen the role of the state, rather than weaken it.

The challenge of globalisation is summarised well by Christopher Coker: 'Economically, globalisation is a fact but not a fate. Markets are created through politics, and that is true of global markets too. It is possible that a recession or global meltdown could lead people and governments to react unfavourably, to close off the open market system, as it did in the 1930s.

'Indeed, the global economic integration of the late nineteenth and early twentieth centuries ended in the chaos of two world wars, and the intervening Great Depression. But even before that, the rise of an array of collectivist ideas – nationalism, imperialism, socialism, communism and fascism – did much to undermine belief in a liberal world economy. Similar forces are seen at work today: anti-globalisation protestors provide the anti-liberal fervour, financial markets the economic instability, terrorism the conflict.

'The principal lesson of history is that freedom depends on human agency through political institutions. Ironically, the primacy of politics is increasingly accepted by many bankers and economists themselves, who since the late 1990s have begun to warn that globalisation is likely to have political consequences that may determine its course in the future. Political protest movements might be strong enough to arrest it, if not put it into reverse, just as economic nationalism and protectionism in the early 1930s changed the global landscape and led to war. The West, too, needs to see globalisation in political terms and work out political strategies to deal with its challenges and threats.'[83]

Assuming that globalisation is a benefit to most in the long term, if properly controlled and 'applied', what should the West do to deal with the acknowledged very serious problems created by it? The first step is to acknowledge the problem fully and then to seek an agreed multilateral political solution to it.

One of the main objectives for the Western community is to ensure that globalisation continues but does so in a way that is consistent with the interests and values of our own citizens. That means pursuing long-term political strategies to address the sources of conflict and instability in the world.

One way to do this was the proposal by Britain's Chancellor of the Exchequer, Gordon Brown, in November 2001 for a new Marshall Plan to eliminate the most egregious effects of global poverty, especially with regard to education and health, within twenty years. This plan would include the doubling of Western development aid to $100 billion per year.

But also, critically, it would involve not only a major reform of international institutions but also dramatic changes in the way in which developing countries manage their own economic affairs and treat their poorest citizens.[83]

There is a broad consensus emerging that a new Marshall Plan is needed to address the impact of globalisation, particularly in the Islamic world. It is very much in the interests of the West to implement such a plan. Many might assume that such aid should be directed mainly at the poorest nations. Recent research on the impact of globalisation, however, has shown that it has in broad terms served rich countries well and poor ones even better but has left middle-income countries struggling to find a niche in world markets. Much of the resources of a new Marshall Plan should therefore be directed at these countries.

Some of these countries will be helped through entry into the EU. The Middle East Partnership Initiative, launched by the United States recently to foster educational, financial, and judicial reform, will also help the middle-income countries of that region. The EU needs to work closely with the United States and the world community to target all middle-income countries, particularly Islamic ones, in this effort.[84]

Next, it is vital that structural adjustment and similar programmes are appropriately tailored or redrafted to ensure they do not disempower governments who are applying them. It is also essential that a full debate is effected within these countries on such programmes, in order to ensure that their citizens do not feel that key economic policies on such adjustment, and other key matters agreed with international bodies, are impositions by outsiders, generating further distrust and hatred.

The international community then needs to focus significant effort in creating jobs in developing countries that are going through economic transition. This may require major policy changes in the United States and among certain international economic and financial institutions. This especially requires the United States and international institutions to stop discouraging the governments of Less Developed Countries (LDCs) providing subsidies to the urban poor. As Professor Mousseau points out, decreased dependency on the state for jobs and other material and social services has in many countries led to increased dependency on extremist groups. Funds from the new Marshall Plan should be used to subsidise local private enterprises, targeting in particular the urban jobless to ensure that they can find living wages locally. Such subsidies are not permanent: they are a medium-term tool used only until local economic development eliminates the need for them. Ireland provides a good example of an open economy which has used a range of state aids to minimise the negative impact on employment and other areas when implementing economic reforms.

The reduction of agricultural and other similar subsidies by the More Developed Countries (MDCs) should be considered if this will increase jobs and income in the LDCs. (Some, research indicates that the elimination of agricultural subsidies, in particular, by the West does not have the expected result and in some cases leads to job and income reductions in LDCs).

The key issue the Marshall Plan and the full economic and political effort of the West should address is subsidising the emergence of market economies in LDCs affected by globalisation. This does not mean immediately deregulating their economies, which would not necessarily help in the development of markets and could in fact hinder such a development.

In that regard, a market economy does not need to be a free-market one: it can be highly regulated, as in Sweden and many other successful developing economies and, in theory at least, publicly-owned. However the economy is owned or structured, the key issues that need to be dealt with, according to Michael Mousseau, include 'impartial enforcement of contracts and common law; destruction of clientalist linkages (corruption); subsidisation of private enterprises (with fair bidding practices); widespread equitable subsidisation of small loans so people can purchase homes or start small businesses; and redistribution to widen the scope of opportunities for market engagement.

'It is not deregulated markets, democracy or an absence of poverty that produces liberal values, however, but rather a market economy. Thus, to reduce the social support of terror, market democracies should use economic aid as both a means and an incentive for governments in developing countries (1) to create and enforce bodies of common law that are vital to the functioning of a market economy, and (2) to equitably subsidise local private enterprises with the goal of widespread employment. The latter is critical during the transition period: the availability of living-wage jobs in the market alleviates insecurity and prevents anti-market rage.'[54]

There is also a liberating message here for the West. Western help in these areas can in the short term improve the living conditions of the people in these regions and over the long term encourage the development of attitudes that will undercut the threat of al-Qaedaism. The West needs to turn globalisation from a threat into a hope to those in the developing world who currently view it as a Western plot to destroy their culture and seize their resources. The mechanisms of globalisation need to be used to achieve this – but under the close political control of world leaders – control that has in the main been absent to date.

RESPONSE 4: HELP ISLAM TO SUCCEED

In the longer term, the world needs to focus on those who support in varying degrees the objectives or actions of al-Qaedaists, particularly in countries that are currently going through significant economic/political dislocation. Al-Qaedaism is attempting to hijack Islam; the rest of the world needs to help the majority of Muslims resist this hijacking, restore their good name and attain a brighter future. This is the only way to defeat al-Qaedaism in the long term This process will take decades to complete.

(i) *The EU (and the United States), working with Asian and appropriate Arab political and religious leaders, through the UN and other fora, should help the Muslim community take the moral high ground with respect to Islam and the manner in which its message is being disgraced by the views and activities of al-Qaedaists, and expose them for what they are – the real enemies of the Islamic world.*

For Islam to recover its former glory, it will need to return to the openness and dynamism of its early years in a manner appropriate to the twenty-first century and with a concept of jihad returned to that of self-questioning and self-development rather than of self-destruction.

Over the long term, this is the most important issue in dealing with al-Qaedaism and also the most difficult one for the West to help with. It needs significant thought and considerable diplomatic, social and economic finesse which only a united West can provide.

The very broad reaction within Islam over the years to a terrible present has been either to return to the roots of Islam or to focus on education. The latter reaction is not widely acknowledged and yet is clearly vital in helping

Islam develop and in challenging head-on the very shaky underpinnings of al-Qaedaism.

Kumar Ramakrishna explains this: 'Radical Islamic fundamentalists possess an extremely literal interpretation of the *Dar al-Harb*, or "the Realm of War". What the West should be doing in this respect is to discreetly back the moderate Islamic clerics who call for the right of all Muslims to exercise *ijtihad*, or "independent reasoning", which would enable them to adopt lifestyles according to conscientious individual interpretations of Islam, rather than slavishly adhere to the authoritarian fatwas of small coteries of radical Islamic clerics who pursue political goals under the guise of religion. As the leading moderate Malaysian Islamic scholar Farish Noor puts it, Islam "is simply too important to be left in the hands of the *ulama* [religious clerics]."

'To expedite *ijtihad* amongst Muslims everywhere requires the modernisation of education across the Muslim world. Certainly, the study of Islamic history and the memorisation of the Sharia law is the entitlement of Muslims everywhere. However, as former Thai foreign minister Surin Pitsuwan, a devout Muslim, laments, the original spirit of inquiry – which led Arab Muslim intellectuals of the past to attain great heights of achievement in science, philosophy and the arts – has long been absent from Islamic education in general. Rather the general principle in too many religious schools appears to be [as Pitsuwan notes], 'memorization, stop thinking, stop rationalizing'. The end result has been the production of generations of young people who are predisposed to see the world as irrevocably divided between the *Dar al-Islam* and *Dar al-Kufr* – or, even worse, in the case of those with a radical Islamic education from the Saudi-financed Wahhabi schools in Pakistan and Afghanistan – as the *Dar al-Harb*.'[6]

(ii) The West must drop its double standards
It is no longer good enough for the West to seek democracy and liberalism for itself and accept despotic anti-liberal regimes, particularly in the Middle East and Gulf region, just because they happen to sit on oil the West wishes to use.

As Malise Ruthven argues: 'Islamism depends for its following on the paranoid perception that the "West" is virulently anti-Islamic. That perception is reinforced when Western governments give their backing to regimes that systematically violate the rights of their subjects. At the same time, public opinion rallies behind regimes seen to be under Western attack, however repressive they are. Islamic solidarity always operates negatively, rarely positively.'[24]

The United States has led the way, at least in theory, in facing up to this issue and its own errors in this area in the past, although there are worrying signs that the continuing problems in Iraq may be leading to second thoughts by many in the United States in this area. The EU, while acknowledging the point, needs to act on it fully and more forcefully educate its peoples to understand the action that is needed in this regard and the risks involved with such policy changes. The risks involved in allowing the current political mess in the Middle East and Gulf to continue are even greater, however. This process will take time and will be a long and very bumpy road, and the final outcome will reflect local characteristics that are not necessarily shared by the West.

The current political situation in the Middle East and the Gulf region has helped produce al-Qaedaism and the current support for it in that region. The status quo, even if there is a solution to the Israeli-Palestinian crisis, will merely continue to provide recruits and support for al-Qaedaism. The underlying structural issues that have produced the current malaise at many levels in this region must be addressed.

In this regard, we need to deal with some important misconceptions. A key one is that, contrary to the image of Islam in much of the Western media, what the West wishes for itself is also what most Muslims wish for themselves in terms of political structures and systems. These issues were raised by the people from these areas in the United Nations Arab Human Development Report, which, as set out above, identified three 'deficits' – freedom, knowledge, and female empowerment – in that region.

In March 2004, this led to a conference in the confines of the Bibliotheca Alexandrina, where Arab intellectuals, academics, members of the business community and NGO representatives produced the 'Alexandrina Document on Reform in the Arab World'. This called for free speech and free elections, the separation of powers, transparent government and fixed political terms.

Many public-opinion surveys in the region confirm the attractiveness of the document's proposals. They challenge al-Qaedaism directly and are suitable objectives for the West to follow with the citizens of these countries.

Malise Ruthven notes: 'There are also increasing numbers of former Islamist intellectuals, such as Rashid Ghanoushi, the Tunisian leader, and Abd al-Wahhab el-Affendi, the well-known Sudanese Islamist writer now based in London, who have come by bitter experience to recognise that the Islamist dream of restoring the Shari'a 'from above' by political action is a recipe for tyranny and violence.

'The reconstruction of Muslim society must start from the unwavering commitment to democratisation and respect for freedom, especially the freedom of association. And when I say democracy I mean exactly that: democracy, the self-rule of the people through their freely chosen institutions and representatives. Not the rule of God, not *Shura* (a Koranic term meaning 'consultation') nor 'Islamic democracy'. Just democracy. Give the Muslim people the right to decide how they want to be ruled, and the power to hold their rulers accountable. It goes without saying that the Muslim people would want to rule themselves according to the values of Islam, according to one's understanding of these. But it is the people who decide what these values are. The moment we start saying that the authority in a polity is for God and not for the Muslims, or allow a class of people to determine for others what the values of Islam are, this means that someone, other than the community (and above it) must decide what the will of God is. Experience has shown that this is a recipe for bringing to power despots for whom the will of God is the last thing on their minds.'[24]

It is also important to understand that while: 'Many sympathise with [Osama] bin Laden and take satisfaction at his ability to strike the United States, that does not mean they genuinely want to live in a unified Islamic state governed along strict Koranic lines. Nor does anti-Western sentiment translate into a rejection of Western values. Surveys of public opinion in the Arab world, conducted by organisations such as Zogby International and the PEW Research Centre for the People and the Press, reveal strong support for an elected government, personal liberty, educational opportunity and economic choice.

'Even those who believe "Islam is the solution" disagree over precisely what the solution might be and how it might be achieved. Radical militants such as [Osama] bin Laden want to destroy the state and replace it with something based on a literal reading of the Koran. However, some political Islamists want to appropriate the structures of the state and, in varying degrees, Islamicise them, usually with a view towards promoting greater social justice and outflanking undemocratic and powerful regimes. An example of the latter would be the Pakistani Jamaat e-Islami (JI) movement, currently led by veteran activist Qazi Hussein Ahmed. JI represents a significant swath of Pakistani popular opinion, and although it is tainted by appalling levels of anti-Semitism, it has taken a stance against [Osama] bin Laden and the Taliban when politically feasible. Often, as in Iraq, Jordan and Turkey, such groups are relatively moderate and can serve as useful interlocutors for the West. They should not be rejected out of hand as Islamists; refusing to engage them only allows the extremists to dominate the political discourse.'[1]

(iii) The West should start dropping its double standards by adopting an approach such as the 1975 Helsinki accords (with the Soviet bloc) to support the growth of economic and human development, democracy and the expansion of civil society in all Islamic states, particularly in the Middle East and Gulf region.

In other words, what the West considers to be best practice for itself, it should now slowly and carefully encourage and promote, and aid and sustain, as best practice in the Islamic world, particularly the Middle East and Gulf region. This will be difficult and will take considerable time and effort, but there is no reason in terms of dealing with the al-Qaedaism threat, the West's own democratic principles, or with regard to basic human decency, for the West not to do so. For once, applying Western principles, carefully and in a helpful and focused way over time, is the right thing to do both morally and strategically.

(iv) The West must accept that dialogue with political strands of islam (Islamism) is appropriate and necessary
As I have set out in Chapter 1, there has been a major (frequently unstated) assumption that Islamism (political Islam) is part of the problem rather than part of the solution, and is in essence anti-democratic. For that reason, the majority of Western governments and most Western experts have viewed any dialogue with Islamist parties as something to be avoided.

At present, in many countries in the Middle East and Gulf region, the (usually) non-democratic government party is the only one the West can dialogue with; opposition is tolerated or suppressed, depending on the circumstances; Islamic 'political' and welfare parties are classed as associations of varying strength, and are usually illegal, although frequently tolerated; resentment then builds up against the party in power, the elite and particularly the West for supporting these non-democratic structures – usually because they are operating on the assumption that an Islamist takeover would be much worse. There has also been an underlying assumption that reform would invariably bring radical and militant Islamist parties to power on the basis of 'one man, one vote, one time'.

Recently, these understandings have begun to be questioned, with particularly challenging work being done by the International Crisis Group (ICG). The ICG has focused on North Africa, but their findings have wider application.

The ICG has reported that: 'Debate over these issues has become bogged down in a welter of fixed but erroneous ideas. One is the notion that posits a simple chain of cause and effect: absence of political reform generates Islamism, which in turn generates terrorism. This simplistic analysis ignores the considerable diversity within contemporary Islamic activism, the greater part of which has been consistently non-violent. It also overlooks the fact that the rise of Islamist movements in North Africa has not been predicated on the absence of reform but has generally occurred in conjunction with ambitious government reform projects. [For instance], the expansion of Islamic political activism in Egypt occurred in the context of President Sadat's audacious economic and political opening – *infitah* – in the 1970s, and the spectacular rise of the Islamic Salvation Front (*Front Islamique du Salut,* or FIS) in Algeria in 1989–91 occurred in the context of the government's liberalisation of the political system and its pursuit of radical economic reform.

'The problem with reform [in the Arab world], therefore, has not been its absence so much as the particular character of the reform projects that have been adopted by North African governments, the political alliances and manoeuvres in which they have engaged in the process, and their complex, unforeseen and sometimes disastrous consequences.

'The problem of Islamism has not been its doctrinal outlook – this has been varied and variable – so much as the difficulty the Egyptian, Algerian and Moroccan states have had in accommodating the more dynamic forms of non-violent activism and, in particular, their inability to integrate a major

Islamic movement into the formal political system. Egypt has refused to legalise the Muslim Brothers. Algeria, having legalised the FIS and allowed it to contest and win two elections, decided it could not cope with the consequences and took the fateful decision to dissolve the party. Morocco has consistently refused to legalise the 'Justice and Charity' movement led by Sheikh Abdesselam Yacine. Whatever justifications have been advanced for these decisions, it is likely that a major element of the rationale has been the essentially pragmatic concern that their special resonance and dynamism rendered these movements so indigestible that their legalisation threatened to destabilise the political system.

'This consideration should not be dismissed. While arguments about stability can be overstated and abused, the way in which democratic reform in North Africa can be achieved without destabilising the region's political systems is a fundamental and entirely valid question which has received far too little attention. A striking feature of the debates in the West and the region alike has been the prevalence of ideological as opposed to political arguments. The various actors have been preoccupied with questions of legitimacy – who are the real democrats, and who has the right to participate in the political game – rather than policy: how should the form of government be changed, and what specific reforms are desirable and feasible. A new approach is required in both Western and North African discussions of political reform on the place and potential role of Islamist movements, not least because of changes in the outlook and behaviour of Islamic political activists in the region over the last decade.

'Where in the past many Islamic movements tended to combine and confuse religious and political objectives, some now explicitly limit their objectives and activities to the religious sphere, while others define themselves as political movements or parties with political, not religious, objectives. Accommodating Islamic political movements within the formal political systems of North African states is still controversial but these movements are not the source of the terrorism problem. One corollary is that the distinction between moderate and radical Islamic activism is of limited analytical value, and the tendency to identify religious activism with moderation and political activism with radicalism is misconceived. The violent forms of Islamic activism are the product of a radicalisation of the most conservative trend in religious activism. Though their objectives may be

[209]

"political" in the broadest sense to the extent that they aim at overthrowing, installing or disrupting governments, they do not seek to win elections or argue for government policy change: their motivations remain essentially religious. Tendencies that dismiss, ignore or simply have no faith in political action are, when stirred up, most likely to resort to violence because they have no other option.

'Islamic political movements in North Africa no longer condemn democracy as un-Islamic or counterpose the idea of an Islamic state to the states which actually exist. In fact, they explicitly reject theocratic ideas and proclaim acceptance of democratic and pluralist principles and respect for the rules of the game as defined by existing constitutions. Their opposition to regimes has accordingly changed, focusing on the demand for justice and the need to apply the constitution properly (or, at most, to revise it) rather than replace it wholesale. At the same time, they no longer counterpose the supra-national Islamic community (*umma*) to the nation-state, but accept the latter both as legitimate and the main framework of their activity. These changes are reflected in their attitude to law. While continuing to demand the application of Islamic law (*Shari'a*), they acknowledge the need for it to take account of contemporary social realities and, consequently, for interpretative reasoning (*ijtihad*) and deliberative processes to play their part in its elaboration. It is becoming inappropriate to characterise these movements as fundamentalist or even as wholly conservative. They defend conservative positions on certain questions but a striking feature is their revival, after a long eclipse, of the ideas of the Islamic modernism movement of the late nineteenth and early twentieth centuries.

'This is important because the central feature of the original Islamic modernist current were precisely its predominantly positive orientation to elements of Western scientific and political thought, its concern to adapt Islamic legal traditions to contemporary social and political conditions, and its close relationship to the nationalist movement. The weakening of modernist nationalism in North Africa was a major factor in the eclipse of Islamic modernism and the rise of conservative and anti-Western Islamic activism. For the recent recovery of modernist ideas within Islamic political movements to bear fruit requires a broader recovery of the national idea in North African political life.'[28]

The crucial lesson from these timely real-world case studies is that dialogue with Islamic parties is essential for local governments and for Western democrats. The key is to consider the policies of such parties carefully. If the parties involved are non-violent and willing to accept the democratic mandate fully, then they should be welcomed into the political process. The lessons of North Africa show that to legalise them then is appropriate, but to allow them to fully control the 'opposition space' is foolhardy. A number of opposition parties and associations will need to be free to build up support over a number of years before a proper and safe democratic choice can be validly made in such states.

The key for the West is the need to support the existing structures through this difficult transition period, which may take ten to fifteen years or more, to allow a proper, peaceful democratic transition rather than a rush to civil war or conflict, as happened in Algeria and Egypt.

It should be clear from the above that this issue is not one of Islamism versus secularism. In the main, most states we are dealing with here, with the possible exception of Turkey, are not secular in the terms in which this word is generally understood, in view of the significant influence religion has in national life. Islamic parties coming to power in these nations must be seen as part of the development of democracy, just as Christian Democratic parties are now seen as a normal part of the political landscape elsewhere.

I must stress that I am not acting on the assumption that the introduction of democracy will eliminate the threat from al-Qaedaism. As discussed above, attempts to introduce democracy can in fact have the opposite effect and can strengthen various trends and developments that lead to more support for al-Qaedaism. But the West cannot suppress the desire of a particular population to express its will in Islamic fashion. Such must be accepted as legitimate and appropriate, and should be helped carefully and with appropriate checks and balances. Handled properly, and remembering the lessons of history in Turkey, the Middle East and the Gulf region, and Indonesia, this effort can eventually lead to the expression through the normal democratic political processes of Islamic grievances and therefore give a rational basis for dealing with them. In addition, we must accept that 'Islamist parties are also integral to democratisation because they are the only non-governmental parties with large constituencies. Without their participation, democracy is impossible in the Middle East.'[85]

With respect to the role of democracy, while I do not see it as a solution to all problems, it should equally not be seen as something which is inapplicable to the Muslim world, which some commentators assume, either implicitly or explicitly. Several Arab countries initiated political reforms in the 1980s in order to permit multi-party elections. These reforms lost momentum because the process itself was mishandled, not because democracy is inapplicable in Arab countries. Nor will democracy, if allowed to develop properly in the Islamic world, necessarily make life easier for the rest of the world. Nonetheless, it will certainly eventually reduce the threat the world faces from al-Qaedaism.

There are ongoing reform efforts and continuing attempts to develop democracy in the Arab and the wider Islamic world at present, many of which are ignored. For instance, King Abdullah II Bin Al-Hussein, the King of Jordan, has said: 'Indeed, reforms in these areas are sweeping our region. Elections are part of political life for more Arabs than ever before; women's participation in government is rising; a new generation is energised and globally aware. Creative thinkers drive this regional change through organisations such as the Arab Business Council, the Alexandria Arab Reform Conference, and the Sana'a Meeting on Democracy and Human Rights. In Tunis last May, the Arab League concurred in the need for reform.'

Referring particularly to economic developments and related successes in Malaysia and Ireland, he says: 'In economic affairs, we have learned from the dismal examples of the twentieth century. Public-sector enterprise alone simply cannot provide adequate opportunities for growing populations. Nations must also look toward the private sector for job creation, innovation and entrepreneurship.'

He concludes: 'At Sea Island, Georgia, last June, the Group of 8 [G-8] countries reaffirmed their commitment to a lasting, comprehensive settlement of the Arab-Israeli conflict, as well as a democratic and sovereign Iraq. The G-8 also strongly supported reform from within the Arab world and recognised the need to help reformist countries. These and other initiatives can help us achieve the result we all seek: a stable, liberalised and prosperous Middle East.'[47]

(v) Learn carefully and appropriately from the Turkish experience in dealing with Islamism

A small but growing number of experts are beginning to appreciate that the leading challenge facing the Muslim world now is the management and political integration of Islam. This is therefore also the leading challenge to the West, particularly Europe. It is not coincidental that dealing with this issue now is the one sure way to reduce the level of support for al-Qaedaism significantly.

It is also a helpful coincidence that over the next decade the EU hopefully will be working with Turkey to welcome it as a member of the EU. Turkey has striven long and hard to become a member of the EU. For a variety of reasons, both the Islamic party in power there – the Justice and Progress Party (AKP) – and reform elements in the military believe that the right course for Turkey now is to become a member of the EU. Strategically, this is an important opportunity for Europe to improve its relationship with the Muslim community worldwide. Europe failed its Muslim community in Bosnia badly a decade ago, and it took US pressure finally to stop the genocide, political rape and ethnic cleansing of the Serbs there. Muslim opinion is very aware of this failure on Europe's part.

Accepting Turkey into the EU does not mean an immediate influx of 71 million Turks into the rest of the EU: the process of accession will take time and can be used to deal fairly with all the issues of concern on both sides. This was the approach adopted for countries such as Ireland and others and should be similarly applied to Turkey.

The EU has much to learn from Turkey in terms of controlling radical Islamists and in the appropriate relationship between the state and Islam in its own societies. Turkey, accepted fully into the EU, and seen as an integral part of Europe, would be of help in achieving success in the policies set out here designed to undercut support for al-Qaedaism.

Some in Europe are worried that Turkey would be a 'Trojan horse' for the United States within the EU. This fear is unfounded. Graham E. Fuller notes: 'Turkey is growing more independent-minded and less enamoured of Washington and has less need for a systemic type of security guarantee because today it lacks enemies who can seriously threaten Ankara's security as long as Turkey remains domestically stable.

'Washington must recognise that Turkey will play an increasingly strong role in the Middle East, but along lines designed to serve Turkish national interests. It will likely be less responsive to Washington's shifting and transient needs at any given moment. The possibility of Turkey developing further in the direction it is currently headed – politically, with its neighbours, in managing a democratic form of political Islam – is more likely to contribute to a stable region in the long term than a Turkey that conducts its foreign policy as a US proxy, as it has largely done in the past.'[3]

In this regard, an issue for many in the EU is the role of the army in Turkey. This issue must, however, be looked at in the light of the realities of Islam and secularism. As Jonathan Stevenson puts it: 'The realities of Islamic doctrine – and indeed, the cautionary example of Iran – may suggest that secular control of the use of force within a Muslim country may be a prerequisite of a more broadly liberal state. ... A greater promise of EU membership . . . might facilitate an accommodation between a tempered form of Islamism and the secular paternalism of the Turkish military that constitutes a shorter leap from the dynamic now prevailing in other Muslim countries. This would make the Turkish model a rich and realistic basis for a range of Western initiatives: from hard counter-terrorism assistance to nation-building to economic diplomacy.'[21]

(vi) The Israeli-Palestinian conflict must be solved, or at the very least defused
While not core to the al-Qaedaism issue, this conflict has a significant knock-on impact, particularly in the Middle East, the Gulf region and certain parts of Asia, which is very damaging and provides support, and to some, justification for actions by al-Qaedaist groups.

Many issues are actually agreed or close to agreement. If agreement in some form cannot be reached now, then at least the killing and terror need to be decreased and time given for wounds to be allowed heal and for appropriate constituencies and structures for peace to be built before final agreement is achieved. Pressure will be required on both sides, as well as increased understanding of the difficulties and concerns of both sides. Following the death of Palestinian leader Yasser Arafat on 11 November 2004, there is now significant hope, at least in the medium term, for agreement between the parties.

A recent book by Dennis Ross, a US diplomat and scholar who has been heavily involved in the negotiations between the Israelis and the Palestinians under a number of US presidents, particularly Bill Clinton, identifies the issues in that conflict that has made peace so elusive, despite huge efforts, including those of Senator Mitchell, who played such an important part in the Northern Ireland peace process.

Ross says that these issues are: 'The lack of public conditioning for peace, the reluctance to acknowledge the legitimacy of the other side's grievances and needs, the inability to confront comfortable myths, the difficulty of transforming behaviour and acknowledging mistakes, the inherent challenge of getting both sides ready to move at the same time, the unwillingness to make choices, and the absence of leadership, especially among Palestinians.'[86]

A recent review of this book summarises the history of these peace talks well and illustrates the current difficulties in a somewhat different light from that in which they are usually presented to much of the world. The review then summarises Ross's suggestions on how to move forward now: 'The Clinton administration persevered, with encouragement from all successive Israeli prime ministers. Ross himself met or spoke by telephone with Arafat countless times. He recounts many occasions on which Arafat assured him of his intention to take some necessary step such as cracking down on Hamas or Islamic Jihad to stop suicide bombings. Each time, however, Arafat – out of fear of provoking a civil war or other motives – failed to act.

'In private, Arafat repeatedly insisted that he wanted to reach an agreement, and he would stress his friendship with and reliance on Clinton. Persuading Arafat to carry thorough on his own commitments, however, was often impossible. As a negotiator, Arafat was frequently infuriating, despite persistent US efforts to secure his cooperation – a persistence testified to by the fact that he was Clinton's guest at the White House some thirteen times, more than any other foreign leader.

'In the end, Arafat proved unable to accept Clinton's proposal for a two-state solution, even though it was the first time a US president had ever assembled a full-blown US plan to settle all aspects of the Palestine problem. Ross does not blame Arafat for the failure of the earlier Camp David meeting in July 2000. Arafat made clear before coming to those talks that they were premature; he was not ready for a deal at that point. The preliminary negotiations leading up to the summit had soured. But Barak insisted on a meeting as soon as possible, hoping to head off impending violence and the collapse of his own shaky coalition by confronting Arafat with a clear "yes" or "no" choice.

'By late December 2000, however, further negotiations had brought Barak much closer to Arafat's supposed bottom line. Clinton then put forward his "parameters" for a comprehensive settlement, taking account of what he and Ross believed were both the Israelis' and the Palestinians' essential needs. Violence had already erupted in the wake of Ariel Sharon's inopportune September visit to the Temple Mount and had expanded into guerrilla warfare that Arafat was doing nothing to quell. Clinton was due to leave office in a month. Barak's chances of defeating Sharon in an upcoming election were rapidly evaporating. Clinton and Ross each made it clear to Arafat that the deal on the table was the best he would ever get. Many Arab leaders, including Egyptian President Hosni Mubarak, also weighed in and urged him to accept it.

'Yet Arafat could not, or would not, say yes. Instead, as usual, he quibbled and procrastinated. And the outcome was nearly four years of bloody violence that has yet to abate. Little wonder, then, that although Ross identifies numerous errors as having been made over eight years of negotiations by many parties – including himself – he puts the ultimate blame on Arafat, a brilliant revolutionary who never compromised enough to become a statesman.

'Ross argues that the only way to renew negotiations now is to build on the Sharon withdrawal plan with vigorous diplomacy by Washington and its European allies. He urges the United States to work closely with Israel in dealing with the Palestinian Authority's leadership (but not with Arafat), as well as with Egypt. Together, all sides should try to make an eventual Israeli withdrawal successful by creating a viable political and security structure in Gaza which would prevent a takeover by Hamas and set a precedent for further withdrawals from the West Bank. Ever hopeful, Ross sees room ahead for creative diplomacy under energetic US leadership, despite its noticeable absence in recent years.'[87]

Ross is not alone in believing that Arafat eventually became part of the problem rather than part of the solution. Many in the strategic-studies community and in the foreign-policy establishment in Europe as well as in the United States became well aware of the need to bypass Arafat – although this was not fully understood by the general public. This explains the efforts to appoint a prime minister 'under' Arafat. Unfortunately, each such effort failed.

The IISS explained this well: 'The hope, if not conviction, was that a prime minister would provide an untainted interlocutor for Americans and Israelis and so create manoeuvring room for diplomatic progress. Other benefits were presumed to ensue from this. Arafat – "the abominable no-man" – who is seen to have done so much to plunge his people into their present parlous state, would be marginalized. With his influence, patronage and status diminished, the chief impediment to a negotiated settlement with Israel would be overcome. An effective prime minister backed by the Palestinian parliament and propped up by powerful outside sponsors like the United States would be in a position to consolidate and streamline the security services, subordinate them to a constitutional authority and use them to choke off the intifada. In other words, such a prime minister would launch the implementation of the road map. Moreover, an acceptable prime minister would begin to push aside Arafat's cronies – the so-called outsiders who accompanied Arafat from Tunis – in favour of younger "insiders" who are said to possess modern sensibilities more in line with democracy, transparency and accountability than the autocratic and corrupt Arafat. This "new guard" would presumably have the vision and credibility to reach a territorial agreement with Israel and meet the security responsibilities that such a settlement would entail.

'The man designated for the job was Muhammad Abbas, also known by his "kunya", or honorific name, Abu Mazen. Abbas had worked at Arafat's side since the founding of Fatah, the dominant Palestinian party and cornerstone of the nationalist resistance. He seemed to be a logical choice: a staunch nationalist, close associate of Arafat, long-time fixture of peace-process diplomacy and a man who abjured violence, believing that terrorism inevitably played into Israel's hands, making Palestinian political gains all the more elusive. That he had no domestic constituency and was seen by many as an apparatchik at best and Israeli stooge at worst was overlooked in view of the foregoing qualities. When the United States and Europe finally girded themselves for the battle for Palestinian political reform in April 2003, they succeeded in getting Arafat's grudging agreement to Abbas's accession to the prime minister's office. The ten tense days of wrangling that resulted in Arafat's concessions regarding Abbas, his portfolio and the composition of the cabinet were seen as a tough but worthwhile prelude to rationalised government and an empowered prime minister. In reality, these ten days allowed Arafat's wrestling act to reinforce the popular view of him as the defender of Palestinian prerogatives in the face of pro-Israeli foreigners, and to plant a perception of Abu Mazen as the willing instrument of Palestine's adversaries. It was a brilliant performance and it had its intended effect. Abbas was hamstrung from his first day in office.'[88]

Following Arafat's death, I believe that, in the medium term, the agreement that the rest of the world needs, as much as the Palestinians, will undoubtedly be signed by a new generation of leaders on the Palestinian side. But, in this regard, what of the two other key players, the United States and Israel?

In November 2004, President Bush stated: 'It is fair to say that I believe we've got a great chance to establish a Palestinian state ... and I intend to use the next four years to spend the capital of the United States on such a state.' He went on to commit the United States to the 'road map' developed by the Quartet (the UN, EU, Russia and United States), and aver that Palestinian statehood could become a reality in 2009. This timetable evidently captured the administration's safest guess regarding the lead time the Palestinians and Israelis would need to stabilise their respective domestic political arrangements and negotiate a final-status accord that would establish an international border, resolve problems related to repatriation of Palestinian refugees, adjudicate rival claims to Jerusalem and determine the future of Jewish settlements in territory to fall under Palestinian jurisdiction.'[89]

'With respect to Israel, the second dramatic development affecting the dynamics of the conflict [the first being Palestinian developments after the death of Arafat] is the apparent transformation of Ariel Sharon. Since his accession to the premiership, Sharon has given the keynote address at a major policy conference held annually in December in the Tel Aviv suburb of Herzliya. It was there that Sharon first announced his plan for unilateral disengagement from Gaza, using, ironically, the Hebrew equivalent of the term King Hussein applied in 1988 when he declared that Jordan had renounced its legal and administrative claims to the West Bank. His speech on 16 December 2004 followed a year of political turmoil set in motion by his proposal to abandon all the settlements in Gaza and four settlements in the northern West Bank. It was preceded in October 2004 by his statement that Israel does not want "to rule over millions of Palestinians forever" and that "Israel, which wants to be a model democracy, cannot sustain the occupation for a length of time".

'This theme, which could well have been authored by Yossi Beilin, the renowned spokesman of Israeli doves, was developed further in the Herzliya speech. Sharon acknowledged that a situation "where one [nation] rules over another would be a horrible disaster for both peoples". "Disengagement", he conceded, "recognises the demographic reality on the ground specifically, bravely and honestly. Of course it is clear to everyone that we will not be in Gaza in the final agreement. This recognition, that we will not be in Gaza, and that, even now, we have no reason to be there, does not divide the people and is not tearing us apart … disengagement from Gaza is uniting the people". By invoking the demographic dilemma – namely, that an Israeli state that disenfranchises an entire class of people cannot be a democracy, while an Israel that enfranchises Palestinians will cease to be Jewish – the architect of the settler movement endorsed the central claim of the left and denied the viability of Israeli occupation not just of Gaza, but of the West Bank. The speech was therefore a pivotal moment.'[89]

So, for once, the three key parties to this conflict seem to be marching in the same direction and broadly to the same tune. It makes strategic sense for all three to reach agreement now. For the United States, a just settlement for both sides, with democratic accountability for both Palestinians and Israelis, is now widely viewed in the United States as a strategic necessity for a wide variety of reasons.

Many will say that we have had these opportunities before. True, but what is different this time is that each of the three key parties has by now tried every other possible alternative – and are left with very clear choices now. I would be concerned, however, about the prospect of the cycle of violence tactically overriding the strategic necessity once again. Dennis Ross addressed this issue recently: 'With the Saudis alone estimating a \$35 billion budgetary windfall this year from the surge in oil prices, there is no reason why the Persian Gulf states could not provide a billion-dollar Palestinian development fund. If Washington's Arab allies are serious about wanting to defuse this conflict and helping all the Palestinians who have suffered, they must assume some responsibilities as well.

'Some may suggest that the United States should be even more ambitious and present plans for resolving the permanent-status issues soon. Clearly, the United States should take advantage of the moment, particularly because of the high costs of failing to do so. But now is the time for realism, not fantasy. There is simply no way a new Palestinian leadership, even one elected by the Palestinian people, can in the near term make concessions on the existential issues of Jerusalem, borders and refugees; no agreement is possible without such concessions by both sides. The leaders of the Palestinian Authority (PA) must first establish their authority by demonstrating their effectiveness. They need to show the people that their government is capable of ending corruption, establishing the rule of law and obtaining freedom of movement and freedom from Israeli military intervention for its citizens – and especially of helping coordinate Israel's disengagement from Gaza.

'Although Sharon was determined not to coordinate the withdrawal when he believed he had no partner to talk to, now his attitude appears to be changing; he recently said Israel would consider coordinating security and withdrawal with a Palestinian leadership "willing to fight terror." Here again, a dialogue to create the right environment for elections must extend to other matters, as coordination holds benefits for both sides. Instead of Israel's just abandoning its land and settlements in Gaza, handing them off to the PA will allow it to gain public credibility; Israel, to be sure, will require the PA to make security guarantees – and detailed plans for implementing the guarantees – for such a transfer to take place. Hamas has wanted to create the impression that its violent tactics forced the Israelis out, 'liberating' Gaza. But the PA must make it clear that Hamas attacks against Israelis will stop, particularly because Hamas violence would be met by a withering response from Sharon.

'International assistance in targeting the areas from which the Israelis withdraw could help ensure security. Rebuilding projects that would benefit the Palestinian people could be tied to the sequence of Israeli withdrawal and PA commitments to preserve calm. For example, high-rise apartments could be constructed in place of the single-family dwellings that the Israelis will dismantle in the settlements. Not only would this help alleviate Palestinians' crushing housing needs, but it would also create an additional reason for Hamas to avoid subverting a peaceful Israeli withdrawal – or at least make it easier for the PA to confront the militants if they did so.

'International assistance for Palestinian civil needs could also be predicated on an orderly withdrawal [of Israeli forces]. The United States, as well as European and Arab nations, could publicly declare that, as Palestinians assume their responsibilities in the evacuated areas, their needs will be addressed collectively. But in the event of attacks against Israelis before or during withdrawal, all assistance would stop. Knowing that attacks could jeopardize help from even their traditional friends would send a strong signal to the Palestinian public to abstain from violence during the withdrawal.

'None of these measures can guarantee success or even security. But the United States faces a moment of profound opportunity. The one inescapable conclusion from the past is that when such moments in the Middle East are missed, the world is always worse off.'[90]

All the opinion polls in both communities show that both want peace and, in reasonable circumstances, are willing to live with each other. However, to achieve this will require movement, change and concessions by both sides; it may be unrealistic to expect these to be achieved in current circumstances or in the near future. But come they will. The impact of such and of the development of democracy in Palestine on the countries of the Middle East and Gulf will, I believe, be very dramatic. The undue focus non-democratic governments there have deliberately placed on Palestine will rebound on them when their people address to them the obvious question: 'Now why not us too?' The impact this will have on the support for democracy in the region has not yet been fully appreciated.

(vii) Re-conceptualise the war against al-qaedaism to what it truly is – a long-term ideological and political war for the hearts and minds of the Muslim international community

Both Europe and the United States are making conceptual mistakes with respect to the nature of the war against al-Qaedaism. (The term 'war' in this situation, in common with 'the war on terror' is probably a misnomer; however, no more so than the expression 'the cold war', which if nothing else stressed the gravity of the situation; it is likewise with the struggle against al-Qaedaism.)

In the United States, although theoretically many know and understand that this is an ideological and political battle, the military component of the war is given priority. In the EU, while European military forces are involved in both Afghanistan and Iraq, conceptually the war on terror is mainly seen as a police action.

Both conceptual errors significantly understate the extent of the threat posed by al-Qaedaism. As François Heisbourg, chairman of the IISS Council and director of the Fondation pour la Recherche Stratégique, has pointed out, just like in the cold war, the current struggle against al-Qaedaism is as much about the values of each belief system as anything else. Soft power is as important as hard power – and in the long run is the only way to win the hearts and minds of the *umma*.[91]

More than two years ago, when he made his comments, the attractiveness of al-Qaedaism seemed minimal: 'Doctor Death', as Heisbourg put it, seemed a good summary of what it had to offer.[91] Two years later, following the invasion of Iraq and various other developments, we are much closer to the civilisational divide that al-Qaedaism seeks, and the West is losing the propaganda war.

As Brian Michael Jenkins has put it: 'The enemy here is an ideology, a set of attitudes, a belief system organised into a recruiting network that will continue to replace terrorist losses unless defeated politically.'[10] Kumar Ramakrishna says: 'The US [led] Coalition must carefully control the use of force and greatly expand efforts within the ideological and political realms. Following Andre Beaufre, the great French strategist, we may say that the Coalition will have to apply an *indirect strategy* against al-Qaeda if it wants to defeat it without sparking a wider civilisational conflict between the West and Islam, thereby rendering the war against Osama bin Laden unwinnable.'[6]

In order to succeed in this effort, the West, and in particular the EU and the United States, need to agree in the widest sense on the nature of the threat and the need to defeat al-Qaedaism mainly through ideological, political and economic effort. They should then agree on a long-term strategy for victory with India, Russia and China, which already fully appreciate the nature of this struggle.

A key element of the struggle will be countering al-Qaedaist propaganda in the short to medium term. This will require working with Islamic governments and encouraging them, particularly in Saudi Arabia and Egypt, to tone down significantly anti-Americanism, anti-Westernism and anti-Semitism in the media outlets controlled or influenced by them – the majority of media outlets in the Middle East and Gulf region. The key message that needs to be countered repeatedly is that the West is involved in a conspiracy to keep Islam down and to exploit it. It will take considerable focused intellectual effort to counter the al-Qaedaist propaganda on Western conspiracies and actions. It should not, however, take much intellectual effort to show that selling oil that costs very little to extract for $40 or $50 per barrel involves the exploitation by the producers in the region of consumers in the West and in the poorer countries of the world and not the reverse.

The activities in Abu Ghraib Prison and in Guantánamo Bay, and media coverage of them, have been a major defeat for the West in general and the United States in particular. Such self-inflicted wounds must be avoided at all costs.

It is also clear that al-Qaedaists use the Internet, Al-Jazeera TV and other media outlets to show videotapes of appalling atrocities for more than just propaganda purposes. This tactic, which has been used in a variety of ways for more than a decade, is designed to show the strength, power and 'action orientation' of al-Qaedaists as well as the weakness of the West, and perhaps more importantly to increase support for al-Qaedaist activities and to boost recruitment to al-Qaedaists groups. The UK government has recently started to target some such websites.

It has been known for some time that early recruitment videos for al-Qaeda were tapes of appalling atrocities being committed in Chechnya and Afghanistan – and that they seem to have been successful. This strategy is clearly winning support for al-Qaedaism. This fact, together with the use by many regimes in the Middle East and Gulf region of anti-American, anti-Western, anti-Semitic and anti-Zionist propaganda as a means of staying in power means that the propaganda battle may in fact be the most difficult battle of the war on terror.

Conclusion

'We have now returned from the smaller jihad to the greater jihad (the
jihad against oneself.)'
Attributed to the Prophet MUHAMMAD[24]

IT IS CLEAR FROM THE ANALYSIS set out above that al-Qaedaism
now constitutes a strategic threat to the world. This is because of its
totalitarian ideological underpinnings, its hyper-terrorism-based guerrilla warfare targeted at civilians, and its clever usage of spurious religious
commentary, symbolism and justification for its actions. As it is al-
Qaedaists' declared intent to cause mass casualties, and as they have used
MMD and wish to use WMD, they clearly pose a major strategic threat to
the West. Reinforcing the threat in the latter area is the continuing lack of
secure control and proper accounting for all fissile material for nuclear
weapons, the availability of fissile material in nuclear-research reactors
worldwide, the continuing erosion of the nuclear non-proliferation treaty,
and the realisation that biological weaponry may be impossible to 'keep in
the box' due to ongoing developments in commercial-research areas.

This threat, which has been developing for the last fifteen to twenty
years, is derived from the thinking of significant figures within Sunni Islam
going back hundreds of years. Manipulating the ideas of those individuals,
and in particular a number of the key concepts they developed (*jihad,
jahiliyya, Kufr and Takfir, Dar al-Islam, Dar al-Kufr* and *Dar al-Harb*, and finally and most importantly the idea of the totalitarian vanguard) led to the creation of al-Qaedaism in its current form.

Al-Quadaism is initially and crucially a significant threat to Islam itself. It carefully draws upon several core concepts within Islam, reinterprets them inappropriately, cloaks them in religious terminology, symbolism, and spurious justification, and then applies them with great élan, backed by very effective ongoing propaganda. To Muslims who have little education or lack a detailed religious education (in other words, many millions of people), this is an extremely impressive, albeit toxic, message.

The long-term objective of al-Qaedaism is the reestablishment of the Sunni Islamic Caliphate of old. This would require the effective destruction of the UN and of numerous states in the Middle East, the Gulf region, Asia, North Africa and Europe. Its medium-term objective is the elimination of all the current governments in the Islamic world and their replacement with Taliban-like regimes. Such regimes would be a major threat to Shiism as well as to most Sunnis and the rest of the world. Al-Qaedaism's short- to medium-term objectives include fundamentally changing or eliminating various aspects of the way of life that many in the world hold dear, including the separation of church and state, women's, civil and human rights, and democracy itself.

To achieve these aims, al-Qaedaists crucially have to convince most Muslims that the West is conspiring against Islam, and thus help set off a clash of civilisations, while cowing the majority of Muslims who do not agree with them. To do this, they use very effective propaganda and ruthless militarism. Due to the nature of their ideology, they can justify killing anybody, including their own vanguard, to achieve their objectives. When it comes to overthrowing existing Islamic governments, they take the view that the support for these governments by the West in general and the United States in particular must be removed and that these governments will then collapse. Applying their interpretation of the concept of *Dar al-Islam* and *Dar al-Harb*, one way of achieving this objective is to 'cleanse' the house of Islam of all 'infidels'. This tactic has been clearly applied in Afghanistan, Indonesia, Iraq, Saudi Arabia, Egypt and various other Islamic states.

After much debate, al-Qaedaists have mainly focused on the 'far enemy' (the West in general, and the United States in particular). They believe that, if they can remove the influence of this enemy (defined in the broadest sense to include all UN, US, Western, and other 'infidel' military, economic and financial aid, and NGO personnel) from Islamic lands, they will quickly take over the then 'defenceless' Islamic governments, the 'near enemy'. Their plan is to force the United States in particular, and the West in general, to withdraw from Islamic lands through inflicting mass casualties on US civilians in their homeland.

As they believe that they defeated the Soviet army in Afghanistan, thereby precipitating the collapse of the Soviet Union, they expect that the United States, being a much weaker 'paper tiger', as they see it, will be much more easily cowed. They plan to do this by waging a guerrilla war against the United States using WMD and MMD where possible. This guerrilla war is directly targeted at civilians in the United States, on the basis that, after significant casualties (the al-Qaedaist target is 4 million deaths), the United States will concede defeat and withdraw to its own homeland, leaving them a free hand in Dar al-Islam. They then expect that Europe and the rest of the world will quickly collapse, as they believe that the West is completely corrupt and degenerate and will 'concede' quite easily when the United States has withdrawn back into one of its recurring periods of isolationism.

Having examined in detail the current failure of Islam – as perceived by many, including numerous Muslims – in many non-religious areas, and having reviewed in detail various explanations advanced for this phenomenon, it is clear that the decline of Islam, from a very illustrious past, was due to issues within Islam itself and did not arise because of the Crusades, Western imperialism or other factors. It is unfortunate that this is little understood within Islam, as this current crisis is one of the foundations for the threat posed by al-Qaedaism today.

Then having reviewed various explanations for the recent rise of al-Qaedaism, my analysis shows that the only explanations for same, in addition to the current relative failure of Islam, that stand up to detailed analysis are the impact of globalisation on these societies and the activation of international Sunni jihadists as a reaction to the rise of Shiite activism in the 1980s and developments in Afghanistan in the 1980s and 1990s.

The best explanation for the recent growth of the al-Qaedaism threat is therefore the combination of the underlying rage within Islam at its current failure (directed at the perceived cause of this failure, the West), the impact on their societies of globalisation (directed at its perceived source, the West) and the rise of Sunni militancy to oppose Shiite activism in the 1980s, which was then ignited by the spark of the totalitarian vanguard of international jihadists from Afghanistan.

The short-term action needed to deal with the strategic threat posed by al-Qaeda is to defend against terrorist attacks of any nature, and particularly from nuclear and biological WMD, while defeating and demobilising militant jihadists. A key element in this effort is to see al-Qaedaists for what they are: not a close-knit group of like-minded fanatics but made up of three very different types of individuals, each of which requires a different approach. Firstly, there is a core of utterly dedicated militants who are capable of anything. This group must be defeated by military force. Secondly, militant activists who can be negotiated with on local and national issues, and who should be separated from the core by the careful use of both hard and soft power. Finally, 'walk-ins' and supporters who have not become active in al-Qaedaist groups and who can be separated from al-Qaedaism using soft power.

The medium- to long-term action needed to combat al-Qaedaism is to recast globalisation so as to empower governments in developing countries, to help them develop market economies and use a range of temporary aid and support mechanisms to create jobs for the urban jobless. This effort will require the equivalent of a new Marshall Plan for the Islamic world – one which is implemented in a careful fashion, after detailed consultation with Islamic governments and their people.

In this effort, the world needs to accept fully that Islamist political parties which espouse democracy, even if they are sometimes anti-Western, need to be carefully encouraged over time to enter government – after it has been ensured that voters have a reasonable electoral choice and not simply a choice between the Islamic opposition and the ruling elite. Only by the expression of the rage and anger of Islam through normal democratic channels will that issue ever be dealt with successfully and without massive bloodshed.

By carefully, over time, encouraging democracy and human development and the expansion of civil society through a mechanism such as the Helsinki Accords, we in the West are capable of helping the *umma* empower itself to defeat al-Qaedaism. Only they can do that: the West cannot defeat al-Qaedaism without their help.

❦

A number of other points I have made earlier are worth reiterating in relation to the activities of and the threat posed by al-Qaedaists. First, there is the growing realisation that the possibility of biological weapons getting into terrorist hands is a very real possibility; there is also growing concern about the security of nuclear weapons and materials. Second is the appreciation that al-Qaedaism is fighting a guerrilla war, against the United States in particular. Thirdly, this guerrilla campaign is targeting US civilians directly with the intent of causing mass casualties through complex hyper-terrorism or the use of MMD or WMD. All of this adds up to a strategic threat to the world.

Various actions by al-Qaedaists shed light on the way in which these organisations think and operate. The al-Qaeda-supported attack on Bali in Indonesia targeted two social areas frequented by many young Britons, Indonesians, Swedes, Americans, Dutch, Germans and Australians: Paddy's Bar and the Sari Club. A total of 202 mainly young people died in these attacks.

In a video released on 3 November 2001 on Al-Jazeera television, Osama bin Laden warned of such an attack: 'The Crusader Australian forces were on Indonesian shores and in fact they landed to separate East Timor, which is part of the Islamic world. ... We should view [these] events not as separate links but as links in a long series of conspiracies, a war of annihilation.'

In these comments he was talking about the role played by Australia in spearheading a UN peacekeeping force which intervened in the civil war in East Timor in 1999 and later helped East Timor gain independence from Indonesia. This UN-approved effort was strongly supported by many in Ireland and throughout the world.

Exactly a month after the attack in Bali, Osama Bin Laden issued another tape, again broadcast by Al-Jazeera. He said: 'We warned Australia before not to join in [the war in] Afghanistan and [about] its despicable effort to separate East Timor. ... It ignored the warning until it woke up to the sounds of explosions in Bali. ... The Islamic nation, thanks to God, has started to attack you at the hands of its beloved sons who pledged to God to continue jihad as long as they are alive.'

Many will remember the 'smiling bomber' convicted for his role in these attacks. Another of the accused laughed and joked with his accusers in a public interrogation and, when he saw members of the press, including many Westerners, pointed to them and said: 'These are the sort of people I wanted to kill.'[92]

We can also learn from the manner in which Kenneth Bigley and Margaret Hassan, both of whom had significant Irish connections, were treated by core al-Qaedaists. The way in which Bigley was chained in a cage would have been understood very well by many as depicting him as no better than an animal who, when the appropriate time came, could be slaughtered without compunction. (This was the attitude that was evident in the instructions to the 9/11 hijackers, as detailed above.) Both were forced to seek political and military concessions from the British government that were never going to be conceded. After a prolonged period of captivity, Bigley was beheaded on video and Hassan was shot. Neither had been involved in military activity, and Hassan was a Muslim who had worked and lived in Iraq for thirty years helping the Iraqi people.

On 31 August 2004, twelve Nepalese men who had entered Iraq to work as cooks and cleaners for a Jordanian company were murdered by al-Qaedaists. One was beheaded and the others were shot in the back of the neck. As usual, pictures and photographs of the killings were posted on the group's website. Their statement said: 'We have carried out the sentence of God against twelve Nepalese who came from their country to fight the Muslims and to serve the Jews and the Christians – believing in Buddha as their God. Our brothers do not feel any mercy or pity for these nasty and spiteful people: they have left their homes and their countries and crossed thousands of kilometres to work for the American Crusader forces and to support their war against Islam and the mujahedin.' No conditions were set for their release: they were presumably kidnapped and murdered solely to deter others from working in Iraq. UN Secretary General Kofi Annan was 'appalled and dismayed' by these murders and was 'particularly disturbed by the cruel nature of these crimes and their use as a public spectacle', his spokesman said.

From these and many similar actions, the 'rules of engagement' used by core al-Qaedaists are clear:

- UN-approved actions, if contrary to their views or interests, are unacceptable and will be greeted with terrorist bombings, murder and similar acts.

- Westerners and all infidels (as defined by al-Qaedaists), be they young bar or club revellers, journalists, aid workers, domestic staff or businessmen, are all legitimate targets.
- Being a Muslim and working for decades to help Muslims is absolutely no defence. Being a Shiite, Sufi or other Muslim minority may in fact be a death warrant.
- Jews, Christians, Buddhists and all others religious and secular civilians, i.e. everyone other than al-Qaedaists, are legitimate targets.
- God is used to justify their actions – their own interpretation of his views – which can be whatever they want them to be.
- The murder of the 'guilty' will be recorded and used as a propaganda, recruitment or terror tool, and to 'cleanse' the abode of Islam.

For al-Qaedaists, God justifies any conceivable action they carry out, including the use of WMD. This attitude, together with their pure hatred of the rest of the world, and their technological and tactical hyper-terrorist capabilities, makes them an extraordinarily serious threat.

❧❦

I set out in the previous chapter the specific actions the West should take to deal with this threat. In broader terms, one can summarise the necessary action under four related points:

I   FACE UP TO THE THREAT FULLY

Neither the EU nor the United States has fully faced up to the extent of the strategic threat posed by al-Qaeda. There has been no real attempt in the EU to counter the ideological threat from al-Qaeda, and there appear to be few plans to do so. With respect to the religious element of the threat, European governments are only now beginning to wake up to the need to respond. The United States has fully faced up to the terrorism element of the threat. The United States has signally failed, however, to face up to the ideological threat from al-Qaedaists.

2 ACT STRATEGICALLY

At the Global Strategic Review conference of the IISS in September 2002, three experts – Robert Kagan, Christoph Bertram and François Heisbourg – debated the strategy the West should adopt with respect to this threat. Their exchange was published in a subsequent issue of *Survival*, the IISS Quarterly Publication.

Heisbourg even then saw that this was a conflict of values. He said: 'As long as it's "the world against Dr Death", chances are that the latter will not be able to conquer state power of significance, with the al-Qaeda-Taliban symbiosis as an upper limit. However, it is still quite possible that this war of values could turn into something rather more difficult to handle. For example, the war of values would become far more difficult to handle if it were transformed into a clash of civilisations, pitting Islam (and notably Islam in the Arab world) against "the Jews and the Crusaders". This is what al-Qaeda seeks, but it could also be the product of US or Western policies in the Middle East.'

We are now facing a serious issue in that regard following the invasion of Iraq, whatever the rights and wrongs of that action and whatever the outcome of the subsequent occupation of that country.

Heisbourg also drew key lessons on the current struggle from the cold war:

- 'Hard power ... worked in ensuring containment ... except where the adversary had a quasi-monopoly on nationalist values.'
- 'Alliance-building played a major role in extending US influence.'
- 'Soft power eventually reigned supreme, whether market-driven ... or state-sponsored.'

He noted: 'The soft power engine of the West's cold-war victory may also help explain why that historical epoch ended with a political whimper rather than with a nuclear bang.' He also pointed out that 'in a valued-based confrontation, ends and means are closely related: if Western values are based on economic liberalism and political democracy, there is more than a little awkwardness in enlisting the support of states which are economically illiberal and politically autocratic.'

Based on this analysis and his concerns about US plans in relation to

Iraq, he suggested a Grand Bargain between the United States and the EU. The United States should slow down with respect to any possible attack on Iraq and build an appropriate legal and conceptual framework for its preventative and preemptive strategies, both with regard to Iraq and in general. The quid pro quo from the EU would be 'in the form of a serious strategy review by America's partners concerning prevention and preemption, insofar as deterrence, containment and reactive self-defense are not adequate to prevent the use of WMD by non-state groups.'[91]

In retrospect, his comments appear wise and should have been listened to by both sides. They point to the need for the EU and the United States to focus fully on the strategic threat now and to agree a clear policy for dealing with it. To act strategically, the West and the world need to act as one. Divisions between the United States and the rest of the world mean that the struggle against al-Qaedaism will be that much more difficult. The world needs to move beyond the stereotypes of Bush and 'defeatist Europe' and focus on a strategy for victory, as set out above. There are some small signs that this may be developing, following the forgiveness of Iraqi debt and the election results there, but these developments are much too slow.

3 HELP ISLAM

We need to help Islam in the West.

The EU needs to change completely its policies vis-à-vis the Islamic community and to welcome them properly into Europe. In the United States, although the policies of assimilation and integration have worked very well, there is a need to expend huge resources – both intellectual and otherwise – to convince the Islamic community there that the United States is not involved in a crusade against Islam.

The West needs to go out of its way to help Islam to succeed 'at home' and to deal with the negative aspects of globalisation as it affects Islamic societies.

This will require a huge, carefully focused programme of improved education and literacy, the promotion of women's and other rights, addressing a series of demographic issues, and assisting the integration of many Islamic states, particularly in the Middle East and Gulf region, into the international economic system on terms acceptable to both them and the rest of the world. This is a massive exercise which only a united West, assisted by China, India, Russia and the UN, can provide.

4   USE TIME PRODUCTIVELY

There are many examples in history of time slowly ameliorating the worst excesses and extremes of various terrorists and ideologists. Even recent history in North Africa shows that, over time, the threat from local militant Islamists was defused. Time gives the West and the rest of the world an opportunity for 'soft power' to work. Time will also be needed to change attitudes in some Islamic societies.

The only area where time is short is with respect to Iran and Iraq. The actions I have set out above with respect to both needs to happen very fast, or two key opportunities will be lost and the struggle against al-Qaedaism will be much more difficult and much more dangerous.

⁂

This combination of a lesser jihad-based, totalitarian vanguard-led ideological assault on the West, using hyper-terrorist methods, and cloaking these methods in spurious religious justification, is a more dangerous threat to the West than any previous ideological assault or 'ism'. If the hyper-terrorist jihad succeeds in getting access to WMD or MMD, the impact, both directly and indirectly through media magnification and astute propaganda, would be immense.

Structural weaknesses in the US economy and the world economy, if targeted by the al-Qaedaists – which they claim to be doing – are of particular concern. It is notable that in his taped message in November 2004, Osama bin Laden referred to a meeting at the Royal Institute of International Affairs which estimated that al-Qaedaists spent at most $500,000 on the 9/11 attacks and inflicted $500 billion worth of damage to the US economy.

This book is not, however, a counsel of despair. Al-Qaedaism can and will be defeated. The al-Qaedaists have already made a number of serious strategic miscalculations:

- Firstly, their assumption that they brought down the other superpower, the Soviet Union, is plainly wrong.
- Secondly, their belief that the United States is a 'paper tiger' is fundamentally incorrect. They are not the first to make incorrect assumptions about the 'degenerate' culture of the United States

(Hitler and Mao being two prime examples), and they are unlikely to be the last.

- Thirdly, the assumption shared by them and many others, that the United States cannot take casualties of any great number, is based on a false premise. A small number of casualties can and has led the United States to withdraw from humanitarian operations in Somalia, Lebanon and other places. However US casualties in Vietnam and Korea were much higher, when the cause was seen as somewhat more impotant, at least for a time.

A US population that fully appreciated the objectives of al-Qaedaism for them would quickly see the true nature of the threat as an existential one for which no sacrifice was too great. Anyone doubting this should read in detail novels or battle reports of the war in the Pacific against Japan to understand the casualties the United States would be prepared to take and the intensity and commitment they would show to win in such circumstances. Many seriously underestimate the United States in this regard.

- Fourthly, the 9/11 attack was carried out by al-Qaeda under a false assumption: that the United States would not attack Afghanistan or, if it did, it would be defeated in a guerrilla war, or, the United States would never find out who did it. Whichever it was, they were fundamentally wrong in their assumption.

- Fifthly, their assumption that Europe is utterly corrupt and ready to collapse and that it will eventually let al-Qaedaists take back 'their' European 'occupied territories' will in time also be seen as a major miscalculation. It may take a huge effort and considerable time to get Europe to fight, but fight it will, in order to stop al-Qaedaism taking over either parts of Europe or the majority of the world's oil resources.

- Finally, the assumption that Islamic governments will quite quickly fall without US or Western support is likely to prove incorrect in a large number of cases. The history of the Middle East and Gulf region would suggest that there may be some bloody conflicts there but that the existing regimes will not give up without a serious battle – and in many cases will win.

We may consider the aims of al-Qaedaism farcical, assume they can never be achieved and therefore ignore them. They will not go away without a bloody battle, however. The dead of New York, London, Egypt, East Africa, Madrid, Casablanca, Istanbul and Luxor show us what the future will be like, multiplied a thousand-fold if NRBC WMD or MMD are used, unless we face up to this threat and act now.

Our objectives in this effort are identical to those of the Arab intellectuals and NGOs referred to above, and of the bulk of the citizens of those countries and of most Muslims. We must not fail either them or ourselves.

Finally, in this effort the words of Hannah Arendt on totalitarian leaders are relevant: 'They constantly underestimate the substantial power of stable communities and overestimate the driving force of a movement. Since, moreover, they do not actually believe in the factual existence of a world conspiracy against them, but use it only as an organisational device, they fail to understand that their own conspiracy may eventually provoke the whole world into uniting against them.'[35]

1. 'Think Again: Al-Qaeda' by Jason Burke, *Foreign Policy*, May/June 2004 (www.foreignpolicy.com)
2. 'Middle East and North Africa Briefing: Islamism in North Africa II, Egypt's Opportunity', the International Crisis Group, Cairo/Brussels, 20 April 2004
3. 'Turkey's Strategic Model: Myths and Realities' by Graham E. Fuller, the *Washington Quarterly*, summer 2004, www.brook.edu (his latest book is *The Future of Political Islam*, Palgrave Macmillan)
4. 'Commentary: Diagnosing Al-Qaeda' by Jamie Glazov, a *Frontpage* magazine symposium on 18 August 2003, with Brian Jenkins, Bruce Hoffman, John Parachini, William Rosenau and Gregory Treverton, of Rand (www.rand.org/about/ index.html)
5. 'Behind the Curve: Globalisation and International Terrorism' by Audrey Kurth Cronin, *International Security*, winter 2002/2003 (www.mitpress.mit.edu/is)
6. 'Countering the "New Terrorism" of Al-Qaeda Without Generating Civilisational Conflict: The Need for an "Indirect Strategy"' by Kumar Ramakrishna, from a collection of articles he edited with Andrew Tan, entitled *The New Terrorism: Anatomy, Trends and Counter Strategies*, Eastern Universities Press
7. 'The US National Security Strategy', September 2002
8. *Nuclear Terrorism: The Ultimate Preventable Catastrophe* by Graham Allison, Times Books
9. Comments made in two confidential draft papers and one confidential draft presentation on the topic 'Next Phases in the Campaigns Against Terrorism and WMD' by Madame Thérèse Delpech, Dr Gary Samore and Sir David Omand at The International Institute for Strategic Studies ('IISS') Global Strategic Review Conference in September 2003
10. 'Countering Al-Qaeda: An Appreciation of the Situation and Suggestions for Strategy' by Brian Michael Jenkins, Rand
11. *Biotechnology and Bioterrorism: An Unprecedented World* by Christopher Chyba and Alex Greninger, *Survival*, Vol. 46, Number 2, IISS (www.iiss.org)
12. 'Weapons of Mass Destruction and International Order', by William Walker, Adelphi Paper 370, IISS. (He quotes Julian Perry Robinson and Matthew Meselson, 'Non-Lethal Weapons, the CWC and the BWC', the CBW Conventions Bulletin, Issue 61, September 2003)
13. 'Al-Qaeda One Year On', *Strategic Comments*, IISS
14. *Allies: The US, Britain, Europe and the War in Iraq* by William Shawcross (Atlantic Books)
15. 'A Secure Europe in a Better World: European Security Strategy', Brussels, 12 December 2003
16. 'Courage to Fulfil Our Responsibilities', Kofi Annan, the *Economist*, 4 December 2004

17. 'The UN and International Security: Threats, Challenges and Change', *Strategic Comments,* Vol. 10, Issue 10, December 2004, IISS;

18. 'The Military Balance 2004/2005', the International Institute for Strategic Studies

19. 'Al-Qaeda, Trends in Terrorism and Future Potentialities: An Assessment' by Bruce Hoffman, Rand

20. The *Irish Times,* 16 February 2005

21. 'Counter-Terrorism: Containment and Beyond' by Jonathan Stevenson, Adelphi Paper No. 367, IISS

22. 'The Islamist Syndrome of Cultural Confrontation' by John Calvert, *Orbis,* Vol. 46, No. 2, spring 2002 (www.elsevier.com/locate/orbis)

23. *Unholy War: Terror in the Name of Islam* by John L. Esposito (Oxford University Press)

24. *A Fury For God: The Islamist Attack on America* by Malise Ruthven (Granta Books, London)

25. *The Crisis of Islam: Holy War and Unholy Terror* by Bernard Lewis (Weidenfeld & Nicolson)

26. *Islamic Liberalism: A Critique of Development Ideologies* by Leonard Binder, Chicago, 1998

27. *Jihad: The Trail of Political Islam* by Gilles Kepel, I. B. Tauris

28. 'Islamism in North Africa I: The Legacies of History (Middle East and North Africa)' briefing, International Crisis Group, Cairo/Brussels, 20 April 2004

29. 'Al-Qaeda: The Misunderstood Wahhabi Connection and the Ideology of Violence' by Maha Azzam, the Royal Institute of International Affairs, Middle East programme, briefing paper No. 1, February 2003

30. *Masterminds of Terror* by Yosri Fouda and Nick Fielding, Edinburgh, 2003

31. 'Islamism, Violence and Reform in Algeria: Turning the Pages', International Crisis Group, ICG Middle East Report No. 29, Cairo/Brussels, 30 July 2004

32. *Al-Qaeda: Casting a Shadow of Terror* by Jason Burke, I. B. Tauris

33. *Globalised Islam: The Search for a New Umma* by Olivier Roy, Hurst, reviewed in the *Economist,* 16 October 2004;

34. 'Manual for a "Rage"' by Kanan Makiya and Hassan Mneimneh, *New York Review of Books,* 17 January 2002, quoted in reference 24

35. *The Origins of Totalitarianism* by Hannah Arendt, Harvest/HBJ Books

36. *The Power of Now* by Eckhart Tolle (Hodder & Stoughton)

37. *Terror and Liberalism* by Paul Berman (W. W. Norton & Company)

38. *The Mythic Foundations of Radical Islam* by John Calvert, *Orbis,* Vol. 48, No. 1, winter 2004

39. *Militant Islam Reaches America* by Daniel Pipes (W. W. Norton & Company)

40. 'Regional Implications of Shiite Revival in Iraq', by Vali Nasr, the *Washington Quarterly,* summer 2004

41. 'Al-Qaeda in Northern Iraq? The Elusive Ansar Al-Islam', *Strategic Comments,* Vol. 8, Issue 7, IISS

42. 'Occidentalism' by Avishai Margalit and Ian Buruma, the *New York Review of Books,* 17 January 2002

43. 'The Clash Within Islam' by Emmanuel Sivan, *Survival* 45, No. 1, spring 2003, IISS
44. 'Bin Laden May Be Fishing for Allies on Europe's Secular Left' by Brian Michael Jenkins, *Los Angeles Times,* 25 April 2004
45. *The Asian Renaissance,* by Anwar Ibrahim (Times Books International)
46. 'The Greater Middle East Initiative', *Strategic Comments,* Vol. 10, Issue 2, IISS
47. 'The Road to Reform' by King Abdullah II, *Foreign Policy,* November/December 2004
48. 'Four Surprises in Global Demography' by Nicholas Eberstadt, *Orbis,* Vol. 48, Number 4, fall 2004
49. *Introducing Islam* by Ziauddin Sardar and Zafar Abbas Malik (Icon Books)
50. *New Jerusalems: Reflections on Islam, Fundamentalism and the Rushdie Affair,* by Daniel Easterman (London, 1993)
51. 'The Western Encounter with Islam' by Jeremy Black, *Orbis,* Vol. 48, No. 1, winter 2004
52. 'The Firanj are Coming Again', Edward Peters, *Orbis,* Vol. 48, No. 1, winter 2004
53. *On War,* Carl Von Clausewitz, Peter Paret and Michael Howard, editors (Princeton University Press)
54. 'Market Civilisation and Its Clash with Terror' by Michael Mousseau, International Security, winter 2002/03
55. *Egypt's Economic Predicament* by Galal Amin
56. *Cruelty and Silence, War, Tyranny, Uprising and the Arab World* by Kanan Makiya (W.W. Norton & Company)
57. *Through Our Enemies' Eyes: Osama Bin Laden, Radical Islam and the Future of America* by Anonymous (Brassey's)
58. 'The Reckless Mind: Intellectuals in Politics' by Mark Lilla in the *New York Review of Books*
59. 'Driven by History and Hate: Islam's Holy Warriors' by Ian Buruma, the *Times,* 3 August 2004
60. *The Black Book of Communism: Crimes, Terror, Repression* by Stephane Courtois, Nicholas Werth, Jean Louis Panné, Andrzej Pacjkowski, Karel Bartosek and Jean-Louis Morgolin (Harvard University Press)
61. 'Strategic Survey, 2001–02', IISS
62. 'The Terror' by Stephen Simon and Daniel Benjaman, *Survival,* Vol. 43, No. 4, IISS
63. 'Al-Qaeda Targets Europe', *Strategic Comments,* Vol. 10, Issue 2, IISS
64. 'The Rise of Complex Terrorism' by Thomas Homer-Dixon, *Foreign Policy,* January/February 2002
65. 'The Day After' by Stephen D. Krasner, *Foreign Policy,* January/February 2005
66. Islamic Republic News Agency, 25 May 2004
67. 'Iran Builds the Bomb' by Ray Takeyh, *Survival,* Vol. 46, No. 4, Winter 2004/05, IISS
68. 'A World Without Israel' by Josef Joffe, *Foreign Policy,* January/February 2005
69. 'CIA Director of Central Intelligence's Worldwide Threat Briefing', 11 February 2003

70. 'Non-proliferation and the Dilemmas of Regime Change' by Robert S. Litwak, *Survival*, Vol. 45, No. 4, winter 2004, IISS

71. 'Iran's Nuclear Programme', *Strategic Comments*, Vol. 10, Issue 9, November 2004, IISS

72. Further detail of the issues addressed here is available in: 'Proliferation Rings: New Challenges to the Nuclear Non-Proliferation Regime' by Chaim Braun and Christopher F. Chyba, *International Security*, fall 2004; 'How To Be a Nuclear Watchdog' by George Perkovich, *Foreign Policy*, January/February 2005; 'Making the World Safe for Nuclear Energy' by John Deutch, Arnold Kanter, Ernest Moniz and Daniel Poneman, *Survival*, Vol. 46, No. 4, November 2004, IISS; and 'Weapons of Mass Destruction and International Order' by William Walker, Adelphi Paper No. 370, IISS

73. 'Was Iraq a Fool's Errand? What Really Went Wrong?' Larry Diamond, *Foreign Affairs*, November/December 2004

74. 'Now We All Must Share a Common Agenda on Iraq' by Kofi Annan, the *Irish Times*, 16 February 2005

75. 'A Sovereign Iraq?' by Toby Dodge, *Survival*, Vol. 46 No. 3, August 2004, IISS, quoting *Sovereignty, Organised Hypocrisy* by Stephen Krasner, Princeton University Press

76. 'Now Iraq Has Tasted Democracy, the Arab Tyrants are Shaking in Their Shoes' by Amir Taheri, the *Times*, 15 February 2005

77. 'America's Role in Nation Building: From Germany to Iraq' by James F. Dobbins, *Survival*, Vol. 45, No. 4, Winter 2003/2004, IISS, citing a study of the same name by James Dobbins, John G. McGinn, Keith Crane, Seth G. Jones, Rollie Lal, Andrew Rathmell, Rachael Swanger and Anga Timilsina, Santa Monica, CA: Rand, MR 1753 RC, 2003

78. 'The UN's role in Nation Building: From the Belgian Congo to Iraq' by James Dobbins, *Survival*, Vol. 46, No. 4, winter 2004/5, IISS, citing a forthcoming Rand study on this topic

79. 'Occupational Hazards: Why Military Occupations Succeed or Fail' by David M. Edelstein, *International Security*, Vol. 29, No. 1, summer 2004

80. 'Iraq: Winning the Unwinnable War' by James Dobbins, *Foreign Affairs*, Vol. 84, No. 1, January/February 2005

81. 'Iraq: The Logic of Disengagement' by Edward N. Luttwak, *Foreign Affairs*, Vol. 84, No. 1, January/February 2005

82. 'Lessons from the Iraqi Insurgency', *Strategic Comments*, Vol. 11, Issue 1, February 2005, IISS

83. 'Globalisation and Insecurity in the 21st Century: NATO and the Management of Risk' by Christopher Coker, Adelphi Paper No. 345, IISS

84. 'Globalisation's Missing Middle' by Geoffrey Garrett, *Foreign Affairs*, November/December 2004

85. 'Middle East Democracy' by Marina Ottaway and Thomas Carothers, *Foreign Policy*, November/December 2004

86. *The Missing Peace: The Inside Story of the Fight for Middle East Peace* by Dennis Ross (Farrar Strauss & Giroux)

87. 'The Receding Horizon: The Endless Quest for Arab-Israeli Peace', Samuel W. Lewis review essay in *Foreign Affairs,* September/October 2004
88. 'Strategic Survey 2003/4: An Evaluation and Forecast of World Affairs', IISS
89. 'Sea Change in Israel and Palestine', *Strategic Comments,* Vol. 10, Issue 10, December 2004, IISS
90. 'The Middle East Predicament' by Dennis Ross, *Foreign Affairs,* January/February 2005
91. 'One Year After: A Grand Strategy for the West? An Exchange with Robert Kagan, Christoph Bertram and François Heisbourg', *Survival,* Vol. 44, No. 4, IISS
92. *The Base, Al-Qaeda and the Changing Face of Global Terror* by Jane Corbin (Pocket Books).

Bibliography

BOOKS

Graham Allison, *Nuclear Terrorism - The Ultimate Preventable Catastrophe*, Times Books

Hannah Arendt, *The Origins of Totalitarianism*, Harvest / HBJ Books

Paul Berman, *Terror and Liberalism*, WW Norton & Company

Jason Burke, *Al-Qaeda: Casting a Shadow of Terror*, I.B. Tauris

Malcolm Clark, *Islam for Dummies*, Wiley Publishing Inc.

Jane Corbin, *The Base, Al-Qaeda and the Changing Face of Global Terror*, Pocket Books

Stephanie Courtois, Nicholas Werth, Jean-Louis Panne, Andrzej Pacjkowski, Karel Barstosek & Jean-Louis Morgolin, *The Black Book of Communism - Crimes, Terror, Repression*, Harvard University Press

John L Esposito, *Unholy War, Terror in the Name of Islam*, Oxford University Press.

Yosri Fouda, Nick Fielding, *Masterminds of Terror*, Edinburgh 2003

The International Institute for Strategic Studies, *Strategic Survey: An Evaluation & Forecast of World Affairs*, Yearly

The International Institute for Strategic Studies, *The Military Balance*, Yearly

Gilles Kepel, *Jihad, The Trail of Political Islam*, I.B. Tauris

Bernard Lewis, *The crisis of Islam, Holy War and Unholy Terror*, Weidenfeld & Nicolson

Kanan Makiya, *Cruelty and Silence, War, Tyranny, Uprising and The Arab World*, WW Norton & Company

Daniel Pipes, *Militant Islam reaches America*, WW Norton & Company

Denis Ross, *The Missing Peace: The Inside Story of The Fight for Middle East Peace*, Farrar Strauss & Giroux

Oliver Roy, *Globalised Islam: The Search for a new umma,* Hurst

Malise Ruthven, *A Fury For God, The Islamist attack on America,* Granta Books London

William Shawcross, Allies, *The US, Britain, Europe and The War in Iraq,* Atlantic Books

Ziauddin Sardar, Zafar Abbas Malik, *Introducing Islam,* Icon Books

ARTICLES

King Abdullah II, The Road to Reform, *Foreign Policy,* November/December 2004

Kofi Annan, Courage to Fulfil our Responsibilities, *The Economist,* 4 December 2004

Maha Azzam, Al-Qaeda: The Misunderstood Wahhabi connection and the Ideology of Violence, The Royal Institute of International Affairs, Middle East programme, briefing paper No. 1 February 2003

Jeremy Black, The Western Encounter with Islam, *Orbis,* Volume 48 No. 1, Winter 2004

Jason Burke, Think Again: Al-Qaeda, *Foreign Policy,* May/June 2004

Ian Buruma, Driven by History and Hate: Islam's Holy Warriors, *The Times,* 3 August 2004

John Calvert, The Islamist Syndrome of Cultural Confrontation, *Orbis,* Volume 46. No. 2 Spring 2002; The Mythic Foundations of Radical Islam, *Orbis,* Volume 48, No. 1, Winter 2004

Christopher Chyba and Alex Greninger, Biotechnology and Bioterrorism: An Unprecedented world, *Survival* Volume 46, Number 2, IISS

Christopher Coker, Globalisation and Insecurity in the 21st Century: NATO and the Management of Risk, Adelphi Paper No. 345, IISS

Audrey Kurth Cronin, Behind the curve: Globalisation and International Terrorism, *International Security,* Winter 2002/2003

Larry Diamond, Was Iraq a Fool's Errand? What Really Went Wrong? *Foreign Affairs,* November/December 2004

James F. Dobbins, America's Role in Nation Building: From Germany to Iraq, *Survival,* Volume 45, number 4, Winter 2003/2004, IISS, citing a study of the same name by James Dobbins, John G. McGinn, Keith Crane, Seth G. Jones, Rollie Lal, Andrew Rathmell, Rachael Swanger, and Anga Timilsina, Santa Monica, CA: Rand, MR 1753 RC, 2003; Iraq

– Winning the Unwinnable War, *Foreign Affairs*, Volume 84, number 1, January/February 2005; The UN's role in Nation Building: From the Belgian Congo to Iraq, *Survival*, Volume 46, number 4, Winter 2004/5, IISS, citing a Rand study on this topic

Toby Dodge, A Sovereign Iraq? *Survival*, Volume 46 Number 3, August 2004, IISS,

David M. Edelstein, Occupational Hazards; Why Military Occupations Succeed or Fail, *International Security*, Volume 29, number 1, Summer 2004

Graham E. Fuller, Turkey's Strategic Model: Myths and Realities, *The Washington Quarterly*, Summer 2004

Geoffrey Garrett, Globalisation's Missing Middle, *Foreign Affairs*, November/December 2004

Jamie Glazov, Commentary - Diagnosing Al-Qaeda, A *Frontpage* magazine symposium on August 18 2003 – with Brian Jenkins, Bruce Hoffman, John Parachini, William Rosenau and Gregory Treverton, of Rand

Bruce Hoffman, Al-Qaeda, Trends in Terrorism and Future Potentialities: an Assessment, Rand

Thomas Homer-Dixon, The Rise of Complex Terrorism, *Foreign Policy*, January – February 2002

International Crisis Group, Middle East and North Africa Briefing: Islamism in North Africa I: The legacies of history (Middle East and North Africa) briefing, Cairo/Brussels, 20 April 2004; Islamism in North Africa II: Egypt's Opportunity, Cairo/Brussels, 20 April 2004; Islamism, Violence and Reform in Algeria: Turning the pages, *Middle East Report* No. 29, Cairo/Brussels 30 July 2004

The International Institute For Strategic Studies, Al-Qaeda: One Year On, Strategic Comments; The UN and International Security, Threats, Challenges and Change, *Strategic Comments*, Volume 10, Issue 10, December 2004; Al-Qaeda in Northern Iraq? The Elusive Ansar Al-Islam, Volume 8, Issue 7; Sea Change in Israel and Palestine, *Strategic Comments*, Volume 10, Issue 10, December 2004; Lessons from the Iraqi Insurgency, *Strategic Comments*, Volume 11, Issue 1, February 2005; Palestine Confounded - the Palestinian Strategic Impasse, by Yezid Sayigh, *Survival*, Volume 44, number 4, Winter 2002/2003; Iran's Nuclear Programme, *Strategic Comments*, Volume 10, Issue 9, November

2004; Al-Qaeda targets Europe – *Strategic comments*, Volume 10, Issue 2

Brian Michael Jenkins, Countering Al-Qaeda: An Appreciation of the Situation and Suggestions for Strategy, Rand; Bin Laden may be Fishing for Allies on Europe's Secular Left, *Los Angeles Times*, 25 April 2004

Robert Kagan, Christoph Bertram and François Heisbourg, One Year After: A Grand Strategy for the West? *An Exchange Survival*, Volume 44 No. 4, IISS

Stephen D. Krasner, The Day After, *Foreign Policy*, January/February 2005

Samuel W. Lewis, The Receding Horizon: The Endless Quest for Arab-Israeli peace, review essay in *Foreign Affairs,* September - October 2004

Edward N. Luttwak, Iraq: The Logic of Disengagement, *Foreign Affairs*, Volume 84, number 1, January/February 2005

Kanan Makiya and Hassan Mneimneh, Manual for a "Rage", New York review of books, 17 January 2002

Michael Mousseau, Market Civilisation and its Clash with Terror– *International Security*, Winter 2002/03

Vali Nasr, Regional Implications of Shiite Revival in Iran, the *Washington Quarterly*, Summer 2004

Marina Ottaway and Thomas Carothers, Middle East Democracy *Foreign Policy*, November/December 2004

Edward Peters, The Firanj are Coming Again, *Orbis*, Volume 48, No. 1, Winter 2004

Kumar Ramakrishna, Countering The "New Terrorism" of Al-Qaeda Without Generating Civilisational Conflict: The Need For An "Indirect Strategy," from a collection of articles he edited with Andrew Tan, titled The New Terrorism: Anatomy, Trends and Counter Strategies, *Eastern Universities Press*

Dennis Ross, The Middle East Predicament, *Foreign Affairs*, January/February 2005

Khalil Shikaki, The Future of Palestine, *Foreign Affairs*, November/December 2004

Stephen Simon and Daniel Benjaman, The Terror, *Survival*, Volume 43, No. 4, IISS

Emmanuel Sivan, The clash within Islam, *Survival* 45, No. 1, Spring 2003, IISS

Jonathan Stevenson, Counter-Terrorism: Containment and Beyond,

Adelphi Paper No. 367, IISS

Ray Takeyh, Iran Builds The Bomb, *Survival*, Volume 46, number 4, Winter 2004/05, IISS

Omer Taspinar, An Uneven Fit? The "Turkish Model" and the Arab World, The Brookings Project on U.S. Policy Towards the Islamic world

William Walker, Weapons of Mass Destruction and International Order, Adelphi Paper 370, IISS.

WEB SITES

www.http://brook.edu

www.http://elsevier.com/locate/orbis

www.http://foreignpolicy.com

www.http://Frontpagemagazine.com

www.http://global-issues.tv.com

www.http://iiss.org

www.http://mitpress.mit.edu/is

www.http://rand.org/about/index.html

Index